Revolutionary Feminists

The Women's Liberation
Movement in Seattle / Barbara Winslow

Revolutionary Feminists

Duke University Press Durham and London 2023

Printed in the United States of America on acid-free paper ∞
Project Editor: Lisa Lawley
Designed by Aimee C. Harrison
Typeset in Minion Pro, Clarendon LT Std,
and ITC Franklin Gothic Std by Westchester Publishing Services

Library of Congress Cataloging-in-Publication Data
Names: Winslow, Barbara, [date] author.
Title: Revolutionary feminists : the women's liberation move-
ment in Seattle / Barbara Winslow.
Description: Durham : Duke University Press, 2023. | Includes
bibliographical references and index.
Identifiers: LCCN 2022045549 (print)
LCCN 2022045550 (ebook)
ISBN 9781478019916 (paperback)
ISBN 9781478017219 (hardcover)
ISBN 9781478024491 (ebook)
Subjects: LCSH: Winslow, Barbara, 1945– | African American
feminists—Washington (State)—Seattle—History—20th century. |
African American women political activists—Washington
(State)—Seattle—History—20th century. | Feminists—
Washington (State)—Seattle—History—20th century. |
Women political activists—Washington (State)—Seattle—
History—20th century. | Feminism—Washington (State)—
Seattle—History—20th century—Sources. | Civil rights
movements—Washington (State)—Seattle—History—
20th century—Sources. | Women's rights—United States—
History—20th century—Sources. | BISAC: SOCIAL SCIENCE /
Women's Studies | HISTORY / United States / 20th Century
Classification: LCC HQ1197 .W56 2023 (print) | LCC HQ1197
(ebook) | DDC 305.4209797—dc23/eng/20230207
LC record available at https://lccn.loc.gov/2022045549
LC ebook record available at https://lccn.loc.gov/2022045550

Cover art: Vietnam antiwar march, Seattle, Washington, 1979.
Photograph by Paul Dorpat. Courtesy of the artist.

This book is dedicated to
Clara Fraser and Susan Stern,
who brought Old and New Left
women together to create a
radical women's liberation movement in Seattle, and to Nina
Harding, for her uncompromis-
ing struggle at the intersection
of race, gender, and class. I also
thank the thousands of Seattle
feminists who made all this
possible. Finally, this book is
for my granddaughter, Cornelia
Winslow Frank, and our next
generation of feminists, who will
continue the struggle.

Contents

Acronyms

ACLU	American Civil Liberties Union
ALSB	Anna Louise Strong Brigade
ASUW	Associated Students of the University of Washington
BPP	Black Panther Party
CAR	Committee for Abortion Reform
CORE	Congress of Racial Equality
CP	Communist Party of the United States
CUOWR	Coalition of University Organizations for Women's Rights
CWL	Campus Women's Liberation
DR	Draft Resistance
ERA	Equal Rights Amendment
FSP	Freedom Socialist Party
FSPB	Freedom Socialist Party Bolshevik
FSPM	Freedom Socialist Party Menshevik
GLF	Gay Liberation Front
IS	International Socialists
LGBTQ(IA)	Lesbian, Gay, Bisexual, Transgender, Queer (Intersex or Inquiring, Asexual)
MEChA	Movimiento Estudiantil Chicano de Aztlán (Chicano Student Movement)
NAACP	National Association for the Advancement of Colored People
NOW	National Organization for Women
NWPC	National Women's Political Caucus
NWSA	National Women's Studies Association
PFP	Peace and Freedom Party
SCCC	Seattle Central Community College
SDS	Students for a Democratic Society

SLF	Seattle Liberation Front
SMC	Student Mobilization Committee
SOIC	Seattle Opportunities Industrialization Center
SWAP	Seattle Women Act for Peace
SWP	Socialist Workers Party
UW	University of Washington
VFU	Voice for the Unborn
WC	Women's Commission of the Associated Students of the University of Washington
WCAR	Washington Committee for Abortion Reform
WL-S	Women's Liberation–Seattle
WONAAC	Women's National Abortion Action Coalition
WSFP	Women Strike for Peace
YMCA	Young Men's Christian Association
YSA	Young Socialist Alliance
YWCA	Young Women's Christian Association

Acknowledgments

I ACKNOWLEDGE THE TRADITIONAL CUSTODIANS OF THE LAND on which King County is located and pay my respects to the Suquamish, Duwamish, Nisqually, Snoqualmie, and Muckleshoot (Ilalkoamish, Stuckamish, and Skopamish) elders past, present, and future, for they hold the memories, the traditions, and the culture of this area, which has become a place of learning for people from all over the world.

I received two research grants from the Professional Staff Congress, City University of New York. I also thank my Brooklyn College colleagues in the Women's and Gender Studies Program, History Department, and Secondary Education Department.

Many thanks to the personnel at the Brooklyn College Library, the Seattle Central Community College librarian, the University of Washington Libraries' Special Collections, the King County Archives and Records Management, the Schlesinger Library on the History of Women in America, and the Sawyer Library at Williams College. I appreciate the helpful critiques I received when I presented my work at the New York City Women's and Gender Historians Writing Group, American Historical Association, Organization of American Historians, Coordinating Committee of Women Historians, Berkshire Conference of Women Historians, and Western Association of Women Historians.

I am indebted to an extraordinary group of feminist activists who founded History in Action (HIA) in 2000. Enraged by the *New York Times*' erasure of women's activism in its reporting on New York State's movement to reform abortion laws, we formed a listserv. For over twenty years, we have argued, agreed, announced, supported, and despaired the writings, history, and practices of global women's feminism. Because of HIA, our intersectional understanding of feminism deepened and our feminist commitments strengthened.

There is no way to adequately thank Grey Osterud, brilliant award-winning writer, editor, sister, and comrade in the early days of the women's liberation movement in Seattle. Her comments, critiques, and encouragement meant the world to me. A special shout-out and thank-you to Juanita Ramos, activist academic colleague and sister in struggle at the 1990 Berkshire Conference on the History of Women. Ivy Barrett Fox Bryan was indispensable and indefatigable in her intellectual and technical assistance. Bonnie Anderson, Carol Berkin, Eileen Boris, Susie Bright, Emily Brooks, Lisa DiCaprio, Stephanie Golden, Trevor Griffey, Beverly Guy-Sheftall, Esther Altshul Helfgott, Nancy Holmstrum, Jessie Kindig, Felicia Kornbluh, Deborah Slaner Larkin, Tess Little, Priscilla Long, Iris Lopez, Teresa Meade, James Mohr, Hope Morris, Annelise Orleck, Margit Reiner, Nancy Romer, Mary Logan Rothschild, Sheila Rowbotham, and Jessica Seigel read portions of the book and gave me positive and useful critical support. Matt Baya, Joseph Feliciano, Andi Jo Pettis, Molly Schultz, Kathleen Sheldon, and Ann Umlauf helped me organize documents and provided me with technical and other forms of support. Seattle sisters and comrades, many of whom I interviewed, helped me track down activists and gave me photos, documents, and encouragement. Thank you, Py Bateman, Paul Dorpat, Joseph Felsenstein, Alan Ginsberg, Marc Krasnowsky, Ed Morman, and Nancy Stokely.

I cannot thank the staff at Duke University Press enough. Gisela Fosado supported this book from first reading to publication. Alejandra Mejía was enormously helpful, especially with the illustrations. I am not up to date on the latest technologies, and Ale walked me through everything with great patience and a generous heart. Christine Riggio did a fine job of drawing the map. The production manager, Melody Negron, and the indexer, Derek Gottlieb, were meticulous and kept the process on schedule.

A number of activists who were involved in the struggle in Seattle have since died: George Arthur, Louise Crowley, Walter Crowley, Dottie DeCoster, Kathi Dowd, Clara Fraser, Nina Harding, Gloria Martin, Lee Mayfield (Cecilie Scott), Susan Stern, Flo Ware, and Melba Windoffer. I want to acknowledge their contributions.

During the 2020–22 crises—the pandemic, the election, the racial justice movement, the economy—I was sequestered in western Massachusetts trying to focus on finishing the book. Every morning my dear friend Bette Craig and I walked our dogs, talked about solving the world's problems, and critiqued theater, movies, and books. Poor Bette, she had to hear almost every detail, phrase, and footnote of the manuscript. But our walks and her friendship saved my sanity.

Finally, I acknowledge with love and loss my dear friend, sister, colleague, and comrade Rosalyn Fraad Baxandall. We were together in women's groups, on picket lines, and in demonstrations; we spoke about the women's liberation movement at conferences and rallies; and we traveled together, played tennis (she always won!), rode bikes, skied, took hikes, and went to the theater, the opera, and movies. She commented on my writings, offering insightful (and inciteful) comments. She died in 2015. Throughout this writing process, every time I faced a dilemma, I wished she were here to help me thrash out the issue.

Introduction

ON JUNE 27, 1967, I happily entered into the oldest dyadic and oppressive heterosexual patriarchal institution—marriage (figure I.1). I was twenty-two and madly in love. I had just come back from a year and a half on a college work-study program in London and Leeds, England. Then, like many middle-class White women of my generation, I followed my husband to Seattle to pursue his graduate studies at the University of Washington (UW). My goal was to finish up my senior year, then go on to graduate school in history.

We spent our honeymoon driving from New York City to Seattle. When we crossed the Columbia River into Washington State, we joyously sang Woody Guthrie's "Roll On, Columbia, Roll On": "And on up the river is the Grand Coulee Dam, / The mightiest thing ever built by a man, / To run the great factories and water the land, / So roll on, Columbia, roll on." We drove west on I-90, through the Cascade Mountains over Snoqualmie Pass, then crossed Lake Washington and arrived in Seattle.

I remember that day vividly. Unlike most days in Seattle, it was not overcast or raining. The sun was bright. Lake Washington was glittering, and both mountain ranges—the Cascades to the east and Olympics to the west—were shining. Even Mount Rainier "was out," as Seattleites say. We drove along Lake Washington Boulevard through the University of Washington Arboretum to our rented houseboat on Portage Bay Place West. We settled in, got a dog, registered for our classes at the UW, and enthusiastically participated in the city's radical politics. Three months later, I joined the women's liberation movement. That movement transformed my life—sometimes I think it saved my life—and gave it direction.[1]

Figure I.1 / Barbara Winslow's
formal wedding portrait, June 27, 1967.
Personal collection.

THIS BOOK TELLS the story of the radical women's liberation movement in Seattle, Washington, from 1965 to 1975. It describes the women who founded these organizations, their activities, their publications, their arguments, the challenges they faced, their disappointments, their short-term successes and lasting achievements. Not very much is known or written about Seattle's Left feminist history. Linda Gordon, a historian and early women's liberation activist in Boston's Bread and Roses, may not have known about Seattle when she wrote about "founding events" illustrating "major areas of women's movement activism." She cites New York as the location of the founding event regarding abortion in 1969, even though women's liberation activists in Seattle had begun organizing for abortion reform in 1968 and participated in the first statewide referendum in the US supporting a woman's right to abortion. She lists the University of Massachusetts Boston's struggle for day care as a founding first, yet Seattle's Left feminists began agitating for day care at the UW in 1968. The "first" rape relief center and the "first" battered women's shelter were founded in Seattle. Two other legendary radical feminist activists and writers, Alix Kates Shulman and Honor Moore, write that the Chicago Westside Group was "widely considered the country's first women's liberation group; but Seattle Radical Women was founded in October 1967."[2] This may sound like Seattle boosterism or nitpicky criticism, but these examples illustrate the need for a book about Seattle's place in radical feminist history. My hope is that this book will inspire others to write their own local histories and discover their communities' "firsts," adding to our understanding of the breadth of the radical women's liberation movement.

In the heady days of the women's liberation movement, we all read Maya Angelou's *I Know Why the Caged Bird Sings*. One phrase from that revelatory book, "In the struggle lies the joy," sums up my life as a women's liberation activist.[3] It was in the struggle—in meetings, arguing, consciousness raising, writing, demonstrating, denouncing, picketing, teaching, sitting in, getting arrested, leafleting, putting up posters, listening and learning, and, sadly, sometimes posturing and pontificating—that we created a movement of comradeship and sisterhood. In my lifetime, the women's liberation movement has transformed every facet of our lives. We changed the ways we work, play, think, worship, organize our families, educate children, vote, reproduce, legislate, adjudicate, make love, and make war. We changed the ways we look at gender. Women's liberation is revolution—but our revolution was different from history's gendered images of charismatic leaders, clashing armies, and forcible seizures of power. In our feminist revolution, we were on the barricades, demonstrated in the streets, led political parties, and even took up arms. Millions more organized this social revolution in the often-ignored women's domains of schools, factories, offices, kitchens, bedrooms, hospitals, libraries, backyards, marketplaces, community centers, and places of worship. Much of this feminist revolution has been local and decentralized, most of our leaders unknown and unnamed.

While women as a group have not (yet) seized power, have not overthrown any government or nation-state, do not control any national economy, and do not dominate any national political party, we have challenged the pervasive belief that women's work is less valuable than men's and that we ourselves are worth less. Women's lives today would be unrecognizable to our grandmothers. At the same time, we know that we have not done enough to confront and resolve the global crises of the environment, White supremacy, inequality, injustice, xenophobia, state violence, and war—all of which are profoundly gendered. We continue to struggle to create an egalitarian society in which liberating relationships subvert the hierarchies of class, race, gender, and sexualities.

The history of the Seattle women's liberation movement is important because there are very few histories of the women's liberation movement in places other than Boston, Chicago, New York, and Washington, DC, all of which were major academic, financial, media, and political centers.[4] Studies of feminist activism in other cities and regions, as well as smaller towns and rural areas across the United States, would shed light on the diversity of those involved, the issues they focused on, and the range of organizations they founded. As in any city or town, Seattle's radical feminism reflected its particular demographic, historical, political, and geographic circumstances.

Feminist historians, many of whom were active in the women's movement, are involved in an ongoing and evolving discussion about the origins of the women's liberation movement. Sara Evans, a women's liberation activist and historian, traced its origins in her pathbreaking book *Personal Politics: The Roots of Women's Liberation in the Civil Rights Movement and the New Left.*[5] Later studies point to the influences of the Old Left and labor movements. In his biography of Betty Friedan, Daniel Horowitz emphasizes that "we already understand how left politics of the 1940s and 1950s shaped the civil rights movement. Friedan's life underscores the fact that the other significant social movement of the 1960s—feminism—also has important origins in the two preceding decades."[6] Rosalyn Baxandall, a trailblazing radical feminist activist and historian, documented the connections between African American women's activism and the women's liberation movement.[7] Baxandall and Linda Gordon compiled an anthology called *Dear Sisters* with original documents from the women's liberation movement that point to the influences of the labor and welfare rights movements.[8] In "'This Battlefield Called Life': Black Traditions of Black Women," historian Robin D. G. Kelley discusses the origins of intersectional feminist activism.[9] Sheila Rowbotham, a British historian and women's liberation activist, reminded us that women's resistance to 1950s and 1960s stereotypes of femininity could also be traced to the impact of the African American rhythms of Motown and the somewhat androgynous sounds of the Beatles.[10] All these factors—the Old Left, the labor and civil rights movements, music—combined to create social upheaval in Seattle as well as across the US.

What made the women's liberation movement in Seattle distinctive was the pivotal role of unabashed socialists, Maoists, Trotskyists, anarchists, antiracists, and anti-imperialists in founding the first Left feminist groups. This took some courage. From the late 1940s through the early 1960s, anticommunists led by Joseph McCarthy had persecuted and largely silenced the Left. In Washington State, the Canwell Committee, the Seattle hearings of the House Un-American Activities Committee, and the Seattle Smith Act trials had terrified leftists and brought organizing to a halt.[11] Hundreds lost jobs, homes, and income; families broke up; some activists were jailed; and a few of those who were targeted committed suicide. In Seattle, however, a handful of gutsy women publicly defied the right wing and founded anti-imperialist, antiracist, socialist feminist organizations. A number of the founding members of the women's liberation movement had weathered the recent Red Scare. The Leninists of the Old Left had never supported feminism, looking upon it as bourgeois. Marxist orthodoxy privileged class over gender, race, and sexuality. It theorized that the primary contradiction in all societies was the class struggle, whose resolution was necessary before all other social problems—race, gender, and sexuality— could be solved. New Left socialist feminists challenged that paradigm, developing analyses that connected gender, class, race, and sexuality, the beginnings of what is now understood as theories of intersectionality. They also opposed the top-down authoritarianism of Leninism. Left, antiracist, anti-imperialist socialist feminists were an active, vocal, and leading presence in Seattle right from the start. They infused the women's liberation movement with a political perspective that was more inclusive in terms of class and race and more aware of women's economic position. Very little has been written about the role of socialists and left-wing organizations in founding the women's liberation movement; they are featured in this history.

The accomplishments of the Seattle women's liberation movement include the passage of Referendum 20 in 1970, the first popular vote that liberalized abortion laws in the US; coalition work involving Black, Latinx, Asian American and Pacific Islander, indigenous, White, and lesbian, gay, bisexual, and transgender activists; the expansion of antiracist feminist health care; and the creation of women-controlled rape crisis centers, divorce cooperatives, shelters for battered women, and lesbian feminist resource centers. Left feminists, all of whom were active in opposing the US government's war in Vietnam, challenged White men on issues of gender, race, and class in the antiwar movement and integrated gender into theories about war, peace, and imperialism.

Women new to political activism described themselves (in the language of the 1960s) as revolutionaries, meaning that they wished to overthrow the existing capitalist, racist, imperialist, and patriarchal order, and they learned how to navigate complicated political structures as they struggled for day care, health care, and Indian fishing rights; supported the strikes of Farah and farm workers; or advocated for the hiring of women of color on the UW faculty. They confronted many difficult questions: Should revolutionary women campaign for reforms and engage in electoral politics? How do radicals work with reformists and not get co-opted? How can revolutionary feminists insulate themselves from the lure of power and privilege that media attention and money can bring? Is it possible to build inclusive intersectional organizations and coalitions? All these challenges faced by Left feminists in the 1960s are being debated today by activists in the Black Lives Matter, #MeToo, reproductive justice, voting rights, and climate movements.

Women of color played foundational roles in the radical women's liberation movement in Seattle, even though the city was 94 percent White.[12] Women of color did not form their organizations in reaction to racism within the White women's movement or in response to sexism within the Black Power movement. In fact, they had had their own organizations for more than a century, even though some may not have been identified as feminist. As early as 1964–65, for example, women in the civil rights movement in the South were engaged in activist work that might later be termed women's liberation.[13]

Here is another reason why local histories are so important to a fuller understanding of the politics of race and radical feminism. In Seattle, the racial-ethnic order was not binary, White/Black, but White/Black/Asian American and Pacific Islander/Latinx/Indigenous. Reading the African American, Latinx, underground, feminist, and college and university newspapers and newsletters; discovering leaflets; and interviewing participants yields insights into class, racial, and gender politics. Contrary to popular mythology, the radical women's liberation movement was not an all-White movement. Women of color were founders of Seattle's first three women's liberation organizations, wrote for radical feminist publications, and formed autonomous coalitions, called Women of Color and Third World Women, at the same time. Nonetheless, most women's liberation groups were overwhelmingly White, and White supremacy, racism, racial cluelessness, tone deafness, and indifference often characterized majority-White feminist groups and activities. But in these early years, Seattle's socialist and anti-imperialist White women tried to be allies. We tried to build coalitions, sometimes successfully and at other times ending in acrimonious splits. Women of color found themselves having to struggle with White women as well as men of color in their families, neighborhoods, and political organizations.

Local history can dispel many of the antifeminist characterizations of women's liberation that have become part of current misogynist mythology. The women's liberation movement has been characterized as hostile to housewives, motherhood, and children. Our early campaigns for childcare dispel that myth. Feminists have been accused of hating men, hating sex, hating lesbians, or being lesbians; they were (and still are) caricatured as humorless, vindictive, vengeful, and demanding of special privileges. And of course, some charged that women become feminists because they are ugly and can't catch a man. The chapters in this book take apart these false characterizations, with documentation and a sense of humor.

This book begins in 1965 and ends in 1975, dates that mark the beginning and demise of the first socialist, anti-imperialist, and antiracist women's organizations. Women's liberation consciousness and organizing did not end in 1975, but later left-wing, socialist feminist, and socialist lesbian organizations had even shorter life-spans than the first groups. By the mid-1970s the political landscape in Seattle and the US was changing. There was an unanticipated and relentless backlash against the women's movement, and the Black movement was decimated by murderous assaults directed by the Nixon administration. Liberals and leftists shifted their focus from local to national priorities. White Christian nationalism, right-wing media, corporate opposition to the social safety nets of Franklin D. Roosevelt's New Deal and Lyndon B. Johnson's Great Society, White opposition to the gains made by the civil rights movement, and misogynist attacks on women's rights kept liberals, progressives, socialists, and Left feminists on the defensive.

I was able to research and write this book because I was a founder of Seattle's first two women's liberation organizations and was very active in radical politics. In 1969, while in England I joined the British International Socialists, an Old and New Left Trotskyist organization, and was a member of the

US International Socialists through the 1970s. I managed to save over four boxes of archival material, including leaflets, pamphlets, photographs, news clippings, and handwritten notes of meetings, speeches, and talks. Ephemeral documents are difficult or impossible to find in archives and have been indispensable in reconstructing this story. I decided to write this book not only because few histories of feminism consider places like Seattle but also because much of what is written about the women's liberation movement is cloaked in left-wing misogyny. No other White-dominated progressive organizations or movements are attacked as vehemently as feminist ones. For example, I have yet to hear or read of male-dominated groups described as the "all-White Students for a Democratic Society" (SDS), the "predominantly White antiwar movement," or the "overwhelmingly White student movement." The SDS chapter at the UW, the UW Committee to End the War in Vietnam, and the Student Mobilization Committee were far Whiter than Seattle Radical Women or Women's Liberation–Seattle. Even feminist writers in the twenty-first century damn women's liberation activists with faint praise. In *The Fire This Time: Young Activists and the New Feminism*, Vivian Labatan and Dawn Lindy Martin acknowledge that their "feminism has *roots* in past feminist work," and then comes the "but." Without distinguishing between mainstream feminism and radical socialist feminism, they charge that 1960s and 1970s feminists "placed a select few issues at the center of what is thought of as feminist activism, neglecting the full range of experiences that inform women's lives." Furthermore, they claim that the movement "operated from a monolithic center" and was inattentive "to racial, cultural and national differences."[14]

I am acutely aware of the difficulties and challenges facing anyone writing about this recent and contested past. In the past twenty years I have read hundreds of critiques of the movement, as well as attending and participating in conferences, seminars, and forums. In comparison to other groups (except perhaps for the civil rights and Black Power movements), few progressive social movements get such intense pushback and criticism. I think that this tendency is partly due to the deep societal resonances of issues related to race, gender, and sexuality, but it is also due to the activists themselves. Some feel and say that no one can write about the movement in which they participated because no one else can write about their experience. The women's liberation movement was intensely personal *and* political, but it has been demonized by both the Right and the Left since its emergence in the late 1960s. Moreover, feminist activists often repudiate and severely criticize their own and their predecessors' mistakes, as if the movement did not need to learn from experience and could have birthed today's intersectional theory as if it were Athena, the goddess of wisdom, emerging fully formed from the head of Zeus.

Seattle's story disproves many of these assertions. Feminists have been more self-critical of the exclusionary character of early women's liberation groups, have recognized that Black feminism developed at the same time, and have formed more inclusive coalitions and organizations than most mixed-gender, predominantly White groups. Much of the writing about the women's liberation movement, except for the collections of its writings, fails to capture the elation we experienced as we created a new world. In the early years of the movement, we were "ecstatic utopians," as Naomi Weisstein, founding Chicago women's liberation activist and musician in the Women's Liberation Rock Band, put it.[15] We were determined, dedicated, and fierce, but we also had fun. Sisterhood was powerful, contentious, difficult, and joyous.

Even with my four boxes of original materials, researching Seattle's radical feminism was daunting. Our groups did not always keep minutes. Very few of us saved our personal documents. Some were concerned about police or FBI raids and did not want to save what might be considered incriminating evidence. We did not realize that our leaflets, speeches, posters, and photos would be important for future researchers. To my knowledge, only Grey Osterud's diary exists as a day-by-day, week-to-week record of a group's political discussions. Today, I beg younger activists to save their emails, tweets, and images for future historians. I interviewed over twenty-five women and spent years trying to find other activists. A few, embittered by past faction fighting, refused an interview, and even though they were important activists I chose not to name them in the book out of respect for their viewpoint. Other women could not remember events or dates, so an interview was not helpful. But most were eager to talk, and their stories are an integral part of this book. Other information came from autobiographies and histories by participants.[16] Online histories such as HistoryLink.org and the UW's Seattle Civil Rights and Labor History Project provided me with local histories as well as interviews with activists.[17] Finally, I was able to access the papers of a number of organizations and participants in the Archives and Special Collections at the University of Washington Libraries. I have deposited my four boxes of materials there as well.[18]

As I researched this period, I was surprised to find myself in more newspaper stories, leaflets, and newsletters than I was aware of at the time, or at least could recall (figure I.2). I did not want to write an autobiography or memoir. My Seattle experiences are included in two anthologies of feminist memoirs.[19] I could not write a first-hand account; although I lived in Seattle

Figure I.2 / Barbara Winslow at a demonstration against the US war in Vietnam, 1969. Photograph by Paul Dorpat.

from 1967 to 1973, I was not in the city from August 1969 to September 1970 and for three months in 1971. Instead, I decided to write a history of a movement in which I was an active participant. I know this presents challenges of emotional involvement and bias. Today historians are urged to interrogate and reflect on their own personal biases and predispositions as they teach, research, and write about historical events. I certainly hope I have.[20] During this period, I was in a Trotskyist group; I hope I have reined in any past sectarian impulses. As I went through the material, I found that some of my recollections of events were simply wrong, and a number of my judgments of some participants and groups at the time were not based on facts.

A word about the language I use. The phrases *women's movement* and *women's liberation* are not interchangeable. *Women's movement* refers to the more mainstream, moderate, reform, liberal, or, in our day, bourgeois women's movement, best exemplified by the National Organization for Women and the National Women's Political Caucus. The term *women's liberation movement* refers to those feminists who identified as anticapitalist, antiracist, and anti-imperialist and called for liberation from all forms of patriarchy.[21] For the most part I use the language of the period. For example, *Chicano/a*, not *Latinx*, because in the 1960s Mexican American youths used *Chicano* as a politically charged self-identification. Activists in the struggle to protect Indigenous lands were involved in a group called Indian Fishing Rights; *Indo-China* was the imperialist term for Vietnam, Laos, and Cambodia. I do not use the derogatory term *Trotskyite* for Trotskyists and rely on the terms used by groups that identified as Maoist or Stalinist. The Weatherman faction considered themselves revolutionaries, and that is how they are described.[22] Three women, Lee Mayfield, Anne Schweisow, and Theresa Williams, changed their names after this period; I use their earlier names because that is how they appear in the documents. I capitalize *White* as well as *Black*. I agree with Nell Painter: "In terms of racial identity, white Americans have had the choice of being something vague, something unraced and separate from race. A capitalized 'White' challenges that freedom, by unmasking 'Whiteness' as an American racial identity as historically important as 'Blackness,' which it certainly is. No longer should White people be allowed the comfort of this racial invisibility; they should have to see themselves as raced."[23]

This book is an accessible, readable, nonacademic history. But there are a lot of endnotes and explanations. I structured it this way in part because much of feminist history is so contested that I felt compelled to prove almost everything I wrote. In addition, extensive endnotes are necessary because we know so little about our local history. With the passage of time, we forget the names of people and movements etched in our memories. For example, how many readers remember going years without eating a grape? Perhaps my endnote fanaticism provides resources for further studies. I try to include the names of as many activists as possible. Too many times women who play central roles in history are left out, ignored, or unrecognized. I want as many as possible included and remembered. I have included a glossary of left-wing organizations and political positions, for the language we used in the 1960s is no longer the language we use today.

Because of my over fifty-year involvement, I decided to end this book with self-reflection, in particular on issues of race, abortion, White supremacy, and beauty. What have I learned? Are there regrets? What went wrong? Did our actions have unanticipated consequences? How has the work of younger scholar-activists influenced my perspective? How has my life changed?

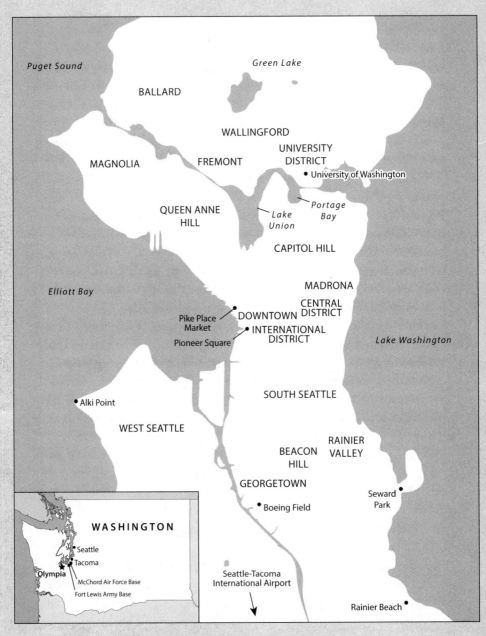

Map 1.1. / Map of Seattle neighborhoods.
Map drawn by Christine Riggio.

It's Reigning Men

1

I MOVED TO SEATTLE IN 1967, before Starbucks, Amazon, and Microsoft dominated the economy. Its population was 550,000. About 200,000 jobs had been lost since the 1950s, largely because of the economic problems facing the Boeing Airplane Company, then the state's largest employer. The city was affordable for students, young people, and white- and blue-collar workers. Our first home was a rented houseboat on Portage Bay, a small body of water between Lake Washington and Puget Sound (map 1.1). At that time, our neighborhood was nowhere near as upscale as the location of Tom Hanks's houseboat depicted in the movie *Sleepless in Seattle*. The renters were artists, students, professors, and hippies or "fringies," meaning people on the fringes of society, an appellation my husband and I embraced. We loved our neighborhood. Up the hill was the notorious Red Robin tavern (not today's franchised one), a raucous and popular bar frequented by New and Old Lefties, fringies, and the University of Washington (UW) rugby team. Under the Freeway bridge was Freeway Hall, headquarters of the Freedom Socialist Party, a popular center for left-wing meetings and parties.

When developers evicted us from our houseboat, we moved to Madrona, a liberal and left-wing enclave in the predominantly African American Central District. With its political radicals and its racial and ethnic diversity, Madrona suited us. We enjoyed its spectacular views of Lake Washington and the Cascades and the eight miles of parks and beaches along Lake Washington. The three-bedroom house we sublet was amazingly affordable for two graduate students. Aaron Dixon, captain of the Seattle Black Panther Party, enthused, "Madrona was a little paradise of Asian, White and Black families, a bit removed from the rest of the city." "Up on Madrona," he remembered, "we kids were largely insulated from the tentacles of racism."[1] We lived just two blocks from the Black Panther Party headquarters, and we knew and worked with many of its members. While Madrona residents experienced a semblance of racial comity, they also suffered from ongoing police brutality and repression. On October 5, 1968, the police shot and killed Black Panther member Welton (Butch) Armstead. The next day, there was a shootout between the Panthers and the police in our front yard while we hid in our cellar. Madrona was not quite "paradise."

WHEN I MOVED TO SEATTLE, its population was 94 percent White. Residents had varied ethnic backgrounds: Scandinavians from the Midwest, Italians and Jews from the East Coast, and substantial proportions of Asians, mostly Japanese Americans but also Chinese, Filipinos, and Koreans. Only 4.8 percent were African Americans, most of whom did not come directly from the rural South but from other cities in the North and Midwest. Latinx people were counted as White on the 1960 census, although in 1970, according to MeChA (Movimiento Estudiantil Chicano de Aztlán, the Chicano Student Movement), there may have been as many as 6,000 Chicanos in Seattle, with about 1,400 children in the public school system.[2] Asian Pacific Islanders represented 3.1 percent of the population, and 0.8 percent were Indigenous—American Indians and Native Alaskans.[3]

In spite of its racial and ethnic diversity, Seattle was a segregated city, as committed to White supremacy as any locality in America. Restrictive covenants on real estate banning owners from selling houses to members of racial and religious minority groups created residential segregation. There were Japanese, Korean, and Chinese neighborhoods. Japantown was obliterated after the United States declared war on Japan in 1941; over eight thousand of its residents were rounded up and incarcerated in Minidoka, Idaho.[4] African Americans lived in the Central District; Scandinavians lived in Ballard. Prohibitions of sales to Asians, Jews, and Catholics as well as African Americans generated marginal pockets of mixed Asian, Jewish, Catholic, and Black families with middle-class incomes or aspirations just inside the boundaries of "good" schools.[5]

One topographical feature that shaped the city is the narrow isthmus between Puget Sound and Lake Washington on which Seattle was originally built. The other key feature is its many hills, which broke up its street grid. Small, closely spaced single-family houses created neighborhoods that were neither classically urban nor contemporarily suburban. Finally, there was a visible contrast between Seattle's rundown waterfront and central business district and its shining cultural institutions, some of them downtown and others in public parks.

During and after World War II, Seattle's economic base was transformed from fishing, lumbering, and shipping to military bases, shipbuilding, and other war industries. With the growth of container shipping, Seattle became the United States' leading port on the Pacific, surpassing the San Francisco Bay Area. Boeing, a key defense corporation, made the B-52 nuclear bomber and missile guidance systems, as well as passenger planes. The city's recent rapid growth and its complex racial-ethnic mix generated a degree of social fluidity. These features created a rather strange combination of social liberalism with a hegemonic military and defense industry on which the people and economy of the city and region were heavily dependent.

The women's liberation movement—its participants, demonstrations, organizations, storefronts, communal homes, and headquarters—centered in a number of neighborhoods in and near Seattle. North of Portage Bay is the UW, often pronounced "U Dub." It had over fifty thousand students, faculty, and staff, and other people came to visit, play, or hang out on its open campus. The university was the second-largest employer in Washington State as well as in the city, so it dominated life in Seattle. Left-wing students, as well as faculty and staff, regarded it as an employer as well as an educational institution, which explains why so many campaigns centered on the campus. Just one unit within the university focused on female students, the Women's Commission of the Associated Students of the UW (ASUW). Formerly called the ASUW Women, it was dominated by the sororities until 1970.[6] The nearby University District (called the U District) was peopled by students, academics, hippies, and street people and included head shops, coffee shops, the "alternative" Id Bookstore, an independent movie theater, and the Coffee Corral, which housed the Free University. On Forty-Fifth Street, which bisected the U District, was the Blue Moon Tavern, a haven for artists and radicals and one of the very few racially integrated bars. It reeked of stale beer and cigarette and marijuana smoke; people danced on the floor and on tables, argued about politics, and hooked up. During World War II it was the only bar outside the Central District to serve African American servicemen. The tavern also provided a haven for UW professors who had been fired and blacklisted during the McCarthy period. Regulars included authors Tom Robbins and

Darrell Bob Houston; poets Theodore Roethke, Richard Hugo, Carolyn Kizer, Stanley Kunitz, and David Wagoner; and painters Mark Tobey, William Cumming, Richard Gilkey, and Leo Kenney. Visitors included Dylan Thomas, Ken Kesey, Allen Ginsberg, and Mik Moore. Indicating the international notoriety of this tavern, in 1991, Mikhail Gorbachev, the last president of the Union of Soviet Socialist Republics, asked his English-language interpreter, Ross Lavroff, "So you're from Seattle. How is the Blue Moon?"[7] After the rise of the women's liberation movement, the Blue Moon lost favor with women because of rampant sexual harassment.[8]

West of the University District were Wallingford, Fremont, and Ballard, affordable neighborhoods that were popular with students, graduates, hippies, and left-wing activists. Downtown was dominated by department stores, as well as the Space Needle and the Monorail built for the 1962 World's Fair. The Pike Place Market, overlooking the Elliott Bay waterfront, was one of the oldest continuously operating public farmers' markets in the United States. Organized in 1907, it enabled small growers and fishermen to sell directly to consumers. In the 1960s it was not the tourist trap it is today. Most shoppers were working- and middle-class Seattleites looking for fresh fruit, vegetables, and seafood.[9] Pioneer Square, site of the first White settlement on the isthmus, was south of the market. Pioneer Square was also called "hobotown" because of its dilapidated, abandoned buildings and the large number of homeless people sleeping on the streets. The Moore Theater, located north of Pioneer Square and the Pike Place Market, was the city's oldest continuously running theater, and it brought popular groups such as the Grateful Dead to perform.[10] George Wallace, running for the presidency in 1968 on an openly racist platform, held a rally there.

The Capitol Hill neighborhood was located on a steep hill just east of downtown. Lesbians and gays began moving there in the early 1960s, and today Capitol Hill is the heart of Seattle's LGBTQIA community. Seattle Central Community College educated those African American and White working-class students who could not go to the UW and was a center of civil rights and feminist political activism. Atop Capitol Hill, Volunteer Park, one of the highlights of Seattle's Olmsted Parks and Boulevards system, was a venue for many antiwar, antidraft, antiracist, and feminist protests as well as gay pride and LGBTQ festivals. Rock bands such as the Grateful Dead, Ike and Tina Turner, and Jimi Hendrix performed there.

To the south was Boeing Field, with many runways, hangars, factories, and administrative buildings. Farther south down I-5 was the Seattle-Tacoma Airport, called SeaTac, which during the war in Vietnam was the second-largest disembarkation point for US troops. Tacoma, an industrial working-class city heavily polluted by the pulp and paper mills, was farther south and west. The state capital, Olympia, lay another thirty miles south. Just west of Olympia were two huge military bases, US Army Base Fort Lewis and McChord Air Force Base, which were centers of antiwar activism.

IN 1967, WOMEN OUTNUMBERED MEN in Washington State. Racial and gender discrimination existed everywhere in the US: in politics, the economy, religion, the family, and society at large. Washington State was no exception. The state government was a male preserve. Dan Evans, the Republican governor, was White and male, as was every governor before him. The lieutenant governor, secretary of state, state auditor, attorney general, state treasurer, superintendent of public instruction, and commissioner of public lands were all White males.[11] The legislature's fifty-member senate was all White and all male. The one-hundred-member house of representatives included nine women, all White, listed according to their marital status: *Mrs.* Kathryn Epton, *Mrs.* Joseph E. Hurley, and, because she was single, Doris Johnson.[12] All nine judges of the state supreme court were White men; so were all of its appointed officers. In 1965, only three women served in any top state administrative positions, which were appointive, not elective: the state librarian, the director of the Department of Licenses, and a member of the Board of Prison Terms and Paroles.

White men governed cities and towns. In 1960, 265 of the state's 267 mayors were men; White men were 934 of the 1,000 city and town council members. Even school board members were 89 percent male. That figure seems startling given the predominance of women among elementary school teachers, but the vast majority of school administrators were men. Gender parity could be found only among municipal treasurers, clerks, and finance commissioners: 128 men, 139 women. Women predominated on library boards; indeed, 98 percent of their members were women, reflecting the gendered character of librarianship and the fact that many public libraries had been established through the advocacy of women's groups and women continued to serve them as volunteers.[13]

In terms of national representation, both US senators were White men. Of the seven Whites who constituted the state's delegation in the US House of Representatives, two were women, Democrat Julia Butler Hansen and Republican Catherine D. May.

Under White male dominance, women had fought for and won political rights. In 1910, the all-male and all-White Washington State legislature voted to enfranchise women. In 1920, the Nineteenth Amendment to the

US Constitution enfranchised all women citizens—but only in principle. As recent scholarship has demonstrated, Black women were often excluded from voting, as race trumped gender.[14] According to the Commission on the Status of Women in Washington State, women in the Pacific Northwest voted in the largest proportion of any region in the country, yet 28 percent of eligible women did not vote in the 1960 presidential election, when John F. Kennedy defeated Richard Nixon.[15] A state law enacted in 1890 prohibited women from holding a statewide elective office until it was repealed with only one dissenting vote in 1963.[16]

In 1967, the mayor of Seattle was a White male. One woman, Myrtle Edwards, sat on the all-White, nine-member city council. The president of the Seattle School Board was a White man; one woman served with four men. The police chief and fire chief were both White men. Although women were over 30 percent of the paid labor force, all of the labor union presidents were male, making the Seattle Central Labor Council all male. So was the Seattle Chamber of Commerce. In 1963, the US Chamber of Commerce testified at a US Senate labor subcommittee hearing that it opposed any and all legislation mandating that women receive equal pay for equal work. There is no record of the Washington State or Seattle Chamber of Commerce opposing the national organization's point of view.[17] Men headed the largest employers, the UW and the Boeing and Weyerhaeuser corporations.

In the 1960s, women citizens in Washington State could vote; could serve on juries and as guardians, trustees, administrators, and executors of estates; and were granted equal inheritance rights. Legally, women were allowed to enter any occupation, vocation, profession, or calling on the same terms as men. Unmarried and married women had the same rights to control property; so did wives and husbands. Legal inequities persisted, however. Women chosen to serve on juries could claim exemption based on sex. In marriage, the husband had the right to manage and control the community property, all the money earned, property bought, and debts incurred during marriage. A married couple's legal domicile, which was used to establish residence for voting, holding public office, jury service, taxation, and probate, was fixed by the husband. In cases where a wife sued or could be sued, the husband, with few exceptions, had to be a party to the legal action.[18] Only heterosexuals could legally marry. Contraception was difficult and expensive to obtain, even for married women. Abortion was illegal. In sum, in terms of public, political, and economic power and civic responsibility, White men dominated and controlled women by accruing all public power, as well as maintaining possession of household resources.

Women were everywhere in the public sphere—but not visible, powerful, recognized, well paid, or appreciated. In 1960, the typical woman working in the paid labor force was a forty-one-year-old high school graduate. Employed women were 31 percent of all workers in the state and 34 percent of the state's female population, and their numbers were rising. One woman in three in the paid labor force was married; Black women accounted for just 3 percent of the paid labor force, yet 37 percent of all women of color worked for wages or salaries and 59 percent of them were married.[19]

The job market was sharply segregated along racial and gender lines. The majority of women were channeled into stereotypically feminine occupations, especially teaching, nursing, social work, and clerical and service jobs. According to the Washington State Department of Labor's statistics for 1960, *all* of the state's engineers were men. Only 8 percent of farmers were women, and just a handful of them were Black, Asian American, or Indigenous. No Black women were listed as managers, officials, or proprietors of businesses. Women outnumbered men two to one in clerical work; no men were listed as secretaries, stenographers, or typists. Most educational leaders were men, although two-thirds of elementary and secondary schoolteachers were women. Only one-fourth of all federal employees in Washington State were women.

While a rising proportion of women were entering the paid labor force, their earnings reflected clear sex and race discrimination. In 1959, Washington's working women had median earnings of $2,351 a year, about 57 percent of those of men. Black women earned only a little more than half as much as White women. All women were economically disadvantaged, although not to the same extent. Men received larger retirement benefits, even compared to women with the same length of employment and rate of earnings. Although in theory women working for the federal government earned equal pay for equal work, the overwhelming majority of women were employed in lower-paid, primarily clerical jobs. Women with employed husbands had to pay higher family health insurance rates than married men. If a woman worked for the federal government, there were no survivor benefits for a husband who had not depended entirely on his late wife's earnings, yet widows received benefits regardless of their financial situation.

Employed mothers faced the greatest obstacles, especially concerning childcare. In 1960, married women made up more than half the female labor force in the state; over half of the 270,000 children under the age of eighteen had mothers in the workplace. A majority of employed women had children under six years of age who did not attend school. Black women made up 4 percent of the total number of employed mothers, and 40 percent of them had children under six. Fully 11 percent of employed Black mothers were the sole wage earners in their households. Black mothers in the paid labor force carried an even heavier burden of family support than did White mothers.

Provisions for childcare were woefully inadequate. In 1960, 185,000 children whose mothers were employed were twelve years of age and younger, and 81,000 were under six. At the same time, there were only seven hundred state-licensed day care homes, with a combined capacity for 1,100 children, and thirty-three licensed private day care centers serving another 1,100 children. Grandparents, older siblings, other relatives, generous neighbors, and caring friends were not enough to fill the gap between childcare needs and childcare resources. The *Report of the Governor's Commission on the Status of Women* admitted that the greatest childcare needs were in low-income, working-class, and non-White communities. Furthermore, children were penalized by the federal tax code, which provided only a $600 exemption for each child in a household. The exemption ended when the child turned twelve, the assumption being that the child no longer needed close supervision. The commission recommended that tax deductions for childcare when both parents were employed be increased from $5,100 to $7,500, and that the age of children who could qualify for day care be raised from eleven to twelve years.[20]

Employers, who were overwhelmingly White and male, admitted to discriminating against working mothers. Their stated preference was for widowed, single, or divorced women who were the sole wage earners in their households. According to employers, a woman who was a sole breadwinner was "more apt to become dedicated to her job" than a woman who might be supported by a husband. They regarded other women as "Until Workers": women who "plan to work 'until marriage'; 'until the house is paid for'; 'until the car is paid for'; 'until the baby comes'; 'until her husband finishes college'; or any other number of 'untils.'"[21]

Women's educational aspirations were constantly demeaned. According to "The Place for Women," published in *Columns*, the UW alumni magazine, "There was a time when it was widely believed—rightly or wrongly—that most women attended the University primarily to achieve a goal not listed in any curriculum, and if in the process they gained a degree, that was pure gravy.... Degrees and husbands are now equally valued by the 'second sex.'" Discouraging women's academic aspirations at the UW had a deleterious effect, but in the early 1960s the gender imbalance was rapidly being reversed. "The data show that the proportion of men to women receiving the baccalaureate was 2:1 in 1960 but declined to roughly 1:1 in 1965."[22]

Women in Washington State were the vast majority of unpaid workers in civic and community organizations such as the League of Women Voters, the Red Cross, the Gray Ladies, the PTA, churches, and groups serving everyone from preschoolers to older citizens. Very few volunteer groups were racially diverse. Women of color expressed reluctance to join with White women because of their encounters with racist hostility, and instead they formed their own community and civic organizations.[23] Men led many fraternal groups that did community service, such as the Lions Clubs. Some had "ladies' auxiliaries" for members' wives and are now gender-mixed. These groups served mainly as a source of business contacts, but women's participation in volunteer work also helped their husbands' careers and established their middle-class status. Aside from joining fraternal groups, leading Boy Scout troops, and coaching boys in sports, men seldom participated in voluntary organizations.

EVEN THOUGH THE SOCIAL AND POLITICAL LANDSCAPE was very White and male, Washington State, and in particular the Seattle metropolitan area, had long been viewed as politically progressive, and its mix of radical and reform activism extended to women's rights.[24] Yet the city and the state had a shameful record of discrimination and violence against Chinese and Japanese residents, as well as against Indigenous communities.

In the late nineteenth century, anarchists, socialists, feminists, trade unionists, and other radicals organized utopian communities, many of which espoused heterodox ideals of gender equality. Many feminist radicals and suffrage leaders visited the state, campaigning for the vote, birth control, and sexual freedom. The Pacific Northwest branch of the National Association for the Advancement of Colored People (NAACP), founded in 1912, was led by Nettie C. Asberry, who was featured in a series on "The First Ladies of Colored America" in the NAACP magazine, *The Crisis*.[25]

The Socialist Party in Washington State was always dominated by its Left wing. Revolutionary syndicalists in the Industrial Workers of the World played a significant role in organizing unskilled laborers, not only in lumbering and shipping but also in manufacturing industries that employed women. During the Seattle General Strike of 1919, Anna Louise Strong, a left-wing journalist, was among its most prominent leaders. The first woman was elected to state office in 1912, just two years after women gained the right to vote in state elections. In 1926, Seattle's Bertha Knight Landes became the first woman elected mayor of a major US city.[26] During the 1930s and 1940s, the Communist Party was the largest left-wing organization and played a significant role in pushing the state's Democratic Party to the left. In fact, Washington State's left-leaning reputation led James Farley, postmaster general under Franklin D. Roosevelt, to issue his famous toast "to the forty-seven states and the Soviet of Washington."[27]

In comparison with other states, Washington's women enjoyed a somewhat more favorable legal status. In 1943, the state adopted an Equal Pay Act, which mandated equal pay for comparable work, although it was seldom enforced after the war ended. (The legislature passed another Equal Pay Act in 1963, but it was not enforced either.) In 1913, state legislators had passed a series of labor laws that provided working women with an eight-hour workday, as well as daily rest and meal periods. This set of "protections and privileges" was originally intended to prevent the exploitation of women and children employed in factories, who at that time had no legal rights, could not vote, and were not represented by organized labor, and therefore needed legal protection. By the 1960s, there was a growing consensus among politicians, policy makers, and some women's rights activists that protective laws should be abandoned because women and minors were no longer powerless and in need of state protection from employers. In Washington State, the move was to apply protection equally to men. The issue of protective legislation became an important debate within the women's movement in Seattle in 1970.

In 1961, President John F. Kennedy came under pressure from Esther Peterson, who directed the federal Women's Bureau, and other women in the Democratic Party who were concerned about the lack of progress regarding women's rights, to establish the Presidential Commission on the Status of Women.[28] It was chaired by Eleanor Roosevelt. The commission's 1963 report, *American Women*, as well as subsequent studies, thoroughly documented pervasive social, economic, and political discrimination against women. In response, several states established their own commissions to conduct statewide surveys on the status of women. Jo Freeman, an early women's liberation activist and the author of *The Politics of Women's Liberation*, wrote, "These commissions were often urged by politically active women and were comprised primarily of women. While many governors saw them as an easy opportunity to pay off political favors, many women saw them as opportunities to turn attention to their concerns." Freeman believed that these federal and state commissions laid the groundwork for the women's movement of the later 1960s and 1970s.[29]

Washington State governor Albert Rosellini, a liberal Democrat, was the second governor in the country to convene a commission to review the status of women.[30] The committee consisted of one honorary male member, seven full-time male members, and twenty-two women, and it was chaired by Mildred

Dunn, a prominent Democratic Party activist. Public meetings were held in the state's largest cities: Bellingham, Kennewick, Seattle, Spokane, Tacoma, Vancouver, and Yakima. All the work of the commission was carried out by the volunteer efforts of its members, which was common for state commissions. The forty-page report, published in December 1963, documented and analyzed women's economic, social, political, and legal position in the state. Its main points were that women's economic and political potential was sorely underutilized, that women in the labor force experienced serious economic discrimination, and that educational opportunities for women, beginning in kindergarten and extending through adulthood, were seriously lacking. What may seem surprising to readers today is that the majority-female commission also blamed women themselves for the economic and legal discrimination they experienced. The report explained that since women did not regard themselves as a permanent part of the workforce, it was understandable that employers would not want to hire women or give them promotions or raises.

Most of the recommendations urged voluntary action to include and involve more women in economic and political life. The report advocated for expanded vocational and higher education for women; called for more studies of the effects of mothers' employment on their children; came out against sex-specific job descriptions, in which job openings were commonly publicized under the headings "male only" and "female only"; encouraged more women to run for office; and urged the two political parties to seek out qualified women candidates. It recommended legislative action to repeal women's exemption from jury service on the basis of sex, to allow a married woman to sue in her own name, and to amend Washington State's protective legislation so that laws regulating conditions of labor would apply equally to all workers doing the same work, regardless of sex.[31] The report did not include information about Indigenous, Latina, or Asian American and Pacific Islander women, nor did it examine the impact of racism on women of color. There was no mention of the effects of the proposed Equal Rights Amendment (ERA) on employed women. Finally, the report lacked any discussion about the politics of women's bodies, such as how maternity benefits, the legalization of abortion, or accessible sex education would affect women's participation in the workforce.

Rosellini promised to act on the commission's recommendations. He pledged to "request that each department head take a good look at his own department to see that women are given an equal opportunity for leadership and equal employment" and "to direct the state personnel director to make an annual survey of positions open to women in the major state employment offices." He agreed to have the Department of Labor and Industries look into male-only and female-only job descriptions and to place more women in apprenticeship programs for the skilled trades.[32] Both the governor and the state legislature acted on a few of the report's recommendations, repealing an 1890 law making it illegal for women to hold public office, and ending the exemption of women from jury duty solely because of their sex.[33] But neither Rosellini nor his successor, Dan Evans, a liberal Republican, did anything more to implement its recommendations.[34]

The activities of the federal and state commissions were part of the beginning of a political awakening. In 1963 Betty Friedan's book *The Feminine Mystique* became a best seller, prompting many women to question the gendered status quo. Jo Freeman argued that the addition of the word *sex* to Title VII of the 1964 Civil Rights Act, prohibiting discrimination in employment, was the "third strand of incipient feminism."[35] These developments were the impetus behind the formation of the National Organization for Women (NOW) in 1965, which soon became the largest and most prominent organization of the women's movement.

All the contradictions of the ostensibly conservative and conformist 1950s were present in Seattle. Thomas Beecham, once the conductor of the Seattle Symphony Orchestra, pronounced the city an "esthetic dustbin."[36] Walter Crowley, an influential political and cultural activist, found Seattle "puny, provincial and puritanical."[37] Puritanism and provincialism were indeed aspects of Seattle's dominant culture. So was segregation, a conservative pro-business press, and a state dominated by rural interests. The growth of the Boeing Corporation, aided by the Cold War and the permanent arms economy, created a smug and self-confident pro-business elite that saw the 1962 World's Fair as its great accomplishment. Ironically, hosting the World's Fair helped bring about social change. Crowley recalled,

> The fair . . . salved Seattle's chronic inferiority complex as a parade of visitors marched through town: the Shah and Empress of Iran, Prince Philip of the United Kingdom, cosmonaut Gherman Titov (who scandalized the town by announcing that he had not seen God in space), astronaut John Glenn, New York Governor Nelson Rockefeller, Vice President Lyndon Johnson, Attorney General Robert Kennedy (who would become a frequent visitor and mountain-climbing companion of mountaineer Jim Whitaker), and entertainers Bob Hope, John Wayne and Elvis Presley. Elvis had not been in Seattle since performing at Sick's Stadium in 1957; and his return to film *It Happened at the World's Fair* virtually paralyzed the city.[38]

The World's Fair was a commercial success. It also began to crack Seattle's insularity. Its legacy included new cultural institutions as well as sports and performance venues.

Along with conformity and conservatism, the 1950s were a period of social, political, and cultural ferment, all of which contributed to the development of a radical women's liberation movement. Most important, the emergence of a radical, militant, Black-led civil rights movement broke the logjam of social and political reaction. As a result of the example set by civil rights activists, people were not as afraid to protest, express political ideas, or challenge authority as they had been since the heyday of McCarthyism. The Seattle branch of the Congress of Racial Equality (CORE) was the city's most prominent civil rights organization. Jeri Ware, a leading member, remembers that in the 1950s, "there were no black firefighters, garbage collectors, cooks in schools, no teachers. Thelma Dewitty was the first black teacher; unions fought against the hiring of black janitors and cooks."[39] Beginning in 1961, CORE led a selective-buying campaign to force downtown stores to hire more African Americans. It staged "shop-ins" at grocery stores and "shoe-ins" at Nordstrom's, one of Seattle's leading department stores, in an attempt to force retailers to change their hiring practices. That November, Martin Luther King Jr. made his first and only visit to the city.

By 1963, political organizing and demonstrations by African Americans and their allies began to force some change in the city's schools and housing. Adding to the militancy and racial awareness of African Americans, in August 1963 the Nation of Islam organized a Seattle chapter. On August 28, while 250,000 Americans marched on Washington, DC, for "jobs and freedom," 1,500 Seattleites rallied at the city's federal courthouse. The next month, between 3,000 and 5,000 supporters of open housing demonstrated at Garfield High School, a predominantly African American school in the Central District. This was the largest civil rights protest to date. After marches and sit-ins, the Seattle City Council agreed to create a human rights commission and to consider an open housing ordinance. Open housing was defeated by a two-to-one margin in a 1964 referendum. Progress in desegregating schools and housing and reducing police brutality against the Black community was very slow.[40] But it was not as slow as in cities such as Chicago, Philadelphia, and Baltimore, where Whites resisted with greater unanimity and more violence. Perhaps the difference was due to Seattle's larger Left and liberal presence, its proportionally smaller African American population, and the racial-ethnic diversity of its residents. Seattle's well-organized Japanese and Chinese communities also fought to desegregate the city.

There were a few striking successes. In 1962 Wing Luke, who was born in China, became the first person of color to be elected to the Seattle City Council and the highest-ranking Asian American elected official in the continental United States. A lawyer, Luke had led the Civil Rights Division in the state attorney general's office before running for the city council and fighting to end racial discrimination in housing. In 1963, the school board of Bellevue, an affluent White suburb of Seattle, named Donald Phelps as its first African American principal. In 1965, Charles Z. Smith was appointed Seattle's first African American judge, serving on the municipal court.[41] Even though the civil rights movement had limited success in ending racial discrimination, it revitalized the African American, left-wing, and liberal residents of the city; gave people courage to organize politically; and opened up new channels of public discussion.

Other strands of political ferment expressed opposition to the cultural status quo. In 1962, Lorenzo Milam, Gary Margasan, and John Gallant established the Jack Straw Memorial Foundation to operate an alternative radio station in Seattle.[42] In December 1963, radio station KRAB (AM 107.7), located in a converted donut shop in Seattle's U District, broadcast its first program. By 1967 there were at least four alternative high school newspapers, the *Advocate*, *Jacobin*, DARE, and the *Voice*.[43] The *University Herald*, a newspaper focused on the U District, warned its readers about the growing number of beatniks, later called hippies and fringies. The police began staging raids in the U District, arresting people for possession of marijuana.

Finally, radical political activity, long dormant because of the fear engendered by McCarthyism, emerged from the shadow of the early 1950s. In 1966, the Seattle chapter of the Trotskyist Socialist Workers Party (SWP), along with a group of high school students, waged a successful campaign to allow one of their spokespeople, Frank Krasnowsky, to speak at Ballard High School. Actor Marlon Brando and Robert "Bob" Satiacum, a member of the Puyallup Indian tribe, were arrested in 1964 during a Puyallup "fish-in" supporting Indian fishing rights.[44] In that same year, students from the UW picketed the Subversive Control Board, which was holding hearings on alleged communist activities in Washington State. The next year over two hundred students at the university attended the first teach-in on the Vietnam War.[45] All of these underground rumblings, marches, and "alternative" music and politics were part of larger changes taking place in the United States. Yet in Seattle, as elsewhere, it was still a man's world.

From the Woman Question to Women's Liberation

2

THE FIRST WOMEN'S LIBERATION GROUP in Seattle was organized in October 1967, when approximately twenty women met in the basement of Susan Stern's home in the University District. The meeting's organizers were apprehensive about whether this disparate group of White women, ranging in age from eighteen to fifty-eight and coming from widely divergent political backgrounds, would be able to find common ground. The main organizers of the meeting were women who belonged to or were connected with the Old Left of the 1930s and 1940s or the New Left of the 1960s.[1] In Seattle, contrary to impressions that are based on other places or on myths propagated by the media, the women's liberation movement did not spring up spontaneously; it did not emerge in reaction to the male chauvinism of any particular organizations; nor did it necessarily arise from women's experiences in the civil rights or antiwar movement. The close relationship between Old and New Left women in Seattle defined the political direction of the early women's liberation organizations, which combined Old Left politics with New Left imagination, audacity, and utopian vision. The early women's liberation groups did not separate themselves organizationally from Old Left organizations until New Left politics came to dominate the Seattle movement scene in 1969. Their links to the past, in particular with the labor, left, Black, welfare, and civil rights movements, grounded these early feminist organizations and enabled them to play important roles in Seattle's political struggles, especially the struggle to legalize abortion in Washington State. Younger women with little political experience but with a strong sense of social justice, enraged at the contradictions between their aspirations and abilities and the reality of their secondary status in relation to men, provided the catalyst and turned the Woman Question of the Old Left into the women's liberation movement of the New.

TO UNDERSTAND THE HISTORY of Seattle's radical women's liberation organizations, a brief account of left-wing organizations is necessary.[2] Depending on one's point of view, the history of the revolutionary Left in the United States is tortuously complicated, humorous, or underappreciated. A basic tenet shared by Marxists of all stripes was that socialism, a transitional form, and communism, its more advanced iteration, had to be international in order to transform the global economic and political order. The socialist and communist parties that existed in Seattle during the 1960s held a variety of differing viewpoints on ideology, organizational structures, and political strategies. Even before the Russian Revolution, European communists split into two camps. The Bolsheviks advocated a small party of revolutionaries who would lead an armed insurrection and would carry this movement across national boundaries. The Mensheviks called for a larger, more inclusive party and espoused a constitutional or parliamentary road to socialism. In the period this book covers, however, the term *Menshevik* was a loose pejorative, meaning that a Menshevik was either a Trotskyite (another pejorative) or a wimpy socialist; in contrast, the term *Bolshevik* signified toughness, bluster, and self-confidence. In the 1960s the men in the New Left who nicknamed themselves Bolshies tended to be strutting and sexist, but no male leftist wanted to be considered a Menshevik.

After the Russian Revolution of 1917, radicals in Europe and the Americas joined the Communist International. The US Communist Party (CP) responded to directives from the International and to distinctive developments in American politics. The CP played a significant role in the labor, unemployment, and Black movements in the 1920s and 1930s and supported antifascist efforts in the 1930s and 1940s. Hounded by the US government and McCarthyism, with many of its leaders jailed in the post–World War II period, the CP's influence declined in the 1950s. When it reemerged in the 1960s, it was less radical.

The 1928 split between the supporters of Vladimir Lenin and of Leon Trotsky left a lasting legacy in Seattle. This schism turned on questions of nationalism and internationalism: the followers of Trotsky opposed Joseph Stalin's insistence on "socialism in one country" and upheld the classical Marxist idea that only an international movement can defeat capitalism. Trotsky's supporters in the US founded the Socialist Workers Party (SWP) in 1938. The SWP and its youth group, the Young Socialist Alliance, had their greatest influence during the antiwar movement of the 1960s. The Trotskyist movement underwent numerous internal splits, with the formation of even smaller groups that all claimed the mantle of Trotsky.[3] Opponents of Trotskyism refer to its supporters pejoratively as Trotskyites, while proponents condemn their antagonists as Stalinists.

The success of the 1948 Chinese Revolution led by Mao Zedong precipitated further fractures. In the US, people who supported the view that peasants and other people outside the industrial proletariat can become revolutionaries called themselves Maoists. As the CP abandoned its support of Black self-determination within the US and national liberation movements swept Africa, Black nationalists and Pan-Africanists left the CP and founded their own militant organizations. Others on the Left modeled themselves on revolutionary leaders such as Cuba's Che Guevara and Vietnam's Ho Chi Minh. These tendencies, which emerged in both the Old and the New Left, offered alternatives to what some had come to see as stale, abstract debates that did not speak to the oppressive situations faced by the working class, women, and Africans Americans and other people of color in the contemporary US.

In this book, the term *Leninist* describes the structure of communist, Maoist, and most Trotskyist groups. They were organized on a top-down basis, called democratic centralism, which meant in practice that the leadership—usually White and male—decided policies and activities that rank-and-file members carried out without question. In addition, orthodox Leninists opposed any left-wing, Black, women's, and youth organizations that they did not control. *Old Left* refers to those left-wing political organizations, including the CP, Trotskyist organizations such as the SWP, the Freedom Socialist Party (FSP), the Maoist Progressive Labor Party, and, in Seattle, those people who professed pre-1960s anarchist politics. *New Left* refers to those radical and revolutionary individuals and groups that emerged in the 1960s, which broke from the hierarchical organizational structures of the Old Left and stressed personal liberation as part of the challenge to global imperialism and capitalism. But even in the New Left, the overarching centrality of class continued, as did fierce debates over the questions of national versus international socialist revolution and centralism versus internal democracy. While the story of the Left is rife with fissures, this is neither unique nor exclusive to socialist politics or socialism. Ideological right-wing and religious groups are as sectarian and factional as any on the Left.

ONE OF THE MOST IMPORTANT DEVELOPMENTS in the revival of socialist politics was the opening of the Free University of Seattle, which, according to Walt Crowley, "collected Seattle's dissidents into a critical mass for the first time in decades" and held classes on "everything from Anarchism to Zen."[4] The impetus for the Free University came from Miriam Rader, a Trotskyist and the daughter of Melvin Rader, a University of Washington (UW) professor who had been the target of anticommunists in Washington State. Activists from the Old Left, including members of the FSP and the anarchist Louise Crowley (no relation to Walter Crowley), were the teachers. According to the *Seattle Post-Intelligencer*, the Free University was "the largest floating university in the country," with over four hundred enrolled faculty and students.[5] Another example of changing times was the publication of Seattle's first (and short-lived) underground newspaper, the *Seattle Barb*, in January 1967. It was known mainly for its use of profanity and its support of sexual liberation and homosexual rights. The local chapter of Students for a Democratic Society (SDS), which was organized in 1965, split down the middle over a series of articles called "To Fornicate Is Divine."[6] Two months later, 1,500 copies of the *Helix*, Seattle's most successful underground paper, were sold on the streets of the University District. While professing to be dedicated to "no cause, no interests, no point of view," the *Helix* reported on the emerging radical and political scene: police harassment of hippies, the burgeoning drug and music culture, the formation of the Negro Labor Council to fight discrimination in Seattle's building trades, advocacy for the environment and Indian rights. It contained articles about psychology, sexuality, love, and Eastern spirituality. Personal ads, then called "unclassifieds" costing ten cents a word, provided needed revenue. A substantial proportion of these unclassifieds sought sexual partners, swingers, and other assorted ménages. Street people and hippies were the main vendors, earning a few pennies for their labors. Key sales outlets were the head shops that sold drug paraphernalia, record stores, taverns, Volkswagen repair stores, and porn shops. Walt Crowley admits that "porn later became an issue with the advent of feminism, but in the early years smut merchants were both reliable advertisers and ... dedicated champions of freedom of speech."[7] Like the Free University, the *Helix* brought together a wide assortment of people from the Old Left and the New Left, hippies, artists, musicians, and intellectuals.

Of all the factors contributing to the emergence of a women's liberation movement in Seattle, the presence of the Old Left was decisive. Some of the people and groups on the city's Left had managed to survive McCarthyism, although in a state of disarray. The CP was made up mainly of older, White members with a core group of younger African American members. Party members continued to work in the labor movement, allied with the older, more established civil rights movement, and participated in the formation of Seattle Women Act for Peace (SWAP). SWAP was organized in 1961 when, according to Anci Kopple, a group of women with ties to the CP and peace organizations wanted to urge President John F. Kennedy to negotiate a treaty banning atmospheric nuclear tests when he visited the city that fall.[8] Not until the mid-1970s did SWAP embrace feminism.

The SWP, a Trotskyist group, was also present in Seattle. In 1966, the entire Seattle SWP chapter quit in disagreement with a number of the national organization's political positions, including its lack of attention to women's rights. New, mainly younger SWP members moved to Seattle that year to start up a separate branch. They were active primarily in the antiwar movement and did not get involved in the women's liberation movement until 1970. Other small, autonomous anarchist, Stalinist, Trotskyist, and Maoist groups as well as individual radicals played various roles in the movement's development.

The FSP, which came out of the resignation of Seattle members from the national SWP, played the most decisive role in the early formation of the radical women's liberation movement. Clara Fraser, who had been a national leader in the SWP and was a founder of the FSP, was a prime mover in organizing Seattle Radical Women (figure 2.1). Born in 1923 to a Russian social democratic mother and Latvian anarchist father, Fraser grew up in the radical culture of East Los Angeles, where she joined the Young People's Socialist League, the youth section of the Socialist Party. Fraser earned a bachelor's degree from UCLA in 1944, worked as a screenwriter, then joined the SWP. In Chicago she took part in a union organizing drive at a department store where she wrote advertising copy. In 1946 she moved to Seattle.

By 1948 Fraser was a shop steward on the top tier graded "A" lined electrician heading a crew on the final assembly line producing such aircraft as B-52s (the planes that carried atomic bombs). She was a leader of the six-month strike of the International Brotherhood of Electrical Workers against the Boeing Company, which was eventually broken by the Teamsters Union under the leadership of Dave Beck.[9] During the strike, she organized a "stroller brigade" of mothers and babies to defy an antipicketing injunction.[10] This was no small feat for a woman, a Jew, and a Trotskyist, especially at a time when misogyny, anticommunism, and anti-Semitism combined with vicious ferocity. After the strike, Boeing refused to rehire her. Blacklisted, she spent the next ten years going from one job to another until 1966, when she was hired by the Seattle Opportunities Industrialization Center (SOIC), a job training

Figure 2.1 / *Left to right*, Clara Fraser, Melba Windoffer, and Gloria Martin, founders of Radical Women and members of the Freedom Socialist Party, Seattle, Washington. Photograph published in 1976 in the *Freedom Socialist*, Seattle, Washington.

center. A mother of two, Fraser was always an advocate for children, and in 1967 she established childcare for the trainees at SOIC.

In 1966, Fraser was among the key members of the Seattle SWP who initiated its split from the national organization, which turned mainly on what the Old Left called "the Woman Question." The Seattle branch argued that feminism must become a priority in the Trotskyist movement. Her work at the Seattle Equal Opportunities Commission and SOIC connected her with the African American community, as many of the SOIC leaders were active in the Congress on Racial Equality (CORE). Fraser had a commanding presence. When she spoke, either in meetings or to the larger public, she exuded fearless self-confidence. She was one of the very few White revolutionaries who could challenge the Black Panther Party on its male chauvinism.

In an interview, Fraser recalled that when the FSP was organized, it had few members and fewer supporters.[11] At the same time, the founders were aware of the growing political activism among young people and wanted a way to connect with them. What made the FSP distinctive on the Left at the time included its ties to the civil rights, welfare rights, and draft resistance movements; its commitment to the Woman Question; and its willingness to work with younger radicals. One reason for holding classes at the Free University was precisely to attract young people to the politics of the FSP.

In 1967 the Seattle FSP split, ostensibly over the divorce of its leading members. As often happens with small political groups, personal disagreements escalated into political differences. Both groups kept the name Freedom Socialist Party. Fraser, the leader of one FSP faction, grandiosely compared the FSP split to that between the Russian Bolsheviks and Mensheviks in 1903. New Left activists humorously called the Fraser-led faction the FSP Bolshevik (FSPB) and the faction led by Frank Krasnowsky and Lee Mayfield the FSP Menshevik (FSPM).

Gloria Martin was the oldest woman at the October 1967 meeting at Susan Stern's where Seattle Radical Women was founded (see figure 2.1). She had been active in the Young Communist League as a teenager and joined the CP when she turned thirty. As a young woman she had been involved in CP-led desegregation activism in St. Louis. After leaving the CP in 1941, she did not belong to any organization until she moved to Seattle, where she resumed her participation in the civil rights movement. Martin was a community organizer in an antipoverty program. Along with an African American friend and coworker, Mary Louise Williams, she formed Aid to Dependent Children Motivated Mothers, which recruited women who received assistance from the federal welfare program, Aid to Families with Dependent Children. She attempted to organize the first labor union for antipoverty program workers. "I didn't join anything," Martin remembered in an interview, "until the [Free] University happened, and we had the classes in women's history and the *Feminine Mystique*."[12] Martin was the main teacher of the six-month class series on women in US society. Other women with connections to the Old Left who organized the classes at the Free University and the first women's liberation meeting included Jill Severn, an eighteen-year-old White working-class single mother and member of the FSP. Judith Shapiro, a twenty-four-year-old "red diaper baby" (meaning her parents were communists) and an assistant professor of economics at the UW, also sat on Stern's floor at that auspicious first meeting.

Stern was equally pivotal to the formation of Seattle Radical Women (figure 2.2). She had few connections to the Old Left, civil rights, or labor movement. She represented the New Left as well as the counterculture. Born in 1943, she was raised in an affluent Jewish household in New Jersey and attended Syracuse University, where she met and married Robert "Robby"

Figure 2.2 /
Susan Stern, a
founder of Radi-
cal Women, Se-
attle, Washington,
1971. Photograph
by Paul Dorpat.

Stern. They moved to Seattle in 1966. In her autobiography, *With the Weath-ermen*, Susan wrote that she was miserable and depressed during her first year in Seattle. While she adored her husband, she always felt inadequate. "Although I was among the top students at the School of Social Work, I com-pared myself to Robby in all ways and always came out inferior." She began to resent her role as student wife: "Almost immediately we fell into a routine. I went to school, held a job, cleaned the house, cooked, and helped Robby type his papers. Robby went to school. As time wore on, I wore thin. It seemed to me grossly unfair that we should both go to school and then I had to do all the housework while he relaxed and watched the news or studied. We both considered housework shit work; why did I end up doing it all?" When she and Robby became politically active, she noticed that "Robby soon began to dominate meetings; although I always attended them with him out of fear of missing something important, I was known mostly as 'Robby Stern's wife.'"[13]

The two broke up for a year and Stern experimented with drugs, the hippie subculture, and political activism; she sang at a local jazz gallery, reunited with her husband, and lived in a political commune in the U District. She met Gloria Martin while doing fieldwork in the Central District and attended the classes that Fraser and Martin organized at the Free University.

In August, Susan and Robby attended the 1967 National Conference for New Politics in Chicago. In her autobiography, Susan commented, "The important thing about the New Politics Convention . . . was that we came into contact with white radical organizers, among them Students for a Democratic Society (SDS). We were impressed by their spirit and polemic and decided to join SDS when school resumed in the fall."[14] At that New Politics conference, Jo Freeman and Shulamith Firestone organized a radical women's caucus but were prevented from presenting the caucus's demands for women's equality at the plenary. According to one of the participants in the caucus, William Pepper, one of the National Conference for New Politics chairs, "patted Shulie [Shulamith Firestone] on the head and said, 'move on little girl; we have more important issues to talk about here than women's liberation.'"[15] If Susan was aware of the radical women's liberation caucus, she did not report on it when she came back to Seattle.

The Seattle chapter of SDS was organized in 1965.[16] Three of the SDS organizers in Seattle, Marc Krasnowsky, George Arthur, and Ed Morman, had direct connections with the Old Left. Krasnowsky and Arthur were high school friends and became active in SDS when they went to the UW. In an unpublished memoir, "Ask Any Fringe," Arthur remembered, "I met my first real-time socialist at David Denny Jr. High School, Marc Krasnowsky, whose parents, Frank Krasnowsky and Clara Fraser, were active in the Seattle branch of the Social [sic] Workers' Party . . . and soon to be Freedom Socialist Party. In short order, I was initiated into the mysteries of Free Way Hall . . . drink tickets, the united vs. the popular front, combined and uneven development, the labor theory of value, male chauvinism, the hidden histories of racism, the Vietnam War."[17] Morman was a City College of New York graduate and at the time sympathized with the Progressive Labor Party (a Maoist and Leninist organization). He learned that the socialist Left traditionally addressed the Woman Question as parallel to, say, the Negro Question or the Jewish Question. What was unusual is that these men first raised the Woman Question within the Seattle SDS chapter.[18]

After the initial women's meeting at Susan Stern's in October, the participants did not take action as a group right away. In November 1967, the SDS chapter invited Clara Fraser (whose public alias was Clara Kaye)[19] to speak about women in society. The leaflet advertised a speech on "The Feminine Mystique." There was a wide cultural, generational, political, experiential, and geographical divide within Seattle Radical Women. Everyone who was not a member of the FSP was on the UW campus as a professor, student, faculty wife (yes, that was an official term then), or staff worker. The FSP members demanded that the group thrash out a wide range of political questions before embarking on activities. The campus-centered members were already exhaustively involved in antiwar, antidraft, Indian fishing rights, United Farm Workers, and antiracist activities, so they found these discussions tiresome.[20] Radical Women met sporadically, but for the most part the meetings centered on programmatic issues largely determined by the older, more experienced women from the FSP.

The politics of women's liberation in Seattle exploded publicly with the appearance of a *Playboy* Playmate. In April 1968, the UW Committee to End the War in Vietnam had scheduled a week of protests. At the same time, the Men's Commission, a university organization controlled by the fraternities, announced that the annual Men's Day would include a display of antique cars, a Phil Ochs concert, and separate programs for men and for women featuring the *Playboy* model.[21] (For Women's Day, which would be scheduled in May, the [always unnamed] wife of the governor presided over a sorority tea.) While many antiwar activists were convinced this was a fraternity plot to dissipate antiwar activism, Barbara Arnold, Grey Osterud, Susan Stern, and a small group of other members of Radical Women decided to protest this blatant exploitation of women and, at the same time, to call attention to the war and racism. During the same week of protests, the Black Student Union began its campaign for the admission of more Black students and the establishment of Black studies at the UW. The men's meeting was held in the student union ballroom (pun intended), with a capacity of one thousand; the women's meeting was in a smaller auditorium.

Radical Women hotly debated tactics for the protest, which had to take place at the meeting for women. The majority agreed to interrupt the meeting with guerilla theater: they would storm the stage wearing paper bags over their heads and conduct a mock funeral for the Playmate and all women who were victimized. Seven members of Radical Women managed to leap onto the stage and start chanting from the script before they were dragged off by the men in charge; some were beaten, kicked, and even bitten. Later, I recalled,

I was involved in the protest. However, either from shyness or disagreement with the tactic of putting a paper bag on my head, I sat in the auditorium during the beginning of the protest. Horrified that my sisters were being attacked, I found myself getting up on the stage, and giving my first speech ever. I tried to explain that women were tired of being treated like sex objects (my mini skirt was shorter than that of Reagan Wilson, the Playboy model); I knew nothing about the politics of feminism but I had just read an account of the militant suffragettes, and I spoke about how women had to struggle to get the vote. What was so astonishing was the fury of the women who came to hear the bunny speak. They screamed at me, "get lost," "get laid," "get a husband."[22]

Hours of screaming arguments, the threat of disciplinary action against the demonstrators, and front-page articles in Seattle's daily papers followed. The *Post-Intelligencer*'s headline read, "Co-Eds Sulk, Guys Gulp at 38–24–36." The UW *Daily* put the protest on the front page: "Playmate Meets Women—Radical Ones" (figure 2.3). Only the *Helix* reporter George Arthur wrote a feminist piece on the protest. Nonetheless, the publicity garnered by the demonstration put Seattle Radical Women and women's liberation on Seattle's political map, and more women joined the organization.[23] This women's liberation demonstration took place four months before the Miss America protest in Atlantic City. Had the Playmate confrontation occurred at Harvard or Columbia, no doubt it would have made the front page of the *New York Times*.

After that, it seemed that almost every event, internationally, nationally, and locally, encouraged support for women's liberation. Seattle activists were thrilled when they heard of the feminist protests at the April 1968 student takeover at Columbia University. On May 1, Florynce "Flo" Kennedy, an African American radical and feminist lawyer, came to speak to the University of Washington Law School. In a meeting with members of Radical Women, she was supportive and encouraging. On Memorial Day, in the midst of patriotic pro–Vietnam War marches and veterans' demonstrations, members of Seattle Radical Women, dressed in black pajamas and wearing Vietnamese straw hats, carried antiwar posters and marched through Seattle's Civic Center, demonstrating solidarity with the women of Vietnam.

On July 4, 1968, Draft Resistance Seattle held a picnic, political rally, rock fest, and "be-in." Draft Resistance, like most of the groups on the Left in Seattle, brought together both the Old and the New Left. Because of the influence of the Old Left, Draft Resistance Seattle spoke about the class nature of conscription, which granted exemptions to college students and thus privileged White men. The organization had a number of African American

Playmate Meets Women—Radical Ones

By KATHY MASSOTH

Women, both radical and non-radical, were not in the shadows during Men's Day on Friday. In the brightest light was red-haired Reagan Wilson, 22, a Playboy Magazine Playmate, who filled the HUB ballroom with 500 men students and filled campus coeds in on her achievements. She also brought the Radical Women into full swing.

As Miss Wilson started an unprecedented question-and-answer period with about 200 coeds in the HUB auditorium, six members of Radical Women emerged from the back of the auditorium to protest what they called the exhibition of womanhood as just a body.

In the midst of the protest, one of the protesters, Barbara Arnold, received minor head injuries that brought accusations of brutality against Men's Day Chairman, Steve Hanson.

Miss Arnold, a sophomore, who led the sack-masked protesters onto the auditorium stage, claims that she was kicked and slapped by Hanson as he and two other AMS officials tried to remove the girls from the stage, after AMS President Jim Rodgers asked them to leave.

Hanson denied that there were any intentional injuries. He said that any injuries incurred by Miss Arnold were accidental. Miss Arnold bit Hanson when she thought she had been kicked.

The protest by the coeds consisted of a burial ceremony with chants of "Here lies the body of *(Continued on Page 9)*

—photo by Jan Shaw

"The effort that has gone into this program could have been better used to protest the war," Barbara Winslow told the Playmate.

Barbara Arnold Herbert *Trey O...*

"Here lies the body of Reagan Wilson," chanted the masked radical women.

photo by Jan Shaw

Figure 2.3 / Barbara Winslow with Reagan Wilson, *Playboy* Playmate, on April 18, 1968. Photograph published in the University of Washington *Daily*, April 29, 1968, Seattle, Washington.

spokespeople, mainly the sons of families who had been involved in the civil rights struggle in Seattle. Finally, because of the influence of members of Radical Women, Draft Resistance spoke out against a popular slogan, "Girls say yes to boys who say no."

In April 1968, Draft Resistance Seattle published a position paper titled "Women and Draft Resistance." This document was written by Jill Severn, a member of Radical Women and the FSP. The July 4 picnic featured Morgan Spector, national leader of SDS and organizer of the 1968 Stop the Draft Week in Oakland, California; Fred Lonidier of Draft Resistance Seattle; Aaron Dixon, who represented the Black Panther Party; and me, identified as an SDS and Vietnam Committee member. I had been told to tie together women's liberation and opposition to the draft, the war, and racism and link them to a Marxist class analysis in a five-minute speech.[24] This was the first time that a woman had spoken about women's liberation at a large antiwar and antidraft rally in Seattle, and unlike what happened in other cities, I was not booed, heckled, ignored, or wolf whistled.

That summer, Seattle Radical Women and the FSP embarked on an ambitious six-week educational series titled The Woman Question in America. Topics included "The Origins of Female Oppression," "Women's History from the *Mayflower* to the Civil War," "Freud and Women," and "Toward Liberation." The well-attended classes provided a rich political education for many younger women who were new to activism and knew little about women's history. During the planning and the classes themselves, political differences between the women in the FSP and the younger, campus-centered women emerged. Stern found the endless debates at planning meetings "hopelessly tedious." "We couldn't agree on our goals. Most of the differences lay between the young, action-oriented women and the older, education-oriented women."[25]

The FSP wanted a women's organization based on a Leninist model, with a socialist program and democratic centralist structure. Gloria Martin wrote, "Inevitably, a tension developed between the Old Left women, mostly FSP members, who knew, from long experience in radical politics, the importance of firm program and structure, and the New Left petty-bourgeois students with instinctive antipathy to any type of formal organization." She added, "Our concepts, with their frankly old left, proletarian, and common sense insistence on formal, organized structure, either dramatically attracted or repelled women."[26] In a position paper drafted by Clara Fraser, Radical Women delineated its differences with the New Left women's liberation organizations, especially with regard to the idea that the "personal is political" and the importance of consciousness-raising groups: "The contention that special soul dialogues and intimate group interchanges are crucial to expanded awareness and energizing is highly doubtful, and perpetuates the image of women as inner-oriented, subjective and psychological as opposed to the objectivity, outer orientation and sociologic capacity of men."[27]

Many of the younger, New Left women withdrew from Seattle Radical Women in the summer of 1968 and founded two new groups, the Women's Majority Union and Women's Liberation–Seattle (WL-S). Seattle Radical Women continued as a radical and feminist organization connected with the FSP. Both new women's liberation organizations also had direct connections with the established Left in Seattle.

In the spring of 1968, the Women's Majority Union ("Or the Order of the Red Balloon") issued *Lilith's Manifesto*, a two-sided leaflet that combined the ideas of personal and sexual fulfillment, power, and revolution: "If you, brother, can't get a hard-on for a woman who doesn't grovel at your feet, that's *your* hang-up; and sister; if you can't turn on to a man who won't club you and drag you off by the hair, that's yours. Keep your hang-ups the hell out of this revolution."[28] The first issue of its mimeographed periodical contained pieces on Valerie Solanas of New York, the author of the "S.C.U.M. Manifesto" who shot Andy Warhol; an article by Judith Bissel on women and the draft;

an article by Janet Hews titled "On Becoming a Radical Woman"; a position paper from the Black Unity Party of upstate New York requesting "the Sisters to not take the pill," along with a response from six Black women from Mount Vernon, New York, which begins, "Poor black sisters decide for themselves whether to have a baby or not to have a baby"; a position paper by Marlene Dixon on radical women in the professions; and finally an article on the word *lesbian* by Elaine Smith. The seventeen editorial contributors included two Black women and two White men.[29] *Lilith* had a circulation throughout the US and in parts of Europe. The Women's Majority Union also published biweekly bulletins containing "Further Notes on the Man Question." *Lilith* folded in 1970, announcing, "We are too few in number, and too lean in resources, to undertake any further publications."[30]

The Women's Majority Union dedicated itself primarily to political writing, rather than organizing activities. Many of the women who signed the original manifesto and wrote for the journal were active in other women's organizations. Nina Harding, for example, was a member of Radical Women. Dotty DeCoster, Flo Ware, Alice Armstrong, and Sheila Kritchman were members of the Women's Liberation Committee of the Peace and Freedom Party (PFP) of Washington State. When the Women's Majority Union no longer functioned as a group, Janet Hews and Madelyn Scott joined Radical Women. Judith Bissell joined SDS and later unsuccessfully tried to join the Weatherman faction and the Weather Underground. Erika Gottfried, a high school student, joined WL-S.

The other group to emerge from Radical Women was WL-S. It had an extremely complicated structure, understood by no more than a handful of its members at the time. The younger, New Left women who left Radical Women were all SDS activists who were opposed to the war, racism, and the draft and supported Indian fishing rights and the United Farm Workers Organizing Committee's boycott of grapes. At the time that Radical Women was splitting, sections of the Old Left—in particular the CP, SWAP, Progressive Labor, and the FSPM—were organizing a Washington State branch of the PFP. The PFP was a radical electoral organization that nominated Eldridge Cleaver, the Black Panther Party leader, for president of the United States in 1968. The PFP attracted a good section of Seattle's New Left. For its short life, it remained a coalition of the New Left and the CP, Trotskyist, anarchist, Old Left. At this time WL-S was a committee of both the PFP and SDS. But WL-S also acted as an independent organization. According to Lee Mayfield, a member of the FSPM and an original member of WL-S, "This got us off to a great start—neither organization could tell us what to do."[31] Mayfield, an engineering technician and mother of two, had been a member of the SWP and then the FSP. She was a central figure in WL-S and played an important role in its political direction. With the exception of Judith Shapiro, the younger women came from the political struggles of the 1960s but were willing to work with and learn from those from the Old Left.

Neither Radical Women (RW) nor WL-S was an autonomous women's liberation organization; both were connected to larger, gender-mixed Left parties or organizations. In that sense, these two women's liberation organizations continued the Leninist principle that mass organizations must be subordinate to the revolutionary party. In contrast to Old Left traditions, however, both groups were all female. While most of the members of Seattle Radical Women and its leaders were also members of the FSPB, the two organizations had no official relationship until 1973, when Radical Women and the FSP announced their formal political affiliation. According to Gloria Martin, "A rock-bottom base of FSP women was always there to pick up the pieces and provide the Marxist and feminist analysis and guidance that enabled RW to recuperate from internal derelictions and external blows."[32]

It is doubtful that, except for Mayfield and Shapiro, members were aware of the Leninist position regarding women's organizations and vanguard parties. For them, connections with SDS and the PFP meant connections with the broader Left. For the most part, WL-S functioned with few problems within the PFP. WL-S wrote its platform on women, and when it was presented to the founding convention, there was neither dissent nor patronizing corrections. Two of the six local candidates were women: Shapiro, who was White and Jewish; and Flo Ware, who was African American, the vice president of Seattle CORE and a sympathizer of the FSPM. The state chair was Alice Armstrong, founding member of Women's Majority Union, who was also the delegate to the PFP National Organizing Committee. The majority of the PFP electors were women. At its founding conference, "Mass Rally and Convention on September 17, 1968," along with others, I spoke at the keynote plenary. Aaron Dixon of the Black Panther Party spoke about the "liberation of the Black community," and I spoke on "the liberation of women."

Women from the PFP demanded changes in Old Left organizational practices. Women chaired all the meetings; they needed the experience because in the past, only men chaired meetings. The chair always had to call on a woman after a man spoke. In these ways, women embraced the more egalitarian ideals of the New Left, in hope of ending the tradition of women's silence, or more pointedly the practice of silencing women.[33] WL-S also challenged male chauvinism within the broader Left, in particular the way in which the antiwar and

GI organizing movements used women as sex objects to talk with soldiers. While the PFP was supportive of its women, it hardly embraced a women's liberation perspective and platform. The only candidate who specifically mentioned women's rights was Shapiro, and her position statement said only that the US government put "employers' advantages over women's rights."[34] WL-S, and the PFP as a whole, never questioned the candidacy of Cleaver or the hostility of the Black Panther Party's male leadership to women's liberation, even though Cleaver was alleged to have coined the phrase "pussy power" and, far worse, was an admitted and convicted rapist.[35] Nor did the Washington State PFP demand that the vice-presidential candidate be a woman.[36]

The activities of members of WL-S, the PFP, and SDS went beyond participating in committee and subcommittee meetings and writing leaflets; they had fun as well. In the fall of 1968, the local newspapers announced a meeting on *Fascinating Womanhood*. Written by Helen Andelin, a Mormon in the conservative antifeminist movement, the book suggested that women be more enticing to their husbands by acting servile and stupid. By demonstrating against this gathering, WL-S members hoped to reach a larger audience. They sent out press releases to the editors of the women's pages and invited Radical Women and the Women's Majority Union to join.

Some women leafletted outside; others, wearing dresses, stockings, and high heels, went into the meetings and asked provocative questions: Why get married? Why be a housewife? They challenged the spokeswomen for *Fascinating Womanhood* to debate the book's call for women to "revere your husband and honor his right to rule you and your children." Male supporters were outside also handing out leaflets. The protesters spoke only to women of the press. The *Seattle Times* sent Joan Geiger to cover the protest. The headline read "Seattle Women Clash over the Right to Slavery and Freedom," but the article was supportive of the radical feminists. Geiger included the obligatory put-down of each side, but she commented positively on the action and spotlighted WL-S.[37]

Women's Liberation–Seattle evolved from an organizationally complicated committee comprising two separate groups but acting in its own right into an autonomous women's liberation group because of a clear break with New Left, rather than Old Left, politics. It attracted more women from the UW SDS chapter, and by the end of the November 1968 election there were more SDS women involved than women from the PFP. The PFP put out a newspaper, the *Western Front*. It carried regular theoretical pieces and news articles about women. The committee brought Fannie Lou Hamer, the civil rights activist and leader of the Mississippi Freedom Democratic Party, who was famous for challenging Lyndon Johnson at the 1964 Democratic Party convention, to speak on women and the civil rights movement.[38] In January 1969, the WL-S committee of the PFP created an abortion rights committee and attended the hearings organized by the Washington State legislature to liberalize Washington's restrictive abortion laws.

In March 1969, the Women's Liberation Committee of SDS and the PFP sponsored a two-day conference celebrating International Women's Day. This was the first time since 1945 that International Women's Day, a socialist holiday that originated both in textile workers' strikes in the US and in the Russian Revolution of 1917, was celebrated in Seattle.[39] Organized around the theme "A Woman's Place Is Not in the Home," the conference focused on childcare not only as a prerequisite for women's "emancipation from domestic servitude" but also as the basis "for a new and equal relationship between men and women."[40]

Preparing for the event, members of WL-S read from Leon Trotsky's *History of the Russian Revolution* about the active role of women on International Women's Day. "The revolution was begun from below, overcoming the resistance of its own revolutionary organization, the initiative being taken by their own accord by the most oppressed and downtrodden of the proletariat—the women textile workers, among them, no doubt, many soldiers' wives."[41] Members of WL-S researched socialist women's history, learning about Clara Zetkin, the leader of the international socialist women's movement; the Russian revolutionary feminist Alexandra Kollontai; and socialist garment workers in New York City. The International Women's Day celebration featured a screening of *Salt of the Earth*, the now-classic movie made in 1954 about the confluence of race, ethnicity, class, and gender during a strike of the International Union of Mine, Mill and Smelter Workers in Arizona. We also learned about the film's socialist and feminist origins. The director and most of the actors had been blacklisted during the McCarthy era. The lead actor, Rosaura Revueltas, was deported to Mexico during the filming. Women's liberation activists rediscovered and popularized this extraordinary film. In 1992, the Library of Congress decided the film was "culturally, historically, or aesthetically significant" enough to be selected for preservation in the National Film Registry.[42]

By the end of March 1969, the PFP had collapsed, and its demise meant that WL-S was a committee solely of SDS. Given the changing politics of the national SDS leadership, however, tensions soon arose between WL-S members and SDS, leading the women to break with the larger group.

Initially the Seattle SDS chapter, unlike so many in the country, was very supportive of the women's liberation committee. Women chaired meetings and were public speakers; women's issues and committee reports were always discussed by the membership at large; the SDS Research and Propaganda groups were named after women, including Harriet Tubman, Sojourner Truth, Mother Jones, Elizabeth Gurley Flynn, and Clara Zetkin. There were always women speakers at the large demonstrations and public rallies. When Don McGaffin, a news reporter for the local CBS affiliate, approached SDS leaders about making a documentary, the SDS chapter insisted that women be interviewed equally with men. Yet in spite of the support for women's liberation expressed by the men in SDS, the chapter was still male dominated. The leadership was overwhelmingly male; it was men who decided which women would be allowed to speak at rallies.

By 1969, women came into conflict with SDS leaders. On January 31, the WL-S committee of the PFP and SDS held a joint teach-in on women's liberation. Over 250 people participated. Three of the four plenary speakers had been involved in the Old Left: Lee Mayfield; Waymon Ware, the husband of Flo Ware, a civil rights activist, and member of the FSPM; and Carla Chotzen, a member of SWAP. Bernardine Dohrn, the national interorganizational secretary of SDS, was the only New Left speaker. It was at this conference that women in WL-S first expressed concern about the SDS leadership. Although Dohrn was a woman, her behavior was appalling. She spent all her time with the men, picked fights with members of WL-S, and criticized the women's liberation movement and the Women's Liberation Committee of the Seattle SDS chapter for not being anti-imperialist enough.

The behavior of SDS's national leaders convinced many members of WL-S that there was something very wrong with the organization. Men in the national leadership would come to Seattle, cavalierly make passes at SDS women, and at the same time show complete indifference to women's activism and feminist politics. In February 1969, Mike James, who was active in Chicago's community organizing program, Jobs or Income Now, came to an SDS meeting to talk about organizing White workers. About 150 people were present. James was explaining how to relate to White workers, speaking in an affected manner in what he thought was a White working-class accent. Explaining how he made alliances with White male workers, he said, "And then sometimes we all get together and ball some chick." There was complete silence. Then Jill Severn from Radical Women (figure 2.4) stood up and asked, "And what did that do to the chick's consciousness?" James was unable to answer the question, began to backtrack, and finally admitted that he never gangbanged women; he just said he did in order to appear tough. It was not lost

Figure 2.4 / Jill Severn, a member of Radical Women, getting arrested at a demonstration of the Building Service Employees Union, Seattle, Washington. Photograph published in the *Seattle Post-Intelligencer*, November 13, 1969. The headline read, "Little Gal Arrested."

on the audience that the only person to stand up to James was a member of Radical Women. The women at the meeting surrounded Severn, praising and congratulating her, thrilled at her timing and presence of mind. Most of the SDS men were embarrassed.

It was the participation of members of WL-S in a strike of women photofinishers that convinced some members of WL-S that continued affiliation with SDS was impossible. In April 1969, a small group of White women, most of whom were in their forties, went on strike against the Perfect Photo Company. This was the first time that any of these women had been involved in any type of labor activity, although they belonged to the International Electrical Workers, a left-wing union. One of the strikers was married to the president of the local American Federation of State, County and Municipal Employees

(AFSCME) union at the UW. A former member of the CP, he had worked with campus radicals supporting the United Farm Workers Organizing Committee. He asked members of WL-S and Radical Women if they would help his wife and the strikers by coming down to the picket line. Radical Women, the Women's Liberation Committee of SDS, and some male SDS members went down to the picket line and started a fight with strikebreakers and scabs. Fourteen people were arrested.

After the picketers were released from jail, an emergency SDS meeting was called to discuss this action and the strike as a whole. SDS leaders, the majority of whom were men, argued that the photofinishers were not fighting against racism and imperialism, but only for themselves. Until they gave up what the White SDS leadership described as their "white skin privilege," SDS should not support the strike. For a core group of WL-S members, mainly those who had been involved in women's liberation from the beginning, it was outrageous that a small group of White middle-class men were snottily criticizing the actions of a group of White working-class women who earned only minimum wage, had been ignored by their union leadership, and were fighting back for the first time in their lives.

The actions of Radical Women, WL-S, and SDS, while well intentioned, proved disastrous. The women lost the strike; the Photo Finishers Union denounced and successfully red-baited all three groups. That was the end of any relationship between women's liberation activists and the photofinishers. The debacle was a profound lesson for its WL-S members. Members realized that as middle-class students or, in today's parlance, "privileged" women, they could not swoop in on a strike and act more militant and adventurist than the strikers themselves. Through reflecting on their arrogance and terrible judgment, women learned how to be better allies and strike supporters in the future.

In reaction to SDS's attitude toward the photofinishers, a group of women, mainly those with Old Left connections, began to argue that WL-S should no longer be a committee of SDS but rather become an independent organization. No one argued that women should leave SDS entirely but instead that we needed an autonomous group for feminist organizing. Judith Bissell and Karen Daenzer, who opposed a separate women's liberation organization, proposed that the "role the women's liberation committee has actually played has practically speaking been phased out." The task for SDS was to develop a program regarding women within "the overall anti-imperialist context."[43] Judith Shapiro, Lee Mayfield, and others argued that the work of ending women's oppression could never be phased out. At a meeting a year earlier, Flo Kennedy had taught the White Left feminists that, just as African Americans had their own independent organizations to fight against racism, so, too, women should have their own all-female organizations to fight for women's liberation. Furthermore, since no one in SDS would dare to argue that Blacks did not need independent organizations, why not allow separate organizations for women?[44] Why should women's work always be relegated to some committee? In a remarkably calm meeting, the majority of the WL-S committee members voted to disband the women's liberation committee. WL-S became an independent radical women's liberation organization.

In fall 1969, there were three independent women's liberation organizations: Seattle Radical Women, Women's Liberation–Seattle, and the Women's Majority Union. These groups had been founded and initially guided by women whose political ties were to the Old Left and with roots in Seattle's activist communities. After SDS's crack-up in the summer of 1969, more women joined these organizations, which maintained a women's liberation activist agenda and mounted a campaign to legalize abortion in Washington State.

In 1970, other women's liberation organizations emerged from the ashes of another New Left formation, the Seattle Liberation Front. Its treatment of and attitudes toward women mirrored those of other male-dominated New Left formations, so eloquently and angrily described by Robin Morgan in "Goodbye to All That" and by Marge Piercy in the "Grand Coolie Dam."[45] These later women's groups did not have connections to the Old Left, nor did the majority of their members have experience in Seattle's past movements. The groups played a smaller role in the most significant struggle of the women's liberation movement of the 1970s, the abortion rights referendum campaign. Obviously, we cannot conclude that only those groups that had connections with the Old Left had longevity, or even that women's liberation groups with deep roots in their communities were more successful in their political activities. Yet in Seattle the women's liberation movement clearly owed its origin and early political direction to the Old Left rather than the New, as the Woman Question was gradually transformed into women's liberation.

Let ~~Him~~ Her Live

3

IN 1970, REFERENDUM 20, a proposition calling for the liberalization of Washington State's restrictive abortion law, was coming up for a vote on the November ballot. Those favoring reform canvased, telephoned voters, marched, picketed, and spoke on television and radio, as did opponents of abortion rights. In Seattle antiabortionists mounted a billboard campaign that had unexpected results. One billboard depicted a male fetus with a gestational age of four months curled up in a large hand. The first time the ad was shown in the papers, it was deemed "offensive" and "obscene" by the courts because the fetus's male genitalia were visible.[1] The word "KILL" in large letters was followed by "Kill Referendum 20 Not Me!" in small type. Another ad showed the same fetus with a message reading, "Let Him LIVE: Be a VOICE for the Unborn, Vote No Ref 20" (figure 3.1). Early one morning at the height of the campaign, Nancy Stokely and three other women who belonged to the Anna Louise Strong Brigade, a Maoist women's collective, took a can of red paint, climbed a billboard displaying the ad, crossed out "HIM" and wrote in "HER." Another group of radical feminists graffitied another billboard with "Happy Mother's Day." Abortion reform activists won that battle of the propaganda war.

Their successful campaign was the single greatest achievement of the Seattle women's liberation movement. The nascent movement was able to get abortion reform off the obituary pages of the local papers, where it had always appeared, and on the front pages. It was radical feminists who urged

Figure 3.1 / "Let Him Live." Antiabortion ad from Voice for the Unborn, whose message was changed by advocates of the decriminalization of abortion during the statewide referendum campaign in 1970, Seattle, Washington. Photograph published in the *Seattle Post-Intelligencer*.

that new abortion legislation be presented as a referendum to the voters. While Washington was not the first state to liberalize its abortion laws, it was the first to do so through a popular referendum. The campaign brought together a wide range of women's liberation activists who fought not only to change Washington State's abortion laws but also to extend reproductive health services to women and to create feminist health networks. By bringing in their own personal experiences, women transformed the debate: rather than approaching abortion as a health-care problem to be solved by professionals, they understood abortion as woman's right that is inextricably connected to issues of bodily integrity, gender, class, and race. This activist, radical, grassroots, feminist movement continued to campaign to keep abortion legal, funded, and accessible to all women regardless of age or marital status. Furthermore, participants began to challenge the racist, eugenicist, and population-control approach to contraception and abortion; agitated for an end to coercive sterilization; and placed abortion rights in the context of a holistic feminist health-care perspective. Radical activists confronted the challenges of coalition work, facing the perennial conundrums of reform or revolution, conviction or compromise. Finally, they learned how to navigate these complicated waters and gained invaluable experience in grassroots organizing and institution building.

Abortion reform galvanized women's liberation activists. Young women who were the backbone of this movement belonged to the generation that had reached sexual maturity when the pill offered women a birth control method they could control. They had experimented with the so-called sexual revolution of the 1960s, only to realize that sexual freedom for women could not be achieved as long as contraception was fallible, unsafe, inaccessible, and expensive and abortion was illegal. The transformation of sexual mores drew women into the struggle for the repeal of restrictive abortion laws. Controlling their own reproduction was essential for women enrolling in colleges and universities and entering the paid labor force in greater numbers.[2]

THE STORY OF NINA HARDING exemplifies the interconnections of class, race, and gender in the struggle for reproductive rights (figure 3.2). Harding was a leading figure in the Seattle women's liberation movement and in the development of Black feminism.[3] Her unhappy marriage, unreliable contraception, and illegal abortion helped bring her into radical feminist politics. Harding's harrowing experience was indicative of what Black and working-class women like her experienced while trying to get an abortion in Seattle. She recalled, "I

Figure 3.2 / Nina Harding, member of Radical Women and founder of Third World Women, Seattle, Washington. Courtesy of the Museum of History and Industry.

had contraceptive foam, which I would certainly never recommend to anybody, and I became pregnant. And now the question was, 'How do I terminate this pregnancy?' In spite of the fact that I am very Catholic, I am a staunch woman feminist in that I control my body. I also did not want to go through 72 hours of labor for another child when I knew I was going to be a single woman and [already] had a beautiful child to raise alone." Harding continued,

> The struggle to identify medical assistance was the most arduous experience I've ever had in my life. Abortions at that time were all back alley. And as I traveled the back-alley route, it was all rich White gals from Mercer Island and Bellevue. I was the only Black woman. I remember I finally had a reference to a doctor. He would only be there once a month on a particular Saturday, and it was $250 or $300, and you had to have cash and carry. And I was there. The nurse took some brief biographical information, and then she came out and preselected women. She said, "You, you and you; and the rest of you can leave."

The nurse rejected "women who appeared to be inner-city women, appeared not to be South End women, appeared to be working-class women. And so she took the East Side, which is well-to-do women, the Mercer Island, Bellevue girls."[4]

Desperate, Harding went to a friend, a practical nurse, who agreed to perform the procedure. The nurse "went to the hospital to get a couple of implements—[in] reality, she was going to steal the items. She was unsuccessful, so we had to do it with what we had, which was nothing." Harding's ordeal did not end there:

> She put the catheter tube like a glove on the tip of a clothes hanger and inserted the tube in the vagina.[5] You were to keep that tube in you for seventy-two hours. Under no circumstances were you to pull it from you. In order to cope with the pain, I had to take the pills and straight gin. I was to heat the gin and drink it. A whole pint of it. Straight. A pint at a time. Had to have a total of three pints. I don't like liquor and I'm not good at drinking. And I cannot to this day stand the fumes of gin. And then you were to have as much activity of moving and jumping and carrying on. You were not to sleep for seventy-two hours. And needless to say the period started to come down, which of course brought the abortion. I bled for approximately ten to twelve days. After I ceased bleeding, I had gone to my ob/gyn, and in those days, you were supposed to be reported.[6] He had done a vaginal check and he was very angry with me. He told me, "Don't you ever do that again, and don't you ever come back to me." And I didn't.[7]

That traumatic experience prompted Harding to support the abolition of restrictive abortion laws.

While abortion was illegal in Washington State, women obtained abortions illegally and quasi-legally. Well-connected women could find psychiatrists and physicians who would recommend a "therapeutic" abortion. Before the campaign to reform abortion laws, doctors made distinctions between therapeutic, or medically essential, abortions and unnecessary or "elective" abortions.[8] Certain psychiatrists provided referrals for some women. For example, a psychiatrist would state that the pregnant woman had such serious psychological problems that an abortion was lifesaving. The problem with this way of obtaining a legal abortion was that the psychiatrist's statements were often used in job references, applications for credit or welfare, and child custody cases. Some women were outraged that they had to pretend to be crazy in order to make a sane, rational decision. Washington State doctors also referred pregnant women to California once that state liberalized its abortion laws in

1967. Most doctors in Seattle, however, would not refer a woman unless she was married or already had a child.[9]

Women obtained illegal abortions locally through underground networks. Dr. Maclarity and Dr. A. Frans Koome were among the few physicians who performed safe abortions despite the real risk of prosecution. Koome publicly surfaced during the abortion campaign, while Maclarity kept her silence.[10]

Some women traveled north to Vancouver, British Columbia, where a clandestine network of nurses performed safe, illegal abortions for just $200.[11] But going to Canada was problematic. During the US war in Vietnam, hundreds, if not thousands, of young men who did not want to be drafted or sent to fight the Vietnamese fled to Canada through Seattle and Bellingham, and cars with young people in them were routinely stopped and searched at the border.

Other avenues were open to middle-class women. It cost $1,000 to travel to Japan to terminate a pregnancy. The cost of the ticket covered a four-day stay, including one day of sightseeing.[12] State legislators who lived away from home in the capital sent women they impregnated to Japan for abortions. It was well known that "some of the same senators who claimed to be opposed for religious reasons had extra-marital affairs with women in Olympia and had arranged abortions for them."[13] Jill Severn, a member of Radical Women, voiced her anger that "along with the nursing home industry, it would appear that one of the most promising and profitable enterprises in the State of Washington is the illegal abortion trade. It is a low-overhead, tax-exempt business, requiring little or no professional training, and, given the apparent cooperation of the Washington State legislature may remain so for years to come."[14]

The situation in the late 1960s, then, was that in Washington abortion was considered a form of homicide, unless the life of the mother was in danger. Nevertheless, the law did not stop abortions, and there was widespread understanding that it was hypocritically applied and disregarded by those in power. The way the law was enforced demonstrated how little women's lives were valued. In 1967, Jack Blight was given twenty years on probation after he admitted to strangling twenty-four-year-old Raisa Trytiak after botching her abortion. Her body was found in a garbage dump.[15] Two years later, Cyrus Maxfield, a homeopath, was given a five-year suspended sentence with one year in the county jail for performing an abortion. His nurse, who admitted to helping Maxfield, was placed on probation for three years. The woman involved asked for leniency, as Maxfield paid her hospital bills and refunded his fee.[16]

THE MOVEMENT TO REFORM Washington State's abortion law began in January 1967, when Dr. Samuel Goldenberg, a Seattle psychologist who was unable to secure a legal abortion for one of his patients, organized the Citizens' Abortion Study Group. Lee Minto, a director at Planned Parenthood, recalled that the study group coalesced after the horrifying case of Sherri Finkbine, a married mother who sought a therapeutic abortion after taking a drug called thalidomide while pregnant.[17] Finkbine hosted a children's program called *The Romper Room* and already had five children. When she discovered the dangers of thalidomide to her fetus, her physician recommended that she have a therapeutic abortion. But when she contacted a local magazine to publicize the dangers of this drug, which were not yet widely known in the US, the abortion was canceled by the hospital and she, her husband, and her ob/gyn received death threats. She finally obtained a medical abortion in Sweden. The fetus was badly deformed and would not have survived. The study group consisted of well-known physicians, psychiatrists and psychologists, ministers, and politicians. Its makeup was clearly professional, majority White, and male, but it also included African Americans and Asians. Roz Woodhouse, a member of the Urban League; Dr. Julius Butler, a Black gynecologist who worked in a Planned Parenthood clinic; and Karen Matsuda, a public health nurse who was a third-generation Japanese American, served on its executive board and remained active in the struggle to legalize abortion. Its goal was to reform Washington State law to make abortion accessible to all women, but to do so quietly and with as little publicity as possible.

In January 1969, the Citizens' Abortion Study Group introduced identical bills in the House and Senate to amend the 1909 law that banned abortion.[18] The amendments had two purposes. The first was to remove the restrictive portions of the old law and enable a physician to terminate a pregnancy after four "lunar months," or quickening. The second was to change the old law's definition that a fetus was a human life.[19]

The state legislature announced committee hearings on the proposed amendments. The study group invited distinguished witnesses to testify, including Dr. Goldenberg, Lee Minto, and Dr. William Watts, then president of the Washington State Medical Association. Opponents of reform also invited medical professionals to speak. Supporters were keeping the hearings and this legislative process hush-hush, in the hope that reform could be quietly passed by the legislature. At this point, none of the radical women's liberation organizations were aware of what was going on.

Within days, however, the abortion issue was brought into the political spotlight by the active intervention of Radical Women. Clara Fraser was the coordinator for community relations at the Seattle Opportunities Industrialization Center (SOIC), an antipoverty program. Part of her job was to study the bills introduced in the legislature to see which ones affected her constituents. Reading what she described as the "fine print" of House Bill 312, she noticed the provisions that would repeal the restrictions on abortion. Fraser immediately called Marilyn Ward to ask if she needed help lobbying for the bill. Ward, a liberal Republican (yes, they once existed) who was married to the state commissioner of commerce and development, was an unpaid lobbyist for a wide range of liberal social causes and was responsible for pushing representatives to introduce legislation on abortion. Year in and year out, she would convince a senator or representative to introduce a bill, only to have it die in committee. Furthermore, no one knew about her efforts. Ward was thrilled that someone called her and offered to help with lobbying. Chuckling, Fraser recalled that Ward had no idea what she had meant by "lobbying."[20]

Fraser then went to her supervisor and told him that HB 312 was directly pertinent to the work of SOIC as too many young women had to drop out of school or leave training programs because they were forced to carry an unwanted pregnancy to term or had been brutalized by a back-alley abortion. Abortion reform would enable young women to stay in school, hold on to jobs, and not risk their health. Furthermore, Fraser argued, a lobbying campaign would be a wonderful opportunity to teach their constituents how to organize the grass roots and lobby their political representatives.

Mobilizing the statewide resources of SOIC meant money for buses, posters, press releases, and banners. On February 13, over fifty women and some men joined in a statewide caravan to Olympia. The overwhelming majority were African American women, a handful of whom were active in Radical Women and Women's Liberation–Seattle (WL-S).

The January demonstration was Nina Harding's first political act. She met Fraser when Fraser was negotiating with the SOIC comptroller for money for the demonstration. She recounted, "As my boss happened to be the comptroller, she had to go through him to get the money for the buses. While waiting on him, she chatted and when I told her, 'Yes, I had an abortion,' she just dropped her teeth because I looked like a prim and proper Bostonian."[21] Fraser convinced Harding to come to a Radical Women meeting where they were discussing articles about illegal abortions and planning slogans and posters for the demonstration. Harding remembered the poster that she made: "I discovered in those readings that women had used any number of instruments in order to abort. And many of those instruments were things I had around my house, like crochet hooks, like knitting needles. I couldn't believe it! I said, 'Well I have those things, well, yes, I'll use a coat hanger.' I still had the coat hanger and catheter tube hanging from it, and I got an older knitting needle, and old crochet hook and an old rusty nail and I scotch-taped it to the sign that said 'Tools of the Trade.'" Harding believed that her sign was the first time that the coat hanger was used as a symbol for the horrors of illegal abortion.[22] At the demonstration, this poster caused quite a furor among Radical Women and with the press. Some people, including Fraser, thought it was too horrifically graphic; others thought it in bad taste. Whether or not this was the first time the coat hanger was used in an abortion protest, it became a symbol for the demand to decriminalize abortion.

The demonstration shook up the state legislators. Fraser believed that the legislators and guards in the capitol were frightened by the presence of African American women: "Hordes of dark-skinned people with placards came to the doors of the rotunda. . . . The guards were terrified. There was hand-to-hand combat between some of the demonstrators and the guards. Our folks had overrun the guards and occupied the rotunda." Ward begged Fraser to remove the sticks from the banners and urge the SOIC contingent not to continue seeking to speak with legislators. Finally, a compromise was reached.[23]

Jill Severn, who attended this demonstration, described what happened. She wrote that the SOIC delegation was "divided into several smaller groups, each intending to speak to one or two of the Rules Committee members. Within a few minutes, Capitol guards were frantically rounding them up, claiming that it wasn't in keeping with legislative decorum for bands of women to be roaming the halls like that. Apparently what they meant was that the visitors' color did not match the decor, and besides, the women were scaring the legislators, who were still a little shaky from a recent visit by the Black Panthers."[24] Everyone was ushered into a committee room where they would be allowed to hear expert testimony.

Lee Minto argued that the present abortion statutes were "coercive, punitive and discriminatory." Dr. Samuel Goldenberg maintained that abortion reform would provide better health care for all classes of society. Dr. William Watts suggested that a heightened awareness of human rights made abortion a personal and not a state matter.[25] Dr. Lester Sauvage, a heart surgeon who opposed reform, asked, "Would you want a physician to have the power to declare you dead just because you can't?" Dr. Gerhard Ahnquist, an obstetrician and gynecologist, argued that abortion reform would lead to a wide range of abuses because patients would want abortions for reasons of "mental health."[26] For the radical women, however, the most terrifying testimony came from a doctor who *supported* reform. He assured the legislators that the medical profession would not be "stampeded into performing abortions at the mere whim of a pregnant female."[27]

After the hearing, the women were ushered into the offices of various legislators. According to the Peace and Freedom Party newspaper, the *Western Front*, "None of [the senators] had any intention of listening to what the women had to say; they all walked in and immediately started defending their various positions on the abortion bill as if they were experts on this question. One particularly brilliant speech about pregnancy and the development of the fetus in the woman's stomach (sic) was delivered by a Rules Committee member who is now a candidate for mayor of Seattle."[28] The infuriated demonstrators jeered and booed the legislators, challenging their power to determine who should have an abortion and why. One group confronted state senators Frank Atwood and William S. Day, both members of the Rules Committee. Atwood admitted that several members of the committee opposed abortion for religious and personal reasons. When Severn told Day that women were tired of being lectured by men and that they sought control of their own bodies, Day objected that women should not have the right to make such a decision. "Women are of varying intelligence," he said. "So are legislators," heckled a demonstrator.[29] The terrified senators hastily announced that the committee room was scheduled for immediate use and the women would have to leave.

This public demonstration in support of abortion reform dramatically transformed the campaign. In one day radical women had learned invaluable lessons about politics. It was clear that abortion reform would not be won through quiet legislative lobbying and deal making. Infuriated at the elitist, White, and male-dominated character of conventional politics, the women were determined to involve as many people as possible in fighting to change the law. The women attending that first hearing and demonstration were outraged and appalled that neither the official voices for reform nor the opponents of reform spoke of abortion as a woman's right. From that day on, radical women began discussing abortion in feminist terms.

The Senate Judiciary Committee pushed Senate Bill 268 into the Rules Committee, known to reporters and lobbyists as the graveyard of legislation. Herb Robinson, a columnist for the *Seattle Times*, wrote that voting on SB 268 in committee was "eminently satisfactory for faint hearted lawmakers" who didn't have the courage to vote on their convictions. The majority of the members of the Rules Committee were middle aged, White, and male; seven of the ten were Roman Catholic. Robinson wrote that these men reflected "the strong anti-abortion views of the Catholic Church."[30] In the House, the bill was stuck in the Committee on Public Health and Welfare.

Bottling the abortion amendments up in committee brought an avalanche of protest by the supporters of reform. Because of the success of the

February demonstration, the Citizens' Abortion Study Group was willing to enter into a coalition with the women's liberation groups. An ad hoc group called Abortion Action Now, comprising the Citizens' Abortion Study Group, Radical Women, WL-S, and fifteen other groups, called for an even larger rally in Olympia to force the two bills out of committee. The study group brought doctors, psychiatrists, and other professionals to speak. Once again, Radical Women and WL-S brought busloads of women, including those from SOIC. On March 28 an estimated 1,500–2,000 people gathered in the capital to demand action on the bills. The radical women marched with banners and placards asserting that abortion was a woman's right. The press treated the demonstration with its usual patronizing manner. Shelby Scates and Susan Payntor of the *Seattle Post-Intelligencer* wrote, "Ladies Day at the State Capitol turned into the politics of confrontation. The delegation of damsels, a rainbow of social types from modish whites to militant blacks showed up with signs and armbands demanding legalized abortion now!"[31]

Jill Severn described the scene:

> This time there were about 1,500 of them and they were better organized. They gathered in the capitol rotunda, gave speeches, and carried signs. And if you thought the legislature overreacted to the Panthers, you should have seen the panic that took hold of the people's representatives when confronted with this! Every door was suddenly locked and guarded. The legislators used their private elevators to get to their private dining room for lunch, and the dining room door was locked, too. There wasn't a legislator to be seen. The source of their fear was unclear. Did they really think the women were going to eat them? Or were they just caught in an indefensible position and refusing to talk about it?[32]

In spite of the large demonstration and the hundreds of letters and telegrams in support of reform, the legislature was unmoved.

Severn believed that the demonstrations shook up the male legislators: "The idea that poor and working women would make such a vociferous and angry demand on the august real estate dealers, lawyers and petty businessmen who run the state's government was stunning to the all-male senate."[33] Frank Atwood, the Republican floor leader, countered, "These people are too aggressive in their lobbying.... If they keep this up, they're going to lose some of the 'yes' votes they already have."[34] In fact, the radical demonstrators had not hurt the cause, as some moderates feared, but brought the issue of abortion and the secretive, manipulative, and sectarian dealings of the state legislature out in the open. The radical women had made "Abortion action now!" and

"Abortion is a woman's right!" the main slogans of the reform struggle, placing *women* at the center of the campaign.

After the second demonstration, Radical Women was no longer in the forefront of campaign activities. As Clara Fraser later explained, Radical Women supported abortion reform and spoke at and attended some meetings, demonstrations, and rallies, but it was not involved in the day-to-day activities of the ad hoc committee on abortion reform.[35] Women's Liberation–Seattle did not do any follow-up work on the abortion issue until it became an independent women's liberation organization, separate from both the Peace and Freedom Party and Students for a Democratic Society (SDS). From January through June, all WL-S members also belonged to SDS, which was involved in a maelstrom of activism. Some members had been suspended or expelled from the University of Washington (UW) or Seattle Central Community College or arrested. Not until the breakup of SDS at its convention in the summer of 1969 did WL-S focus its attention on the abortion issue.

That summer, WL-S created the Abortion Rights Committee, which met once a week to discuss and draft a strategy for the reform struggle. The impetus came from Lee Mayfield, who had had two abortions herself and, while a member of the Socialist Workers Party and later the Freedom Socialist Party Menshevik, was involved in taking women to Vancouver, Canada, to get abortions. She authored and printed a pamphlet titled *I Came into the World Crying and Each Following Day Teaches Me Why*. In this pamphlet she brought to life the letters collected by Margaret Sanger, the foremost champion of birth control and a founder of Planned Parenthood, from her 1928 book *Motherhood in Bondage*. Women and some men from urban and rural areas all over the country had written to Sanger seeking advice on reproductive matters and marital relations and imploring her to tell them how to avoid more pregnancies. Those letters still spoke to women in need of abortions forty years later.

Mayfield contributed an eloquent analysis of the contemporary women's liberation struggle:

> While women's liberation groups fight for abortion, other sections of the radical movement either oppose this struggle or abstain from it. We are told it is irrelevant to the poor in their struggle for survival. Yet poor women, black, white and brown are the ones who suffer from illegal abortions. It is the working-class wife that lives with domestic drudgery. Without control of her body, she and her sisters on welfare face solitary confinement or a continuation of paid labor without adequate, paid maternity leave and without decent child care. The revolutionary movement will be stronger,

though, if it bases itself upon women who reject their subjection and feel that their bodies are their own.[36]

This viewpoint attests to the more comprehensive perspective of radical women with ties to the Old Left. Fraser's and Mayfield's activism linked them to working-class women and women of color like Nina Harding, which helped to make the Seattle movement more inclusive.

Early that summer, the Abortion Rights Committee made two important decisions. One was that its members should join and work with the Citizens' Abortion Study Group. In this way, members of WL-S could stay abreast of what was going on and try to influence the direction of the committee. The study group had commissioned a poll to determine whether voters in Washington State would approve a referendum on abortion. The poll showed that if a vote were taken it would be very close. Based on these results, the study group continued to push for a legislative vote. Members of WL-S, however, still wanted a referendum. Karen Foreit, an anthropology graduate student at the UW, was the WL-S delegate to the study group's meetings. She argued that regardless of the poll's results, abortion reform supporters should push for a statewide referendum. Foreit pointed out that the poll could not be an accurate reading of public opinion regarding abortion because little, if any, information regarding abortion had been disseminated to the public. She said that if the facts were available, the voters would favor abortion reform. After all, WL-S's research had shown that one in four women in the state had or would have an abortion. Foreit and many other activist women were optimistic about the spirit of positive change that seemed to pervade society at that time. Most radical women felt that anything was possible, *especially* abortion reform. After much discussion, the study group finally agreed to push for a statewide referendum to reform the existing abortion laws.[37]

WL-S members' second decision was to draft a pamphlet based on its research on abortion in Washington State. The end result was the pamphlet *One Out of Every Four of Us Has Had or Will Have an Abortion*, which placed abortion in a feminist context and explained why reform was necessary. The first edition was mimeographed, but the second edition was printed on an offset press with a run of five thousand and sold for twenty-five cents, with a discount for bulk orders. Both editions sold out. The pamphlet proved to be effective propaganda, influencing the study group as well as the public.

IN NOVEMBER 1969, the Citizens' Abortion Study Group renamed itself the Washington Committee for Abortion Reform (WCAR) and continued meeting to discuss the wording of the bill that would be sent to the next session of the state legislature. It was able to get support from the Washington State Medical Association and crafted another bill that provided abortion on demand.

That month, the self-imposed silence of those involved in the abortion struggle was once again shattered when Dr. A. Frans Koome wrote a letter to Governor Dan Evans with copies to the press. Koome informed Evans that he had been performing between fifty and seventy illegal abortions per week and would continue to do so. He announced that he would open the Reproductive Crisis Clinic in Renton, next to the Seattle-Tacoma airport, which was accessible to residents of both cities. Koome explained that illegal abortions led to the "vicious chain reaction of early forced marriages and divorce with everybody suffering including the children, adoption is no solution, unwed mothers we have enough already on our welfare rolls, overpopulation is a serious threat." His patients were not stereotypical welfare mothers, he said. "I saw mainly girls in their late teens and early twenties, many studying in college, eager to educate themselves, many daughters of respectable citizens."[38] In the first week after the publication of his letter, Koome performed twenty-two abortions and scheduled twenty-nine for the next week. In spite of the fact that he had flagrantly defied state law, he was not prosecuted. He continued performing illegal operations with impunity, although he was continually harassed and sued for malpractice.[39] His public stance demonstrated the futility of Washington's restrictive abortion law.

Beginning in January 1970, members of WL-s began to work actively in coalition with WCAR. This experience was very difficult, even distressing. Writing in *And Ain't I a Woman*, the WL-s publication, Lee Mayfield explained the political differences. She noted that WCAR "was uncomfortable about defending women's right to abortion and therefore relied heavily on the 'every child should be wanted' theme.... WCAR, motivated by strong distrust for human emotions, relied on 'experts' medical and legal, to carry their arguments."[40] It also recruited doctors' wives. These women, who came to Olympia well dressed and well rehearsed, did not testify about their own experiences and ideas, but buttressed their husbands' viewpoints. Marilyn Ward remembers discouraging the younger and more radical women from attending and warning them against speaking about personal experiences with abortion.[41] She never again asked Clara Fraser to organize a busload of SOIC constituents to come to Olympia. Members of WCAR were only interested in the voices of the professional middle class.

While the radical women's liberation movement stood for abortion on demand as a woman's right, WCAR continued to organize all-male panels to discuss women's rights and women's bodies. According to Mayfield, a "low point in the campaign" occurred at a meeting where Dr. Nathaniel "Ned" Wagner, a professor of psychology and obstetrics-gynecology, spoke on one such all-male panel.[42] Wagner said he was very "unhappy with the ladies" because polls showed more women opposing Referendum 20 than men. "They are a minority group and, as such, have some of the minority group's characteristics, such as self hatred." He claimed that women's self-hatred was manifested in women disliking other women more than men dislike other men.[43]

Members of WL-S and other radical women activists successfully overcame WCAR's reluctance to campaign for a referendum on abortion.[44] The study group's original strategy was to push the legislature to pass a bill that would be signed by pro-choice Republican governor Dan Evans. The members of WCAR were mindful that other Republican governors, notably Nelson Rockefeller in New York, John A. Burns in Hawaii, and even Ronald Reagan in California, had signed liberal abortion bills. Some abortion reform advocates were concerned about putting the question to the voters, who were not accustomed to discussing the matter. Members of WL-S continued to press for the referendum and volunteered to do the grassroots work involved.

Women's Liberation–Seattle advocated militant mass demonstrations to force the bill out of the Rules Committee. On January 12, 1970, WCAR organized buses and caravans to the state capitol. Once again, the sheer presence of several hundred young, militant, radical women who refused to be talked down to, be patted on the behind, or leave the legislators' offices when asked was too much for the lawmakers. In other words, these radical women persisted.

On January 24, the state legislature voted the bills out of the committees, but restrictive amendments were added: (1) a time limitation (the pregnancy must have lasted less than four lunar months), (2) a requirement of the husband's consent, (3) a requirement of parental consent for a minor, (4) a ninety-day state residency requirement, (5) establishment of a physicians' committee of review, and (6) exemptions for doctors, nurses, and hospitals that did not wish to perform abortions. The legislature scheduled a February 4 vote on the proposal.

Supporters of Referendum 20 were presented with a difficult set of choices. These restrictions ran counter to the belief that women alone should control their reproductive health decisions. Knowing they would face opposition from the more radical feminists, Ward and WCAR accepted the bill's limitations, believing it was the only way to win over more conservative legislators. Activists in WL-S were furious. In opposition to WCAR, they handed out their own leaflets to legislators and spoke about access during the hearings: "Abortions should be free; there is no other way of preventing them from becoming the privilege of those who can afford expensive private medical care. Abortion, like birth control, should be given to those who cannot afford to pay for it. And secondly, there is no need to perform abortions in a large hospital. This only increases the cost and gives hospital boards the power to decide whether or not to have abortions performed in their operating rooms."[45] The decision by WL-S activists to publicly raise criticisms and offer amendments aroused the ire not only of members of WCAR but also of Radical Women. Both groups argued that criticisms should not be aired in the open, which would encourage the enemies of reform. The debate that ensued takes place in almost all struggles for social justice. Marilyn Ward summed it up perfectly: "Are we going to lose on principle or win on compromise?"[46]

By the end of January, women's liberation activists decided that it was not in their best interests to continue working in the coalition with WCAR. Part of the reason was that WCAR refused to openly attack the restrictions on women's right to abortion. Members of WL-S believed that the bill should be criticized, even in the context of supporting it: "Women's Liberation–Seattle opposes section 2 of the referendum. Any restriction on the termination of pregnancies discriminates against a certain number of women, and leaves the door open to a number of illegal butchers to operate underground, or for those women to put themselves in danger of taking their own lives under the guise of a 'home remedy' operation."[47] In addition, WL-S disagreed with WCAR's focus on families, rather than women's rights. Most galling was WCAR's resistance to mass mobilizations of women. In one instance, Ward tried to prevent a demonstration of African American women's liberation activists from the Central District who supported the bill, for fear of alienating White conservative legislators.

Early in 1970, largely through the efforts of the University Young Women's Christian Association (YWCA), a group of women coalesced to organize a more radical and feminist group called the Committee for Abortion Reform (CAR). "The Committee for Abortion Reform was launched by women who recognized the need for a real campaign and who had found WCAR unable or unwilling to lead such a campaign," explained Mayfield.[48] Although many of the women on the YWCA's board did not initially identify with the women's liberation movement, they were soon imbued with the spirit of feminism. The YWCA has historically been both Progressive and progressive. Founded in 1858 but burgeoning in cities during the early twentieth century, it is today the largest women's organization in the world. It is committed to women's economic empowerment, racial and gender justice, and women's health and safety. Both the national YWCA and the University YWCA supported abortion reform. The YWCA had also worked with Dr. Ned Wagner in an abortion underground railroad sending women to see Dr. Koome.[49] As the campaign began, the YW became the meeting place for the newly formed CAR.

The University YWCA shared a building with the University Young Men's Christian Association (YMCA), which charged the YWCA rent. By the summer of 1970, the University YWCA decided to separate from the YMCA and stated that they were "reestablishing ourselves as an autonomous women's movement." This was a courageous step for the YWCA because it would mean losing funding from the YMCA and the national YWCA and YMCA organizations, as well as from Seattle United Way. Having been promised support from the women's liberation movement, the University YWCA became independent, devoting all its resources and personnel to the abortion reform effort in particular and the women's movement in general. According to Jean Knudson Krause, a board member, "The split with the University YMCA was much like a divorce, and the reasons reflected on a larger scale much of what characterizes male-female relationships in this society: budget, pay and status differentials, unequal division of labor, unequal power and access to policy making."[50]

The core group working in CAR included members of WL-S, whose political positions tended to prevail. In early 1969, when WL-S was still a committee of SDS and the Peace and Freedom Party, it had drafted its first statement on abortion:

> ABORTION IS A RIGHT. The right to control one's own body is a fundamental right of all human beings. The right to be wanted and the right to be provided for is a fundamental right of all children. The denial of legal abortion is part and parcel of the overwhelming pattern in this society to deny women freedom and equality. It condemns women to raise children they cannot afford. It condemns girls to give birth to children they cannot raise. It condemns children to physical and emotional deprivation, and in many cases to the stigma of "illegitimacy." Furthermore, the absence of legal means often drives women and girls to expensive and illegal abortions, in unsanitary places by unqualified persons, often resulting in permanent physical damage or death.[51]

This early position on abortion focused on gender and individual rights. There was no reference to race or class, and no challenges to the eugenicist, population-control rhetoric of much of the WCAR literature.

THE UNDERSTANDING OF WL-S MEMBERS on the issue broadened over time, as did the struggle itself. By January 1970, WL-S had drafted a leaflet that stated, "Abortions should be free; there is no other way to prevent them from becoming a privilege of only those who can afford expensive private medical care. Abortion, like birth control, should be given to those who cannot afford to pay for it."[52] This leaflet recognized the class dimension of access to abortion and birth control services. Another leaflet, written in September 1970, introduced broader issues of race and reproductive freedom into the abortion debate: "We know the inadequacy of current health care and realize that there is a whole struggle necessary to insure that no woman will be denied an abortion for lack of money. We realize that we as women will have to guard ourselves and our sisters from hospital review boards that may try to continue to force women, especially poor and black women, to beg, plead or submit to sterilization as the price for ending one unwanted pregnancy. But then, that's what the women's liberation movement is about."[53] These shifts register the impact of what Black feminists were saying to White feminists who were listening.

The issue of forced sterilization was taken up in earnest by WL-S. Two events were catalysts. In February 1969, the local Peace and Freedom Party brought Fannie Lou Hamer, the legendary activist of the Black Freedom struggle, to speak at the UW. First a member of WL-S spoke about the abortion campaign. Hamer commented that the presentation was very interesting. She went on to say that she had never really thought much about all the issues raised, but she thought she opposed abortion. She then told about a time when she had been beaten by the police so severely that she had to be hospitalized. After her release and much later, she found out that she had been sterilized—against her wishes. The entire audience gasped. Hamer's experience was profoundly shocking. The predominantly White audience had never learned about the coercive sterilization of African American women, even though the practice was so prevalent that it was referred to as the "Mississippi appendectomy."

The second incident involved a member of WL-S. In 1969, Theresa Williams, a White working-class woman who was heterosexually active, on welfare, a student at Seattle Central Community College, a founding member of the first Seattle Central Community College women's liberation group, and the mother of a multiracial child, had gone to Dr. Koome and used her welfare money to pay for an abortion. In early 1970, she again found herself pregnant. Discouraged and feeling inadequate and stupid, she decided not to spend her money this time but rather to go through the Group Health Cooperative of Puget Sound, an HMO-type provider that paid for therapeutic abortions.

Group Health agreed that Williams was a candidate for a therapeutic abortion because she had proved that she could not handle her own life. Now think about that statement. Group Health did not critique the availability and efficacy of contraception but rather demeaned and punished women who were heterosexually active. An abortion was recommended, but only if she agreed to be sterilized. Utterly desperate, Williams agreed.

She told her story at a WL-S rap group, or consciousness-raising meeting. In order to help Williams, Kathy Dowd, Sue Picard, and Mayfield went to see the executive director at Group Health Hospital and asked him about its procedures regarding abortions and sterilizations. He proceeded to justify the policy, citing another case involving an African American woman. Aghast, the three women realized there had been other victims. Williams was infuriated. In her mind, her sterilization was akin to being raped.[54]

Women's Liberation–Seattle publicized this case. It was written up in *And Ain't I a Woman* and in the abortion primer *One Out of Every Four* as one price women were forced to pay for a legal abortion. For members of WL-S, the personal was very political, and this particular outrage taught the women more about issues of race, class, gender, and sexuality than any study group ever did. This incident also demonstrated that for the radical women's liberation activists, the rap groups had a twofold purpose. One was for women to discuss their personal experiences and develop an understanding of women's oppression, and the second was to translate that understanding into political action.

By the spring of 1970, WL-S articulated a broader class and gender perspective on the issue of abortion, which it raised consistently at CAR meetings, on leaflets, and in larger meetings and demonstrations. But the centrality of race to the abortion reform movement was always problematic because of the issues swirling around race, gender, Black nationalism, and feminism. Nina Harding explained, "I had many Panther women friends, and we agreed on the issues, but it came to a screeching halt when it came to the issue of abortion. Because the party line is that abortion was White folks' genocide of Black people. And in order to perpetuate the race we had to continue to produce babies. And of course it played to their whole notion of sexuality because to produce babies obviously means that you have to have sex [so] the only viable sex for a Black woman was with a Black male."[55] The issue of genocide concerned many people in the Black community, and it had to be addressed then, as it still does today.

Many African American women who had been leaders in the civil rights movement supported Referendum 20 but admitted that the younger militants would not listen to their arguments. According to Jeri Ware, Harding, and Fraser, many women in the Black Panther Party had abortions and supported abortion rights but remained silent about the referendum campaign. Ware, a longtime community activist, later spoke about how she tried to convince younger militant women to support abortion reform, but to no avail.[56] Linda Corr, an African American trade union activist who was a member of the Communist Party at the time, remembered that while the party supported Referendum 20, it did not mobilize its Black members and supporters around this issue, which it regarded more as a matter of democratic rights than women's rights.[57] Johnetta Cole, then an assistant professor at Washington State University in Pullman who was active in the militant Black Freedom struggle, did not remember doing anything about Referendum 20.[58]

For the most part, women from the women's liberation movement tried to answer the charges of racism and genocide and to find ways to integrate race and gender in their approach to the struggle for abortion reform. Radical Women, which was at that time the most racially diverse of all the women's liberation organizations, spoke to the issues of class, race, contraception, abortion, gender, and genocide. In March 1969, Radical Women participated in an "Afro-American Abortion Assembly" at Franklin High School. Jill Severn of Radical Women; Patty Starkovich, a Franklin High School student and daughter of radical parents (her mother was the strike captain of the photo-finishers; her father was the president of the American Federation of State, County and Municipal Employees local at the UW); and two other students were panelists. African American students spoke on both sides of the issue.[59] Severn had a radio talk show on a popular quasi-underground station, KRAB, in which she addressed the issues of Black nationalism, genocide, and a woman's right to abortion, answering the calls predominantly from African American men who charged that abortion and birth control amounted to genocide against the Black community. The spokeswoman on the issue for Radical Women was Nina Harding.

At the time of the abortion referendum, none of the groups involved in the campaign, from the reformist WCAR to the radical groups, approached Black organizations and newspapers. Ward admitted that she was more worried about alienating White conservatives than attracting African American allies. Not one Black organization supported the referendum.[60] There was not one single article about the issue in either of the two Black community newspapers, *Fact* and the *Medium*, nor did WCAR place ads in them. But the antiabortion group Voice for the Unborn (VfU) placed an ad in *Fact* on October 23, 1970, and in the *Medium* on October 29.

Both newspapers were influenced by the Black nationalist position that Black women should not use contraception or have abortions but instead have babies for the revolution. There were no references in either newspaper, or for that matter in the WCAR publications, to the Black feminists, such as Shirley Chisholm, Flo Kennedy, members of the Mount Vernon Women's Group, or those of the Third World Women's Alliance, who challenged the argument that abortion and birth control were genocidal and argued that Black women should be able to decide whether to have a child and receive appropriate medical care.

Dr. Julius Butler, an African American physician who was on the board of WCAR, wrote a personal reply to the ad that was printed in *Fact*. He countered the antiabortionists' argument:

> How is it that they are concerned about Black children and Black family life? Where was their moral outrage in our attempt to get rat control legislation, better housing, better health care, and better jobs? The Voice for the Unborn further asks, "Should being unwanted be punished by death in our society?" The answer to that question is that this racist society does punish the unwanted member, and often by death. The murders at Jackson State was an example of this. Where is the moral outrage for the daily killings of Blacks that take place in this society and has taken place historically for three hundred years?[61]

Yet this eloquent statement seemed to fall on deaf ears.

The predominantly African American Central District precincts of King County (Seattle) gave the referendum halfhearted support or rejected it outright. Neither the Black press and the major city newspapers nor the feminist, left-wing, and underground media reflected after the fact on the salience of race in the referendum campaign. The failure on the part of reproductive rights activists to engage with communities of color about the multifaceted meanings of abortion, contraception, and coercive sterilization was yet another example of racist indifference. Two recent articles analyzing the referendum campaign, one written for the Seattle Civil Rights and Labor History Project, "Washington's 1970 Abortion Reform Victory: The Referendum 20 Campaign," by Angie Weiss, and the other from HistoryLink.org, "Abortion Reform in Washington State," by Cassandra Tate, do not touch on the issues of race, the opposition of voters in African American communities, or the ongoing debate about the racialized aspects of the struggle over reproductive justice.[62]

THE FOOT SOLDIERS FOR THE ABORTION REFERENDUM included the radical feminists who joined CAR. Hundreds of women walked in and out of its second-floor backroom office on University Avenue for endless meetings, mailings, and strategy sessions. Some dropped in for a cup of coffee or tea or for some sisterly support. In the fall of 1970, these radical feminists discussed, analyzed, and debated strategy and tactics; the mimeograph machine never stopped running. At the UW YWCA, CAR organized leafleting and speaking assignments. From September until November 3, radical feminist activists rang countless doorbells and spoke at churches, synagogues, union meetings, community groups, high schools, colleges, and universities. Some WL-S members spoke at the monthly Veterans of Foreign Wars meeting. They leafleted at the major department stores where women shopped and at workplaces where many women were employed, such as the phone company. Some were gutsy enough to leaflet at UW football games, which attracted huge crowds.

During the 1970 campaign, the VfU and other antiabortion activist groups were not mainly composed of Protestant fundamentalists but rather were largely Catholic. Unlike the tactics of antiabortion organizations today, the VfU's campaign tactics did not further its cause. Committee for Abortion Reform activists subjected the VfU's propaganda to ridicule. For example, the VfU's billboard showed a fetus in a person's hand with the headline "Let Him Live." "Let *Him* Live?" abortion rights activists snarled. "Ha! Male chauvinists are really trying to control women's bodies."[63] The VfU rented a trailer in which it displayed fetuses of goats, monkeys, cows, and other animals—though not those of humans. They brought what they called the Life Van to the UW in an attempt to "educate" students as to the realities of abortion. Students renamed the Life Van the "pickled fetus mobile," and it was soon the butt of so many jokes that it moved on.

Karen Foreit recalled, "I remember one demonstration downtown, in which a young woman nervously approached me and asked if she could join us. She then said that the reason she had come downtown was that an anti-referendum canvasser had visited her at home. During the conversation, her young child came to the door and the visitor stopped talking, stooped down and said to the child, 'Aren't you glad your mommy didn't have an abortion?' Our new member said that she sent the canvasser packing on the spot, and when she saw the notice of our demonstration, decided to join us."[64] Despite the negative reaction to the fetus mobile, the VfU continued to use tactics that backfired.

The VfU did not have the sophisticated understanding of the media that the antiabortion movement does today. In fact, people on both sides of the issue believed that the VfU propaganda actually helped the supporters of Referendum 20. In October, when the VfU called for a rally, WCAR decided to ignore it, but WL-S called on all women's liberation groups to stage a joint counterdemonstration in order "to expose and oppose the nature of this campaign and use this opportunity to reach as many people as possible."[65]

The VfU march was inauspiciously called for October 31—Halloween!—and a large contingent of women from the women's caucus of the Seattle Liberation Front came appropriately dressed as witches. Lee Mayfield described the VfU march: "It was very scary. Suddenly, marching down the hill from the Westlake Mall came hundreds of rosy-cheeked parochial school students, mainly young boys, carrying signs that said KILL KILL."[66] The VfU's signs had "KILL" in huge letters and "the bill" in smaller letters. The impact was dramatic—young people marching to KILL.

The VfU's contingent was no match for the five hundred or so exuberant women's liberation activists. When the young boys tried to sing "He's Got the Whole World in His Hands," the radical feminists chanted back defiantly, "That's the problem!" The antiabortion forces were outyelled, outdanced, outmarched, and outnumbered. After a while the scene got a bit ugly. A group of demonstrators started yelling at and hitting women. Clara Fraser and other radical feminists were chased down a street and hit over the head with picket signs. One young man kept asking Fraser if she believed in God. He was so dumbstruck when she told him she was an atheist that he dropped his picket sign and ran away. The voices of the "unborn" were muted when the antiabortion demonstrators met a contingent of witches marching down Fifth Avenue, beating their drums and chanting. By all measures, the counterdemonstration was tremendously successful. Voices for abortion reform and for women's liberation made the front pages of both Sunday papers and were the lead stories on all three major news shows. Women's liberation had won this battle of the streets and the media. Mayfield believed that the success of this demonstration "was the only point in the campaign where we got some inkling of the potential strength of our movement, as a militant and forthright connection between abortion reform and women's liberation."[67]

The next Tuesday, November 3, the voters went to the polls and ratified Referendum 20 with a majority of 56.5 percent. In King County alone the referendum garnered 60 percent of the votes. Many factors contributed to the referendum's success, including a supportive political climate. Both statewide Republican and Democratic Party leaders supported the bill, including Dan Evans, the liberal Republican governor. So did the major newspapers. In 1970, Washington was a progressive state politically, and it was not dominated by Catholic voters. The WCAR reform waged a carefully thought-out and inclusive campaign for reform from above. But the women's liberation activists must also be credited with the victory. They had been more than energetic foot soldiers, and they changed the political dimension of the abortion struggle. Abortion was now "a woman's right," not just a solution to a problem worked out by a woman with her doctor's or minister's approval. Furthermore, the women's liberation movement had vowed to expand access to abortion, to fight to reduce abortion costs, and to oppose restrictions even if that meant violating the law. It later made good on these pledges, including setting up a modern-day "underground railroad" called the Abortion–Birth Control Referral Service. The movement raised the issue of coercive sterilization and continued its fight for expanded access to birth control for economically disadvantaged, unmarried women and teenagers. It laid the basis for a network of feminist reproductive health centers that was established after the success of Referendum 20. Finally, the abortion campaign galvanized the women's liberation movement and drew thousands more women into the struggle.

Freed Up and Fired Up

4

SEATTLE WAS A HOT TOWN in the summer of 1969. In May, the Black Student Union led a militant strike and walkout at Seattle Central Community College. Police responded to a rock music festival at Alki Beach and to street demonstrations in the University District with tear gas and arrests. The New Left was on the verge of collapse with the split in Students for a Democratic Society (SDS) in June and the explosive disintegration of the Seattle Liberation Front (SLF) in 1970. An angry, confident, and energized Left feminist movement emerged from the tatters of the New Left. Women rejected the male domination of New Left organizations, criticized the exclusion of issues that were important to women from radical analyses and agendas, and formed organizations of their own where they could develop their ideas and priorities without having to debate men who were either uninterested or hostile.

The radical women's liberation movement did not abandon the Left, despite the allegations made by some journalists at the time and by some historians in retrospect.[1] In Seattle many feminist activists had developed within and remained connected to the Old and New Left, rather than coming to political consciousness for the first time around women's concerns. In contrast to many other cities, Seattle also had women's groups that were affiliated with Old Left organizations and conducted their own campaigns on women's issues, which brought them into contact with younger women in New Left organizations. Finally, most of Seattle's autonomous women's organizations, like others across the country, maintained close ties with gender-mixed antiwar, anti-imperialist, welfare rights, antiracist, trade union, and working-class coalitions and campaigns.

In the 1960s, the term *radical* applied to feminists in two contradictory ways. It was claimed by feminists who were separatists, who refused to work with men in any way. They thought that women's oppression was *the* fundamental form of oppression; did not connect race, class, and sexuality with sexism; and did not see themselves as part of the Left. Radical feminism was also claimed by socialist, anarchist, antiracist, and anti-imperialist feminists who sought to combat all forms of oppression. They continued to think of themselves as part of the Left and as revolutionaries; worked intensively in antiwar, anti-imperialist, antiracist, and working-class campaigns while addressing women's issues; and brought a gendered perspective to the Left's analysis.[2] With the exception of Radical Women, which still exists today, Seattle's Left feminist and anti-imperialist women's organizations were relatively short lived.

STUDENTS FOR A DEMOCRATIC SOCIETY, the major national organization for student radicals, was founded in 1960 by members of the youth organization of the social democratic League for Industrial Democracy. Its early politics were hardly revolutionary, but SDS incorporated its analysis of US foreign policy, racism, and economic and social inequality into a coherent critique of what its leaders called "the system." SDS was concerned about the "alienation" that pervaded American society and culture in the 1950s and early 1960s and advocated "participatory democracy" both within movements for change and as a better way of organizing society and politics. In addition, SDS broke with the entrenched anticommunism of the post–World War II period, which had paralyzed progressive movements and decimated their leadership and membership for over a decade. Individuals and organizations affiliated with Marxist-Leninist organizations and parties were not excluded, ending the poisonous legacy of McCarthyism.

In 1965, SDS burst onto the national scene when it organized a militant demonstration in Washington, DC, protesting the escalation of the war in Vietnam. Over twenty thousand people listened to SDS leaders denounce the war as imperialist and racist. The organization's support for the Black Freedom struggle, opposition to the war in Vietnam, and embrace of youth culture, dismissively summarized by others as "sex, drugs, and rock and roll," attracted tens of thousands of college students. In the wake of the global upheavals in 1968, SDS leaders became convinced that their organization must declare itself revolutionary and commit to a Leninist, antiracist, and anti-imperialist program. Various Maoist and Stalinist organizations joined SDS to promote their particular points of view. In June 1969, its national convention in Chicago degenerated into screaming chaos, with hostile factions expelling one another and each claiming victory. Their nod to the women's liberation movement consisted of one faction chanting "fight male chauvinism" when Illinois Black Panther Party member Rufus "Chaka" Walls, speaking from the podium for the other faction, used the term "pussy power" and charged that "Superman was a punk because he never fucked Lois Lane."[3] The end result was tragic. For all intents and purposes, the largest anti-imperialist student organization in the US, which began with such promise and quickly mobilized a generation, was no more.

In Seattle, the breakup of SDS had little impact on the existing women's liberation groups. No members of Radical Women belonged to SDS. Women's Liberation–Seattle (WL-S) was by then an autonomous organization. Most SDS women went into either the Weatherman faction, a self-styled anti-imperialist, revolutionary organization committed to acts of violence against property and the state, or the Revolutionary Youth Movement, a self-styled Stalinist and Maoist organization that did not advocate individual or collective acts of violence against people. Both organizations agreed that radical women in the US should be in the vanguard of anti-imperialist activity. In Seattle, Weatherwomen displayed their militancy by tearing through the University of Washington (UW) Air Force ROTC building, throwing ink bombs, spray-painting the walls, and fighting with ROTC cadets. A handful of women who had been in SDS gravitated to the International Socialists, a Trotskyist organization that argued that the communist countries were not really socialist but rather a new form of class society.[4]

The local successor to SDS was the SLF. It had a shorter life than SDS, but its bust-up had greater implications for feminist organizing. It was founded in January 1970 by Michael Lerner, a Berkeley activist and visiting UW philosophy professor who came to Seattle for the express purpose of creating a community-based socialist organization. Four charismatic Cornell student activists, Michael Abeles, Jeff Dowd, Joe Kelly, and Chip Marshall, moved to Seattle and soon joined with Lerner. The Cornell four, affecting the styles of Che Guevara and the Sundance Kid (based on the antiauthoritarian hero of the 1969 movie *Butch Cassidy and the Sundance Kid*, portrayed by Robert Redford), were proponents of Weatherman-style politics and tactics. They came to Seattle fleeing potential arrest and FBI questioning.

Hundreds of young people, enraged by violent racist repression and the US escalation of the war in Vietnam, Laos, and Cambodia, joined the SLF. Its organizational structure consisted of collectives located in a number of Seattle neighborhoods. Reflecting the combination of revolutionary politics and youth culture, the collectives were named the East Is Red, Red Avengers, Tupamaros, Stonerage, and Long Time Coming. The mothership collective was called Sundance. Walt Crowley brilliantly identified the causes of the SLF's self-destruction: "This loose, theoretically participatory democracy was an open invitation to a dictatorship of the ego-tariat."[5]

The SLF immediately leaped into the national spotlight by calling a demonstration, dubbed "The Day After," to protest the verdict in the Chicago Seven trial and the shackling and jailing of Black Panther Party leader Bobby Seale. On a cold and rainy Tuesday in February 1970, over two thousand people showed up in front of the federal courthouse in Seattle. The overwhelming majority of demonstrators came to protest angrily and peacefully, but a handful was determined to provoke. The authorities responded with overkill. Helicopters buzzed overhead, snipers stood on roofs, riot squads fired tear gas, and police in full military body armor clubbed nonviolent demonstrators along with bystanders. Hundreds were injured. Fourteen were charged with federal crimes, and many others faced the usual charges of failure to disperse, failure to obey police authority, disorderly conduct, and profanity.

Two months later, the federal government charged five members of the SLF and two people affiliated with Weatherman with inciting or intending to incite a riot. The SLF used the trial to organize opposition to political repression. There were constant vocal disruptions and walkouts during the Seattle Seven trial, and SLF supporters demonstrated regularly in front of the courthouse. The prosecution's case was weak because government witnesses testified that they would go to any lengths to jail the radicals. Judge George Boldt, aged and clearly out of his league, declared a mistrial on December 10, citing all defendants for contempt of court. He summarily found them guilty, sentenced them to six months in prison, and refused to grant bail. The defendants eventually served three months in prison.

At the same time, local SLF collectives were involved in grassroots organizing around tax reform, welfare, and unemployment. Always bubbling under the surface was the seething rage of SLF women, furious at their marginalization and subjection to the crudest forms of male chauvinism. Some activists, such as Py Bateman, a former SDS member and later a rape prevention activist and founder of the Feminist Karate Union, noticed the leadership's disdain for women at the outset. "Well, I was very tuned into the way they treated women, particularly the way they treated me."[6] Although the third point of SLF's Fifteen-Point Program was "WE WILL STRUGGLE FOR THE FULL LIBERATION OF WOMEN AS A NECESSARY PART OF THE REVOLUTIONARY STRUGGLE," SLF members were seldom active participants in the ongoing campaigns around women's issues.[7] The women complained bitterly that the SLF ignored both gender and race. For example, one male SLF member provided the organization with pages of research on employment at Boeing that never mentioned African American or women workers. Its unemployment and antiwar leaflets entirely disregarded women. Some SLF women refused to participate in what they deemed "just another male defined, male-led demonstration."[8] One SLF member admitted, "There exists in Seattle today no women's group which has spoken with effectiveness, a sense of urgency and a full political understanding of how the liberation of women relates to the ongoing worldwide struggle for liberation from the coercive oppression of capitalism."[9] This tone-deaf comment about the politics and effectiveness of the existing Seattle women's liberation groups no doubt did not endear the SLF to members of Radical Women and Women's Liberation–Seattle.

Women SLF members voiced their grievances about the position of women in their collectives. Echoing sisters in movement collectives across the country, they fumed that women did all the household and secretarial work as well as providing men with sex. Left feminists who had read William Hinton's *Fanshen*, which highlighted the stories of Chinese village women speaking about their oppression, used that account as the basis for their consciousness-raising or rap groups. In China, "speaking bitterness" meetings were public gatherings in neighborhoods and villages in which women denounced the oppressive behavior of specific men (and some women) who exercised power over others. These denunciations discredited the men and usually resulted in their removal from positions of authority, including in the Chinese Communist Party. Here, the SLF women found the inspiration for direct, public denunciations of male SLF leaders who abused and oppressed women in the organization. Women quickly realized that male chauvinism was at the heart of the Sundance leadership's ideology and practice. Michael Lerner made a habit of sleeping with his students. He believed that SLF members needed to get over their "sexual hang-ups and secret longing for one another by having some sort of group sexual political experience. After that, with secret sexual longings out of the way, one could get down to business better. . . . The collective meeting degenerated into an aborted game of strip poker."[10]

Many women found the movement's social life oppressive, especially in the bars they frequented. SLF members patronized the Roach Tavern, popular with Seattle bikers, which proudly displayed a sign reading, "This is a man's bar. Women will be tolerated only if they refrain from excessive talking." A group of Left feminists, including members of Radical Women, was assaulted after they tried to tear down the offending sign. Men in the SLF defended the sign and opposed feminist activism. "After all fascism is going to come down soon," said one member; "we can't afford to alienate the bikers."[11] Women began sharing horror stories about the cavalier sexism of the leadership. "Our humanity was denied to us. Michael Lerner could talk about the availability of a woman for his bed and joke about using sex to recruit women, 'Well boys, I guess it'll take a gang rape for this one.'"[12] Women in the SLF charged that Mike Abeles "could fuck a sixteen-year-old virgin, give her the clap, not tell her and leave her. And he couldn't understand what he had done." Abeles protested, "I don't see how you could be oppressing someone when you're socking it to them." Abeles was also charged with threatening women: "You bitch, I'd like to smash your face in. You're not oppressed. We're the ones that are dying in Vietnam and dying in the jails." When asked about overcoming male chauvinism, Chip Marshall was quoted as saying, "It means you don't treat your girlfriend like a sexual object."[13] Stephanie Coontz, a leading antiwar activist, remembered "one of the Seattle Seven jumping up and down in front of me saying that my blood was going to run in the streets because I was a revisionist bitch." This misogynist rhetoric was extreme, even among left-wing men: "Only SLF men would call another comrade, another woman, a bitch."[14]

A series of rapes at the 1970 Sky River Rock festival was the last straw. Sky River Rock, founded in 1968, was a relatively violence-free, druggy, boozy, nudity optional, friendly, open-air concert featuring performances by nationally known as well as local bands. In 1970, in part to organize for the Seattle Seven defense, the SLF decided to sponsor the rock festival, promising to provide politics and security. Women were appalled at the decision to sponsor the concert after the violence at the 1969 Altamont, California, rock festival. At that event, headlined by the Rolling Stones, the Hell's Angels were in charge of security; one gang member stabbed a concertgoer; three other people were killed; and numerous women charged that members of the security team sexually assaulted them. The SLF's Hydra Collective said that it opposed male chauvinism and could provide adequate protection.

When the news of rampant sexual assaults and gang rapes at Sky River got around, women were incensed by the SLF men's blasé reactions. One said,

"Well it depends on the circumstances, but I never saw anything wrong with a little fucking myself." Another contended, "I don't believe there were any gang rapes . . . the women got what they deserved." Women in the SLF wrote a detailed open letter that began, "The Seattle Liberation Front sponsored the Sky River Rock Festival. Three women were raped. One woman was stabbed attempting to escape. A fourth rape was prevented by a female 'Chauvin patrol.'"[15] At a general meeting that fall, SLF men were confronted by furious women who ordered Mike Abeles, Rick Alba, Jeff Dowd, Joe Kelly, Mike Lerner, John LeLand, Chip Marshall, and Bob Orum to get out of town. The outside of Lerner's house was trashed with graffiti: "Male chauvinist pig lives here"; "Get out of town Lerner"; "No more fucking for you" (figure 4.1). One of the collectives, named for the Mexican revolutionary Emilio Zapata, left the SLF in support of the women. Louise Crowley wrote a lengthy denunciation in *Lilith*. The Fanshen Letter, as it was called, was widely circulated within the Seattle Left as well as nationally. *And Ain't I a Woman*, the mimeographed publication of WL-S, reprinted the Fanshen Letter in its entirety, naming names and thanking the women for "refusing to shut up and 'wait until after the Revolution,' and for reminding us again that any male-dominated revolution would simply reinstitute oppression under another name."[16] Not all the men left town, although Lerner did. Many of the authors of the Fanshen Letter formed a feminist communal house called Fanshen. Even though they declared that they hoped their comments would convince men to be better supporters of women's liberation and strengthen the Left, the document sealed the fate of the SLF.

The existing women's liberation groups participated in the raging debates about the SLF. Louise Crowley supported the SLF women when they confronted the men. "I've been in the movement a long time and every time it came right down to the women's issue, it was pushed aside because there were politically more important issues."[17] The main question that members of Fanshen, the Anna Louise Strong Brigade (ALSB), Radical Women, and WL-S debated was whether to support the accused members of the Seattle Seven. According to Louise Crowley, members of Fanshen and the ALSB, as well as unaffiliated former SLF members, were sorely disappointed that much of the Left dismissed the Fanshen Letter's charges. Crowley commented, "As might have been expected," the Fanshen Letter "was widely printed in the women's-liberation press and virtually ignored everywhere, as though anything women have to say could be of concern only to other women."[18] Radical Women, while highly critical of the SLF for its adventurism, male chauvinism,

Figure 4.1 / Michael Lerner's house, with graffiti painted by women's liberation activists in the fall of 1970, Seattle, Washington. Photograph by Joseph Felsenstein.

and lack of serious programmatic work, nonetheless supported the defense campaign.

Women's Liberation–Seattle was divided on the question. The WL-S members who did not want to defend the indicted Seattle Seven had for the most part never been in mixed-gender Left organizations. They argued that their male chauvinism and repulsive treatment of women made it impossible for feminists to support them. The WL-S women who had just founded *Pandora*, a feminist newsletter, asked "whether women could support the Seattle 8 as allies."[19] "For women who think of themselves as part of a broader movement for social change, are men allies because they too are struggling for human liberation? When 'women's issues' conflict with the male-dominated left, should women defer and leave feminism for a quieter time?" Then the women threw down the gauntlet of feminist resistance: "If we are ever to succeed in the struggle for women, we can no longer join with men who refuse to recognize our humanity or the political importance of women's liberation. Regardless of the potential for uniting people for human liberation, there is no alliance possible with male supremacy. In light of this, we need not apologize for our reservations or our outright unwillingness to defend the Seattle 8." Finally, they warned their sisters: "Throughout history we have been considered secondary. Many times women have given up our own battles for others and a growing feminist movement has died away. We now have another chance. But if we don't take ourselves seriously, and if we continue to defer to others, we will fail again."[20]

Those who argued in favor of supporting the legal defense of the male SLF leaders either were members of Marxist organizations or had experience on mixed-gender defense committees. They argued that the defendants were arrested for organizing social protest, not for being terrible sexists. They contended that women's liberation would not be well served by supporting or ignoring the consequences of a repressive state. In a close vote, WL-S voted to support the Seattle Seven's defense. Those who dissented left the group, the first split in WL-S. This debate about whether to support unrepentant male supremacists who had been arrested for antiwar, antiracist, and anti-imperialist activities demonstrated the unconscious imprint the Marxist Left had on its most feminist members. Those women in mixed Left organizations were willing to give tepid support to male supremacy in return for the "greater good" of opposing the state. The *Pandora* founders made clear that male supremacists were not allies and should not be welcomed as a part of the "broader social movement." *Pandora* continued as an important voice for both the mainstream women's movement and for Left feminists.

IN RETROSPECT, it is clear that 1970 marked the high point of the radical Left women's movement. Out of the implosion and explosion of SDS and the SLF, thousands of women joined and participated in radical, militant socialist feminist organizations. They included groups that were inextricably tied to the Old Left, such as Radical Women, which was linked with the Freedom Socialist Party Bolshevik; Campus Women's Liberation (CWL), which was tied to the Socialist Workers Party (SWP) and the Young Socialist Alliance; WL-S, which had links to the Freedom Socialist Party Menshevik and the International Socialists (IS); and groups with ideological connections to the Stalinist, Maoist, and anti-imperialist Left, such as Fanshen, the Red Mountain Collective, the Sisters of Than Hoa, and the Anna Louise Strong Brigade. While there were substantial political differences among these groups, they agreed that capitalism was the problem and some form of socialism was the solution. Efforts to confront male chauvinism, racism, and imperialism were essential components of their outlook and program. Members of all these groups eschewed conventional electoral politics, and especially opposed working within the Democratic Party. In Seattle, they transformed existing institutions, organizations, ideologies, and relationships and built new ones. Significantly, all of this was done through a wide range of women's organizations rather than a single umbrella group or coalition, in contrast to women's liberation activists in Boston and Chicago.

Fanshen, the ALSB, the Red Mountain Collective, and the Sisters of Than Hoa shared political perspectives on Marxism, Leninism, Stalinism, Trotskyism, Maoism, and anti-imperialism. All these groups were composed solely of White women. It is very difficult to write about some of these groups in detail, for there are very few remaining records; they did not produce much written material, and little was written about them in either the Seattle newspapers and the UW *Daily* or the Left press and radical feminist publications.[21]

The only surviving information about the Sisters of Than Hoa is that the group was formed to organize a conference in Canada, bringing together women from the US, Canada, Vietnam, Laos, and Cambodia. In 1971 it hosted an International Women's Day event and an all-day festival in Seattle's Volunteer Park.[22]

Fanshen, an all-women's communal house, attained national attention with the Fanshen Letter, which circulated throughout the women's liberation and Left press.[23] The statement's impact was similar to that of Robin Morgan's "Goodbye to All That," the iconic polemic against the male chauvinism that dominated the New Left, as a theoretical justification for refusing to work in mixed groups.[24] Fanshen women were known for directly confronting individual men on the left and encouraging other women to do the same. Members were active in the antiwar movement and in organizing for day care, health care, and abortion rights. The collective dissolved in 1971.

The Red Mountain Collective included women who had been in SDS, the SLF, or both. A number had lived in the Magic Mountain, a mixed-gender political commune.[25] It had fewer than twenty members, who held weekly educational meetings focused mainly on Marxism, Leninism, and anti-imperialism; and engaged in militant, confrontational actions. In 1972, members broke into and seized the KNBC news station to protest the ongoing US bombing of Cambodia. They were very supportive of Referendum 20, helped to create women's health centers, and engaged in guerilla theater, dressing up as doctors supporting women's reproductive freedom. In another instance, Red Mountain members wore witches' costumes, went down to Pioneer Square, and trashed bars where women danced topless. The collective broke up in 1972 over left-wing factional disputes.

The Anna Louise Strong Brigade was named after the socialist feminist activist who had been a journalist for the labor-owned daily newspaper, the *Seattle Union Record*, and a participant in the 1919 Seattle General Strike. In 1921, Strong traveled to the Soviet Union and reported on the progress of its revolution; in 1936, she went to Spain to report on the civil war between fascists and antifascists. Expelled from the USSR after World War II because of her sympathy with the Chinese Communist Party, she moved to China in the 1950s. Strong was the first Western journalist to interview Mao Zedong, whom she famously quoted as describing US imperialism as a "paper tiger." The Chinese Communist Party named her an honorary member of the Red Guard. According to Py Bateman, members of the ALSB corresponded with Strong from the late 1960s until her death.[26]

In 1969, the SDS chapter wanted to commemorate the fiftieth anniversary of the Seattle General Strike. It was able to get three men who had been strike participants: Harvey O'Connor, author of *Revolution in Seattle*; Frank Wright, who had been a member of the Industrial Workers of the World (IWW), the Communist Party (CP), and the SWP, as well as an FSP Menshevik sympathizer; and Arne Swaback, also a member of the IWW, the CP, and the SWP before he became a Maoist and joined the Progressive Labor Party. (He appeared as a witness in Warren Beatty's movie *Reds*.) The SDS chapter wanted to have women speak. While Strong was alive and in China, there was no way that she could come to the US, so a woman SDS member represented her. The title of the talk came from one of her columns, "I Must Be a Socialist."

The ALSB defined itself "as an 'anti-imperialist' women's group ... and it is apparent that we women of the Anna Louis Strong Brigade see a relationship between the existence of U.S. imperialism and our own oppression as women."[27] Like the women involved in Fanshen and the Red Mountain Collective, ALSB members were active in antiwar, abortion rights, day care, and health-care activism. Unlike members of Fanshen and the Red Mountain Collective, members did not live collectively, but like their sister groups, they engaged in systematic, intense theoretical discussions. According to Grey Osterud, first a member of Radical Women and then the ALSB, "We were trying to figure out how to integrate Marxism and feminism in such a way as to advance both. I recall reading and discussing Mao's writings and applying his concept of contradictions to women's position in order to identify the dynamic forces that would stimulate mobilization for social change. I also recall analyzing Marx's and Mao's concepts of consciousness to see how they might work in the present, particularly among an oppressed group like women who nonetheless lived in a white supremacist society at the peak of imperial power." Osterud reflected, "It was challenging to try to theorize how women's consciousness was formed and could be transformed under those contradictory conditions. We also read about women's groups in China, which we thought of as a model for grassroots organizing. At least for me, ALSB was more of a study group and an affinity group that participated in women's liberation and antiwar actions collectively."[28]

The diary that Osterud kept in 1970 demonstrates the intellectual caliber of these discussions. They rivaled any advanced graduate seminar on Marxist-Leninist politics. Members read from Karl Marx, Friedrich Engels, Vladimir Lenin, Joseph Stalin, Mao, Frantz Fanon, Fidel Castro, Che Guevara, and Clara Zetkin, to name a few. They used these readings to debate theoretical questions, especially the origins of capitalism, imperialism, racism, and women's oppression, as well as how to apply their theoretical understanding to the antiwar and women's movements. Members of the ALSB were critical of the Trotskyism of Radical Women, as well as what they saw as the failure of WL-S to make anti-imperialism and the fight against White supremacy a priority. A number of members, however, were very supportive of WL-S's work on abortion and women's health. They were self-critical of their own "failure to work as a group," leading to their "stagnation, decline of members' commitment and the weakening of ALSB as a 'force' in the Seattle women's movement."[29] The ALSB dissolved in 1972.

The three other Left socialist women's liberation organizations at the time—Radical Women, Women's Liberation–Seattle, and Campus Women's Liberation—all had left-wing Trotskyist origins. The largest was WL-S, originally a committee of two mixed-gender organizations, SDS and the Peace and Freedom Party. From its inception as an autonomous women's liberation group in 1969 through 1972, it had approximately one hundred members who were overwhelmingly but not all White, predominantly under the age of thirty-five, childless, and either in college or college educated. The original members of WL-S had been active in a wide range of political causes and organizations, including Indian fishing rights, Black and White Concern, the United Farm Workers' boycott, and opposition to the US war in Vietnam. Some belonged to socialist organizations; others were red diaper babies. By early 1970, WL-S was attracting new members who had not been politically active in Left, antiracist, and anti-imperialist organizations before and whose primary commitment was to women's liberation.

In 1970, some members of WL-S lived in the Magic Mountain. For about five years the Magic Mountain had been a semicommunal rooming house, but "it found its true and noblest *métier*... as a Women's Liberation Commune."[30]

For a brief period it became a center for WL-S and housed its office. Members repainted a room, installed a telephone, secured a mimeograph machine, rented an electric typewriter, and began collecting books and periodicals for a library. The Magic Mountain shared its office and its food with those in need. During the February "Day After" demonstrations at the federal courthouse, the household called itself the February 6, 1919 Collective, marking the date of the Seattle General Strike. Three collective members were arrested at the demonstration.

When the commune was first organized, four men, along with "six women, three children and fourteen cats," lived in eleven bedrooms dispersed over four floors. Writing in *And Ain't I a Woman*, WL-S members explained why they wanted men in the house and discussed the problems they faced dealing with male chauvinism. The experiment lasted about nine months. There was no collective explanation for the commune's end. Some people moved to other living quarters; others left the city.

Women's Liberation–Seattle had a loosely defined organizational structure. It never had officers, but at its peak membership in 1970 it had a five-person steering committee to coordinate its multifarious activities. Meetings took place in people's homes or at the University YWCA. Activists met weekly. One day a month was a general meeting open to all WL-S members, where activists reported on their committee work, as well as making announcements about activities and issues in Seattle. Committees working on specific issues or projects met once a month. These included welfare rights; Referendum 20; the Staff Women's Forum, an organization of women employed in nonfaculty jobs at the UW; Women's Liberation at Seattle Central Community College; the newsletter committee; and the Working Women's Committee. In 1971, the Working Women's Committee published a mimeographed leaflet called "Traffic Jam," which was aimed at women members of the Communications Workers of America who worked at Pacific Northwest Bell. The WL-S women, some of whom who worked at "Ma Bell," leafleted the company's workplaces for about three months.

At monthly WL-S educational meetings, members discussed a wide range of political works, including Marx and Engels's *Communist Manifesto*, Fanon's *The Wretched of the Earth* and *Black Skin, White Masks*, Anne Koedt's *The Myth of the Vaginal Orgasm*, and articles and manifestos on topics such as housework, US imperialism, women in the Chinese revolution, racism in the US, and the Black liberation struggle. Finally, each month WL-S organized consciousness-raising or rap group meetings. These meetings tended to be small, with no more than twelve women present, and everyone participated in discussions of personal and political issues ranging from orgasms, sexualities, rape, and self-defense to housework and relationships with mothers, husbands, men, and other women.

Members of WL-S disagreed with Radical Women's critique of rap groups as overly personal and contended that consciousness-raising groups empowered women by generating new understandings of the politics of gendered relationships. Instead of believing that women's powerlessness in the family, at work, in government, and in the community was their own fault, they discovered that their situation was not solely individual but also collective and rooted in basic social structures and institutions. So were the solutions. Sisterhood nurtured in small groups was believed to give women the strength and spirit to fight.

Beginning in 1970, WL-S published *And Ain't I a Woman*. Members sold the newsletter at the Pike Place Market, at the UW, in the U District, and at Seattle Central Community College, as well as at demonstrations and political events. It cost fifteen cents for women but twenty cents for men "until there is equal pay." The gendered price differential was an effective consciousness raiser, provoking spirited discussions and arguments about equal pay. The ten issues covered the ongoing struggles around Referendum 20, day care, the Equal Rights Amendment, and protective legislation. Articles dealt with internationalism, racism, support for the emerging lesbian and gay liberation movements, and opposition to the war in Vietnam. Critiques of movies, television shows, magazines, and feminist writings broadened its appeal. Although WL-S devoted an issue of *And Ain't I a Woman* to the Free Angela Davis campaign, it said very little about the racial animus that targeted her and the Black Power activists she supported, and even its analysis of women in prison did not center race.

Women's Liberation–Seattle was one of the first radical feminist groups to support the emerging gay and lesbian liberation movement. Several WL-S members had been publicly "out" before Stonewall and in 1970 were cofounders of the Gay Liberation Front and the Gay Women's Alliance; after 1970 they formed Leftist Lezzies and other lesbian liberation organizations. In contrast to a number of women's organizations in other cities, there was no split between lesbian and straight women in feminist organizations in Seattle.

The second-largest Left feminist organization was Radical Women (RW), which had the most racially and ethnically diverse membership of all the Left feminist organizations. After 1969, Radical Women was led by the FSP. As one of its founders, Gloria Martin, put it, "In RW's formative stages, FSP's leadership prevailed on an unacknowledged level, given RW's still shaky developmental status. Nevertheless, as RW sharpened its socialist feminist program, a closer and more open alliance with the FSP emerged."[31] In 1973, the FSP announced that Radical Women was its affiliate, which meant that Radical Women was no longer an autonomous women's organization. It had a more formalized structure with elected leaders. Its headquarters and meeting space, Freeway Hall, was a center for movement and community events, replete with a library, kitchen, and meeting and party rooms. The hall was a base for the antiwar movement, women's liberation, the Congress of Racial Equality (CORE), the Black Panther Party and the civil rights struggle, labor defense work, community organizing on behalf of Chicano and Native American rights, and much more. It hosted hundreds of lectures, forums, fund raisers, debates, symposiums, and classes on every pertinent subject and housed childcare, parties, dances, cultural events, movies, theatrical productions, banquets, and rummage sales.[32]

Radical Women members were politically active everywhere. In 1971, they organized a UW campus branch, which was active at the UW, the ASUW Women's Commission, in the day care campaign, and in campus antiwar protests. In addition, Radical Women members supported the Black Panther Party, GI antiwar organizing, and various Great Society antipoverty programs. In the early 1970s, they helped to organize a strike and a union of low-paid employees, most of whom were women of color, at the UW. After 1970, the group supported many lesbian and gay struggles. In 1973, after the collapse of most of the other Left feminist organizations, collectives, and communes, Radical Women emerged as the leading voice of socialist feminism. A number of its members went into traditionally male-dominated trades. At the publicly owned power company Seattle City Light, Clara Fraser crafted and implemented a plan to train women as utility electricians. For these efforts and her prominent role in a mass walkout at the company, Fraser was fired and successfully fought an intense, seven-year legal battle that ultimately affirmed the right of free speech in the workplace and won her reinstatement.

In addition to its involvement in ongoing women's struggles in Seattle, Radical Women participated in citywide as well as national groups and campaigns, including the Feminist Coordinating Council and the Coalition of Labor Union Women.[33] It was involved in the defense committees for Joan Little and Inez García, women of color who were arrested for killing their rapists. Radical Women also defended Yvonne Wanrow, an Indigenous woman accused of shooting a man who was abusing her son. It held workshops on topics ranging from public speaking to how to get a divorce, convened public educational conferences, and hosted countless movement fund raisers and other parties. Radical Women and the FSP continued to attract working-class women of color, who have held prominent positions in the organization. Detractors have pointed to the group's dogmatism and sectarian behavior. Martin's book chronicling the first ten years of the FSP Bolshevik and Radical Women attests to that. Nonetheless, Radical Women was one of the very few activist multiracial socialist feminist organizations with women of color in the leadership.

Campus Women's Liberation (CWL), the last group to be organized, was perhaps the least imaginative, innovative, and radical of all the groups. Its lack of creativity may have resulted from the sectarian infighting that marked the organization from its inception to its demise. Beginning in 1970, members of the Young Socialist Alliance (YSA), the youth group of the SWP, began to attend WL-S meetings. Members of WL-S were aware of the SWP/YSA's change in policy toward feminism, in which they dismissed the women's movement and denied the existence of sexism in their own organizations. The group's modus operandi across the country was to have its members join existing women's liberation groups, achieve a voting majority, and then determine the organizations' policies and actions based on SWP/YSA perspectives. The infiltration usually led to an intense faction fight and a split.[34] Beginning in the fall of 1970, unbeknownst to the membership of WL-S, YSA members who had joined WL-S announced that there would be a UW campus chapter. Hundreds showed up at the initial meetings. Members of WL-S did not wish to fight with the YSA over who organized the meeting and was in control of the group, so its campus members pulled out. During its first year, CWL was very active. It held weekly educational, rap group, and public meetings; organized a teach-in on women's liberation and a feminist film series; brought in speakers; and hosted potluck picnics and baseball games. Three days a week, members distributed literature and talked with students in the student union. The stated purpose of CWL was to "unite around the common bond of sisterhood. We can act together towards the liberation of women, to achieve equal pay for equal work, childcare, abortion reform, to re-educate ourselves and others."[35] Members also worked in a number of coalitions with other Left feminist and mainstream feminist groups.

Within a year, sectarianism killed the campus organization. In July 1971, CWL sent delegates to the first Women's National Abortion Action Campaign (WONAAC) conference. The SWP, which was the major organizing force behind WONAAC, held positions on how to organize for abortion rights that went against those developed by Left feminists. Left feminists had always called for free abortion on demand, an end to sterilization abuse, free childcare, and "freedom of sexual expression," which at that time meant support for lesbian and gay rights. Members of CWL had voted that WONAAC support all the Left feminist demands. But at the convention, the YSA delegates voted against the CWL position and for the SWP position, which spoke only to liberalizing abortion laws. These actions by the YSA members infuriated the majority, so those affiliated with the SWP were expelled. This split was the culmination of long-simmering grievances against the YSA's behavior in CWL. Radical Women, WL-S, and the ASUW Women's Commission defended CWL's action.[36] But the organization collapsed by the end of 1971.

In 1970, there were three other organizations that came out of the radical women's liberation movement and supported Left feminism, although they were not expressly left-wing. The University YWCA worked with women of all political affiliations, advocated for women's rights and sexual liberation, and was antiracist and antiwar, but it never explicitly opposed US imperialism or capitalism. The ASUW Women's Commission was an integral part of the structure of the ASUW. For a while it was staffed by left-of-center feminists, but it always had to operate within the limitations set down by the academy. The stated purpose of *Pandora*, the journal founded by women from WL-S and edited by Erin Von Bronkhorst, was to "maintain communication and sisterhood among the various groups and give fair and accurate coverage to events and projects which concern women's struggle for equality."

THE VARIOUS WOMEN'S LIBERATION GROUPS were not particularly friendly toward each other, given their significant political, organizational, and personal differences. Still, they managed to work together around a number of critical issues. Individuals from these groups participated in meetings and demonstrated in support of Referendum 20. They engaged in actions against bridal fairs, as well as wet T-shirt or hot pants contests at local bars. When waitresses at the Iron Bull Tavern were fired for refusing to wear skimpy "go-go outfits," women from all the groups picketed the tavern. Their leaflet linked women's liberation and workers' rights: "Women will either work with conditions that they control or the Iron Bull's Tavern will be closed."[37]

They all played central roles in making March 8, International Women's Day, an inclusive, citywide celebration. Throughout the US, Left feminists' discovery of the history of International Women's Day led to public celebrations, and eventually March of every year became Women's History Month.[38] In March 1969, the Women's Liberation Committee of SDS and the Peace and Freedom Party held the first International Women's Day celebration in Seattle since 1945.

The next year, WL-S, Radical Women, CWL, and the ASUW Women's Commission organized a daylong teach-in. The speakers reflected Seattle's diversity and inclusiveness. Men were welcome. Topics included women and socialism, the "superexploitation" of working women, the history of women in trade unions, and struggles for women's liberation. Janet McCloud, a spokeswoman for Native Americans whose grandmother gave her the name Yet-Si-Blue, "the woman who talks," discussed the ongoing struggle for fishing rights, which she publicized in *Survival News*.[39] In 1974, after reaching out to Indigenous nations across the continent, she cofounded Women of All Red Nations. That same year, US district court judge George Boldt reaffirmed the treaty rights of Washington State's Indian tribes not only to fish in accustomed places but also to keep half of the state's steelhead and salmon catch. In addition, Alice Spencer spoke for the Black Panther Party. Other speakers included Clara Fraser from Radical Women, Sue Shinn from CWL, and Lee Mayfield and Judith Shapiro from WL-S. The guest speaker was Margaret Benston, a well-known socialist feminist from Vancouver, British Columbia, who analyzed the political economy of women's liberation. What is most striking is how well these women and organizations worked together in issue-oriented coalitions, advocating abortion reform, supporting women workers, and opposing the war in Vietnam, as well as addressing other aspects of women's rights.

Left feminists in Seattle all recognized that, while they spoke about a universal "we," women were divided by class, race, and empire. A constant theme was "the Jackie debate." If women are a class or caste, does that mean that Jacqueline Kennedy Onassis is oppressed under capitalism? Does Lady Bird Johnson, the wealthy White wife of Lyndon Johnson, the president who was escalating the war against the people of Vietnam, have anything in common with Vietnamese women? What does a Black maid share with the White woman who employs her? These discussions were groping toward the intersectional theory that left-wing Black feminists such as Flo Kennedy and the Combahee River Collective were advancing and was articulated in the 1980s by Kimberlé Crenshaw.

Most of these groups were opposed to participating in the Democratic Party's electoral activity. Repulsed by the Democrats' support for the war in Vietnam and other imperialist foreign policies, outraged by the United States' rampant racism, and in revolt against pervasive sexism, women's liberation activists believed that grassroots and confrontational politics produced more socially progressive results. Some left-wing groups, such as the Peace and Freedom Party, the Socialist Workers Party, and the Black Panther Party, participated in electoral politics. But elections were not front and center on any of the groups' agendas; instead, they focused on issue-oriented campaigns.

Their approach to Democratic Party politics was best demonstrated in October 1972 when Margaret Sloan, an African American civil rights activist and *Ms.* magazine editor, and Gloria Steinem, an internationally renowned feminist activist, came to Seattle. The two women spoke at a dinner sponsored by the Washington State National Women's Political Caucus, an organization founded by Steinem and others, held at the University YWCA, and at an event sponsored by the ASUW Women's Commission held at the UW. These gatherings highlighted the Whiteness of radical as well as mainstream feminism. Most of the newspaper coverage in the *Seattle Times*, the *Seattle Post-Intelligencer*, and the UW *Daily* focused on Steinem and did not cover meetings with women of color. At all their talks, Sloan and Steinem emphasized the interconnections between race and gender as well as the importance of building a movement that included all women. The audiences were overwhelmingly White and supportive.

At the UW meeting, however, activists from the Women's Commission, the University YWCA, Radical Women, CWL, and unaffiliated Left feminists, many of whom had been in WL-S, the ALSB, and other groups, leafleted the audience and vocally challenged both Steinem and Sloan for their support of George McGovern, the Democratic Party's presidential nominee.[40] They accused them of not supporting Shirley Chisholm strongly enough and argued that McGovern did not support abortion rights and was "part of the capitalist ruling class." They addressed their questions mainly to Steinem rather than to Sloan, perhaps reflecting not only White leftists' reluctance to challenge a Black feminist but also Steinem's greater prominence. Sloan and Steinem argued that a McGovern presidency would be far better for women than a continuation of the Nixon administration. "For women on welfare," Steinem said, "the difference between McGovern and Nixon is a difference of life or death."[41] Later that night, Steinem invited a group of women back to her hotel room, where the argument about "lesser-evilism," grassroots activism versus electoralism, and the role of the Democratic Party continued to no avail; no minds were changed.

With the 1973 US Supreme Court decision in *Roe v. Wade* legalizing abortion through the second trimester, much of mainstream feminism looked to the Democratic Party and the courts as the defender of women's rights and overlooked the grassroots activism that had led to these victories. The debate about the possibility of a progressive or socialist third party and the perils of working within "the system" began long before 1972, and it has not ended even today.

The sisterhood and solidarity of these Left feminists is all the more impressive in light of the fact that FBI Director J. Edgar Hoover ordered his agents to infiltrate, investigate, and disrupt civil rights, Black liberation, antiwar, student, and women's liberation groups under the name COINTELPRO (Counterintelligence Program). Ruth Rosen, author of the *World Split Open*, wrote in the *Nation*, "Never, in my wildest bouts of paranoia, did I imagine the extent of that infiltration. The FBI, it turns out, viewed the women's movement as a serious threat to national security. (Of course, the women's movement was dangerous, but not in the way the FBI assumed.) Many feminists, for their part, worried that agents and informants were among them, contributing to a climate of fear."[42]

Seattle was no exception. According to an FBI Informant Report from Special Agent Marion Ray Mathis, the FBI had been infiltrating Seattle's Left feminist groups since 1969. They attended citywide as well as regional conferences, picking up the various groups' leaflets and pamphlets. What is astonishing, given that the FBI could find no illegal, subversive, or treasonous activities among any of the feminists or their organizations, is their extensive surveillance of many women who are mentioned in this book. By July 1970 the FBI had collected thousands of pages of information about feminist activists, especially Clara Fraser. But there is no evidence that the FBI played a direct role in subverting radical Left feminist organizations in Seattle.[43]

These Left feminist groups made lasting contributions to politics in the city, the state, and the country. The successful abortion referendum, the expansion of feminist health care, the struggle for day care, the creation of women's studies programs, and challenges to legal and structural discrimination originated from the activities of these fierce left-wing feminists. Furthermore, they planted the seeds for the next generation of feminist organizations. As many of the sisters would paraphrase Mao, they let a thousand flowers bloom.

The Rising of the Women

5

ONE OF THE MOST IMPORTANT FEATURES of the radical women's liberation movement was the creative explosion of ideas, actions, and debates. Like their sisters across the country and around the world, Seattle's radical women confronted and sought to change all the institutions, laws, and concepts of rights that treated people unequally because of their sex or gender, race or ethnicity, and class. Every gendered word, idea, and role was challenged. In a movement that was profoundly intellectual as well as activist, feminists developed theory through practice, for little feminist theory was available and applicable to the situations they faced. Women researched history, literature, politics, psychology, sociology, biology, anthropology, and the law. Finding that traditional disciplines had excluded women and marginalized their concerns, they created new fields.

Feminist study groups were at least as rigorous as any graduate school seminar, and more intense because more was at stake. They asked, What is a woman? Are women an oppressed group, similar to a class or a caste? What are the connections among gender, race, class, and sexualities? How is sexism connected with racism, colonialism, imperialism, and war? These women were "organic intellectuals," a concept developed by the Italian revolutionary Antonio Gramsci. In contrast to traditional intellectuals, who serve the interests of the dominant class and reinforce its hegemony, organic intellectuals, such as Nelson Mandela and Ella Baker, develop within oppressed groups and critique the entire social system. Other intellectuals may come from outside subordinated groups but choose to serve a revolutionary cause, as did Karl Marx and his socialist feminist daughter, Eleanor Marx.[1]

The early theorists of the women's liberation movement belonged to organizations such as Boston's Bread and Roses; the Boston Women's Health Book Collective, which wrote *Our Bodies, Ourselves*; the Chicago Women's Liberation Union; the Combahee River Collective; Lavender Menace; the Mount Vernon Women's Group; the National Black Feminist Organization; New York Radical Feminists; the National Welfare Rights Organization; Radicalesbians; Redstockings; the Third World Women's Alliance—and the Left feminist groups in Seattle. As they built a movement, formed organizations, and changed existing institutions, women's liberation activists developed a new language as well as new academic disciplines. They grappled with a problematic faith in and search for a "universal we" that would guarantee sisterhood and solidarity among all women in spite of the myriad differences and inequalities of power between them.

In Seattle, Left feminists challenged and transformed athletics, redefined the meaning of legal equality, fought for day care, and developed analyses and organizations around care work, health, sexuality, and reproductive rights. Alliances between White women and women of color, and between heterosexual women and the gay and lesbian community (as it was then called), deepened the meanings and extended the reach of feminism and began laying the basis for an intersectional understanding of race, class, gender, sexuality, and all forms of oppression.

ONE LASTING ACHIEVEMENT WAS IN WOMEN'S ATHLETICS. Professional and amateur sports were (and still are) one of the most profitable consumer-oriented institutions in the post–World War II United States. As players, coaches, and team owners, White men reaped the profits and privileges.[2] At the University of Washington (UW), sports were dominated by football, which was controlled by the UW administration, Alumni Association, and highly paid coaches, all of whom were White men. Rik Sortun, a former All-American player for the UW Huskies, contended that athletics mirrored the racism, profit orientation, and violence in US society: "The athletic field or floor, particularly in football, is perhaps the most regimented, brutalizing institution outside the Army or the workshop floor."[3]

Women in Seattle participated in sports when they were allowed to do so. Only a few sports were regarded as acceptable for White, gender-conforming women: archery, diving, golf, gymnastics, skating, swimming, synchronized swimming, and tennis. Significantly, all were sports in which athletes competed for points, rather than games in which teams played directly against one another. Direct competition and physical contact were regarded as unfeminine. Until 1971, there were very few professional athletic associations for women, except for the Ladies Professional Golfers Association. Olympic sports that required teamwork or specialized forms of physicality, such as track and field, were not considered "ladylike," and in the United States they were dominated by African American athletes, who were already racially excluded from normative femininity. In the 1950s, amid the gender anxieties that marked the Cold War, criticism was directed at the "masculinity" of the female athletes from the Soviet Union and East Germany who excelled in the high jump, long jump, shot put, or javelin.[4] High-achieving female athletes were cautioned that physical activity could have an adverse effect on their marriageability and fertility. Behind the warnings about being too masculine lay the unspoken but powerful fear of lesbianism—an identity that was too dangerous to name.

Girls and young women learned that there was something very wrong with female athleticism, especially in school. Girls rarely played active sports during recess. Physical education classes were strictly segregated. Even in high school, young women were seldom taught to play competitive team sports, especially those with a risk of physical contact, so they often found PE boring. Although fitness had become a national priority, it was not fashionable for girls or connected with ideas of feminine beauty. Boys' sports, especially football and basketball, were always highlighted. In some communities, adults, girls, and younger children would come out to watch the boys play on Friday nights. Parents rarely watched their daughters compete.

The squad of cheerleaders who led pep rallies and cheering at men's games received much more attention than female athletes. With little public and institutional support, young women who were determined to compete in athletic events or play team sports were marginalized. They had to raise their own money through bake sales or carwashes, wear their school gym suits or make their own uniforms, and play in front of empty bleachers. Women's teams played softball, not baseball. Until 1970, girls' basketball had different rules from boys', based on the sexist assumption that women lacked the physical capacity to cover a basketball court with five players. Female college athletes were not given scholarships, facilities, or institutional support comparable to those enjoyed by their male counterparts. Joan Bird, a member of Women's Liberation–Seattle (WL-S) and the captain of the first UW women's crew team, recalled that her coach had suggested "the team be hostesses for the men's crew."[5] Lyn Colella, an undergraduate who later won a silver medal in the two-hundred-meter butterfly at the 1972 Munich Olympics, kept going after many other women had dropped out of the UW's competitive swimming program. She recalled that women swimmers had "no incentive ... to keep going. A boy has the possibility of scholarships, and in some sports a professional career. . . . There aren't opportunities like that for women." Colella's brother, also a swimmer, had a full scholarship to the UW.[6] Black women athletes had some financial assistance, but it was called "work aid" rather than a sports scholarship. It offset the cost of tuition while requiring the women to wash dishes, tend the post office, do secretarial work, and perform other stereotypically feminine tasks.[7]

In 1970, the UW invested millions to rebuild its sports facility, which was dubbed "the People's Palace for Physical Culture" in the quasi-Maoist jargon used by student radicals at the time. It was not lost on women that almost 90 percent of the space and equipment was reserved for men. Like most big state universities, the UW took in hundreds of thousands of dollars for sports from students' fees, half of which came from women. But less than 10 percent went to women's athletics.[8] In May 1973, *Sports Illustrated* highlighted the discrimination against women in sports, pointing out that at the UW, where women formed 41 percent of the student body, less than 1 percent of the sports budget went to women's athletics.[9]

In 1971, Rik Sortun, a UW graduate student, member of the International Socialists, and offensive lineman for the St. Louis Cardinals, worked with the UW football players protesting the well-documented racism of the coach, Jim Owens.[10] In addition, Sortun was a committed feminist.[11] At one International Socialists meeting, he proposed that the organization cosponsor a teach-in on sports and society with the Black Student Union. He invited African American athletes who were leaders in the movement against racism in sports to participate. Dave Meggyesy, Sortun's teammate on the Cardinals, was also an antiwar and antiracist activist. Harry Edwards, a Black liberation activist and sociologist, had organized the protest in which two African American medalists raised their fists in the Black Power salute at the 1968 Olympics. Tom Greenlee, who played for the Chicago Bears, had been a member of the Black Student Union and a UW All-American football player. Jack Scott, a sports critic, activist, and educator, founded the Institute for the Study of Sports and Society in 1970.[12]

In 1970, Scott had been offered a position at the UW to teach courses on sports and society and athletics in higher education. He was originally approached by Professor Ruth Abernathy, head of the Women's Physical

Education Division, who told Scott that the UW "had one of the poorest physical education departments in the country." She was determined to bring in faculty like Scott to rebuild the women's division, whose seventeen members voted unanimously in favor of hiring him. But opposition from Jim Owens and four White male professors in the men's division convinced the administration to veto his hiring. Scott sued and received one year's pay as a settlement. Robert Morford, who was offered a job as chair of the combined Department of Men and Women's Physical Education, turned it down, saying that "no one in their right mind would go there now."[13] The teach-in was an educational intervention in an ongoing controversy.

Members of WL-S wanted women's participation. Many suggested Billie Jean King but had no idea how to reach her.[14] Knowing of no other female athletes of King's stature and celebrity, Joan Bird was invited to speak. So was I, even though I was never a serious tennis player. The women speakers were very nervous as the opening plenary began. We had no idea what Edwards, Scott, or Meggyesy thought about women's liberation; we worried that we might be demeaned or treated condescendingly. Instead, Edwards got up from his chair, greeted us warmly, shook our hands, and said he was so glad that women and sports was being discussed. Edwards, Scott, and Meggyesy spent a good deal of time dealing with sexism in athletics. Scott reported that only one sports scholarship was given to a woman in 1971. Meggyesy deplored the fact that women were paraded in skimpy outfits before major televised football and basketball games in the guise of cheerleading. When Bird recalled the enormous challenges faced by women athletes at the UW, the men responded with praise, support, and encouragement.

Over one thousand people attended this extraordinary event. Along with the UW *Daily*, the *Seattle Post-Intelligencer* profiled a number of women athletes at the UW, yet when covering the teach-in, the reporter dismissively called the women speakers "Women's Lib activists."[15] Members of WL-S created an all-women soccer team (there was no women's varsity soccer at the time) and played during the summer months. In 1971, the Women's Commission of the Associated Students of the University of Washington (ASUW) brought a lawsuit against the university charging massive sex discrimination; the athletic program was a major target.[16] By then the strength of the women's liberation movement and the courageous leadership of Billie Jean King had begun to transform the position of women in sports.

STRANGE AS IT MAY SEEM, not all Seattle Left feminists supported the Equal Rights Amendment (ERA) when it was reintroduced to the US Congress in

1969. Legal strategies for ensuring gender equality have long been debated among feminists and opposed by antifeminists. In 1923, three years after the ratification of the Nineteenth Amendment granting women's suffrage, Alice Paul, suffragist and founder of the National Women's Party, and Crystal Eastman, a socialist feminist, drafted the ERA.[17] This proposal provoked a split between the National Women's Party and Progressive feminist reformers who had fought for protective legislation that applied specifically to women workers. These laws, which limited their hours of labor and prohibited night work and heavy lifting, were enacted when women could not vote in most states and were seldom represented by trade unions. This disagreement reflected a wider debate among early twentieth-century reformers regarding alternative approaches to women's equality. One approach emphasized the similarities between the sexes and demanded rights based on a universal vision of humanity. The other emphasized women's differences from men in order to obtain recognition of their specific needs as mothers. The amendment failed in Congress and was never sent to the states for ratification. Although it was reintroduced at every congressional session from 1923 to 1970, it never reached the floor of the House or the Senate.[18]

The National Organization for Women (NOW), founded in 1966, demanded greater government action to enforce the Equal Pay Act and Title VII of the Civil Rights Act, and in 1967 it announced its support of the ERA. In 1969, Shirley Chisholm, a Democrat from Brooklyn who was the first Black woman to serve in Congress, voiced her support for the ERA with her famous speech "Equal Rights for Women" on the floor of the House. In its latest incarnation, the ERA read, "Equality under the law shall not be denied or abridged by the United States or by any state on account of sex. The Congress shall have the right to enforce, by appropriate legislation, the provisions of this article."

With the ERA under serious consideration, radical women's liberation activists found themselves revisiting past debates as they looked to the future. In Seattle, Radical Women and WL-S, the only two Left feminist organizations that considered the issue, took opposing public stands: Radical Women supported the ERA, while WL-S opposed it. The newsletter of WL-S, *And Ain't I a Woman*, announced that the organization "has come out against the Equal Rights Amendment as it now stands because of its possible consequences for working women and protective legislation."[19] *Sabot*, a short-lived New Left newspaper, published both pro- and anti-ERA positions in its women's issue on October 10, 1970. That fall, WL-S and Radical Women held a public forum, with Melba Windoffer presenting arguments in favor of the ERA and Diane Eggleston explaining why those who supported women's rights should oppose it.

The debate echoed fifty-year-old arguments. Protective labor laws, all of which were state laws, still mattered to many women who worked in manufacturing and service industries. Some laws were downright stupid. In Washington State, for example, one law prohibited women from sitting on bar stools in cocktail lounges, but not in taverns where only beer and wine were served. This law was enacted to "protect" women by preventing them from going to bars alone, where they might be accosted by men or accused of solicitation.[20] Other protective laws benefited women and minors employed in food processing, health care, manufacturing, and office work. Their provisions guaranteed meal periods of at least thirty minutes and two ten-minute breaks in an eight-hour day; set standards for ventilation, lighting, and safety; restricted how much weight workers could be required to lift; required the provision of sanitary toilets; and set a minimum wage.

Radical Women argued that "because protective legislation laws exclude most women workers, the cry to retain these laws simply perpetuates special privilege for the few and does nothing to open up equal opportunity for the many."[21] The group contended that an ERA was necessary "to formalize women as equal citizens. Without the protection of the law, we are always dependent on the goodwill of husbands, landlords and employers. And usually, such goodwill has to be paid for in one way or another."[22] An interesting and perhaps ironic aspect of Radical Women's support for the ERA was their argument that it would protect women as housewives and mothers who were in the process of divorce—the very same issues that Phyllis Schlafly, the extreme right-wing antifeminist, used to mobilize White married women to defeat the ERA.

Members of WL-S pointed out in *And Ain't I a Woman* and its leaflets directed at women telephone workers that the proposed ERA would make existing protective laws unconstitutional. Washington State's attorney general, Slade Gorton, announced that protective laws were already invalid under Title VII of the Civil Rights Act, which prohibited discrimination by reason of sex as well as race. Several large employers announced that they would no longer offer pregnancy leaves and used the proposed ERA as the reason. A spokesperson for one company said, "All employees are equal and we won't give a man a leave of absence to have a baby."[23]

WL-S and Radical Women did agree that protective legislation should be extended to everyone in the labor force. In *Sabot*, Radical Women explained,

"Working people, of course, must have decent working conditions, but women shouldn't have to remain second class citizens to keep protective legislation. It should be...extended to all workers regardless of sex."[24] WL-S, too, stated that protective laws were generally beneficial; their provisions "are basic human rights and should be extended to all workers."[25] In February 1971, over one hundred women and men met to discuss the debate over the ERA and protective legislation. Radical Women and the newly founded Seattle chapter of NOW spoke in favor, while WL-S expressed support of the ERA only if protective laws were extended to cover everyone.[26] The main organizations that campaigned for the ERA were NOW and Campus Women's Liberation, which was influenced by the Socialist Workers Party.

For most left-wing women's liberation organizations, the ERA was much less important than creating feminist health clinics, expanding women's access to reproductive services, opposing the war in Vietnam, defending the Black Panthers, supporting women on strike at Farah, and setting up rape crisis clinics.[27] After 1971, radical feminist organizations supported the ERA but did not make activism around it a priority. Members of WL-S leafleted at Bell Telephone, which was dubbed "Ma Bell" because it exercised an intrusive authority over the behavior of its women employees. The operators, who were overwhelmingly female, and the installers, who were overwhelmingly male, were members of the Communication Workers of America. In spite of weekly leafleting, the operators demonstrated very little interest in supporting or opposing the ERA. In Seattle, as in other cities, left feminists criticized NOW for privileging the ERA over other crucial issues, especially reproductive rights. The radicals saw making demands on the state and founding women-controlled services as complementary rather than contradictory ways of organizing women and as better ways to mobilize masses of women than advocating abstract legal reforms.

By 1971, the campaign for the ratification of the ERA had spread nationwide. For Seattle's Left feminists, this brief struggle introduced women to the history and complexities of the meaning of equal rights. Historians of women and labor critiqued protective laws. Whom did they protect, and from what? Wasn't a restrictive and patriarchal state as bad as an exploitative employer? After World War II, many women workers found that protective laws were used to discriminate against them. Limits on the weight women were allowed to lift excluded women from higher-paid jobs, even though the men who held them had machinery to help with the heavy lifting. The prohibition on nighttime work, which was ostensibly to help mothers, meant that some jobs were not open to women who could only work nights because they had to take care of their children during the day. By the 1970s more women were demanding and gaining access to higher-paid, unionized jobs that had been monopolized by men in industries such as mining, steel making, automotive assembly, and trucking, and they were rejecting protective laws that had kept them in lower-paid jobs reserved for women. By 1972 members of WL-S realized that their position was untenable. Protective legislation was Progressive in the 1910s, but over time these laws were increasingly used to exclude women from equal participation in a changing labor force. Furthermore, feminist theorists and historians demonstrated that a patriarchal state never advanced women's interests in the guise of protecting them.

When the Washington State legislature made ratification of the ERA contingent on a statewide referendum held in March 1972, radical and liberal women's groups all supported it. The voters endorsed it, but only by a tiny margin: 617,936 for and 616,945 against. The legislature officially ratified the federal ERA in 1973, but agitation to rescind its approval began almost immediately. Anti-ERA groups mounted campaigns warning voters of the threats the ERA posed to married women, the dangers of unisex toilets, the possibility that women would be drafted into the armed forces, and the destruction of what they called "traditional" family values.[28] Washington never rescinded its ratification, but organized opposition led to a confrontation between pro-ERA and anti-ERA forces at the statewide International Women's Year Conference held in Ellensburg in July 1977. This debacle ultimately led to the demise of the Washington State Women's Council, a state agency independent of the governor that had been established in 1971.[29] Nationally, the ERA expired when it was not ratified by two-thirds of the states. Some state legislatures even repealed their previous ratification as a result of the counteroffensive by right-wing antifeminist activists and politicians.

PROVIDING QUALITY CHILDCARE, which would be nonracist, nonsexist, twenty-four-hour, staff- and parent-controlled, was always central to Left feminist organizing, in Seattle as well as across the country. In *The Feminist Memoir Project*, Rosalyn Baxandall, a feminist activist, theorist, and historian, reflected that "most books on the women's liberation movement neglect the early feminist day-care efforts."[30] In 1967 Baxandall was one of the founders of Liberation Nursery, the first feminist day care center in New York City. Twenty years later, she complained that "even Ellen Willis," who was also a feminist activist, "wrote an article for the *Village Voice* . . . bemoaning the fact that our movement never addressed child care."[31]

But we did. The demand for childcare was an essential part of the women's liberation program and early marches called for child care. . . . In fact, women in the movement established many day care centers. Other mothers started half a dozen in New York City and dozens of others throughout the country. In order to get more space for day care we occupied unused dilapidated buildings, held teach-ins and cultural events to win community support, and repaired those buildings to make them fit for day care and women's centers. Day care was a demand of both the Columbia and Harvard University strikes of 1968. . . . We had a coalition of centers and held conferences that included women from Boston and Connecticut.[32]

It seems strange that this demand and program of the radical women's liberation movement were forgotten, but the contention that feminists did not care about the needs of mothers was part of the antifeminist narrative put forth by right-wing groups.

In an article in *Feminist Studies*, Baxandall reminded readers that African American feminists always saw day care as crucial. "Surveys done in the early 1970s show that in general black women were more feminist" than White women "in their attitudes toward specific issues such as day care." She pointed to Black feminist organizations including the New Rochelle/ Mt. Vernon Group, Mothers Alone Working, the Third World Women's Alliance, and the Sisterhood of Black Single Mothers, which organized day care centers and fought for community and government subsidies for childcare.[33] By 1969, the Black Panther Party (BPP) had made a major political shift from confrontational politics to community-based programs, most of which served children. In Seattle Aaron Dixon, leader of the local BPP, wrote that they were now devoting most of their attention "to creating the innovative and groundbreaking Survival Programs," including a Breakfast for Children Program and a Liberation School. The party's free breakfast program in Seattle was not necessarily predicated on the belief that communal childcare would liberate women, as Dixon acknowledged: "Eventually we were able to get mothers in the community to take over the duties of cooking breakfast and feeding the kids."[34] Recent scholarship on women in the Black Panther Party emphasizes women's leadership of these grassroots programs.[35] In 1971, the Black Student Union at the UW, which included many members and supporters of the BPP, sponsored Mahali kwa Watola, "a children's place," a day care center located in Seattle's Central District. Wanda Hackett, who chaired the Black Student Union day care committee, said that the center was started "in an effort to get black students involved in the black community."[36]

Public or publicly supported care for children has historically been a demand of both progressives and the socialist Left. Late nineteenth-century reformers such as Jane Addams and Julia Lathrop advocated state-supported childcare, and the issue was raised during the New Deal and World War II. In order to recruit women with children to work in defense factories, the federal government, through the passage of the Lanham Act, provided childcare for approximately 550,000–600,000 children. In the South, the day care centers were racially segregated. The program was disbanded with the end of World War II.[37] John F. Kennedy's Presidential Commission on the Status of Women argued strongly for the expansion of federally funded day care centers as essential for women's participation in the paid labor force. President Lyndon Johnson's Great Society programs linked federal support for childcare to policies designed to encourage poor and low-income women to enter training programs or take jobs outside the home. The goal was to reduce the number of Americans receiving "welfare," which was stigmatized as dependency.[38]

In the nineteenth century, socialist utopian communities had experimented with various ways to raise children collectively. *The Origin of the Family, Private Property and the State*, written in 1883 by Friedrich Engels, offered a pathbreaking analysis of the connection between gender and capitalism. Engels situated women's oppression within the context of private ownership of property and the monogamous patriarchal family. He wrote that women's emancipation under capitalism was predicated on their entrance into the paid labor force and the socialization of housework and childcare. Under socialism, "with the transfer of the means of production into common ownership, the single family ceases to be the economic unit of society. Private housekeeping is transformed into a social industry. The care and education of the children becomes a public affair; society looks after all children alike."[39] This understanding of the significance of childcare has been part of the theoretical basis for socialists' views of women's emancipation ever since.

During the late 1960s, women's liberation activists read and studied this classic text. Practically every left-wing organization's platform called for public childcare, although whether they acted on it is another story. The Freedom Socialist Party's political platform called for twenty-four-hour childcare centers on or near job sites, with educational, recreational, and medical facilities, and free nursery schools and day care centers on every college and university campus. In addition, it articulated children's right to free child life centers, open twenty-four hours a day to all children regardless of their parents' socioeconomic status, with professionally trained staff, as well as to summer camps during school vacations.[40]

Even though the majority of activists in the Seattle women's liberation movement were young and did not yet have children, their words and actions demonstrated their awareness of the importance of childcare to women's liberation. Radical Women and wL-s both provided childcare at all their organizational and public meetings. The children were often cared for by members' teenage children. Men in the movement who expressed nervousness about or antipathy toward children were often told that their punishment for these sentiments was to watch the kids. Looking back, these solutions to the challenge of childcare were inadequate, ridiculously moralistic, and not in the best interests of children. Adults smoked while they babysat!

The obvious need for childcare as mothers enrolled in higher education or entered the paid labor force was even more compelling than the theoretical commitment to the socialization of housework. Dotty DeCoster, a single parent of two children, explained how she became a day care activist: "In 1969, I was on welfare and was able to go to trade school at Seattle Central Community College." One of her most serious "headaches" was that she "could not find day care." Licensed childcare centers cost more than she could afford with the minimal support she received from her federally funded job-training program. "We found out that there were a great many men and women who were very concerned about the need for childcare but didn't speak up because they didn't have any childcare."[41] DeCoster devoted her considerable organizational skills to this cause. The problem was plainly laid out in a 1970 article she coauthored in the campus newspaper, the *City Collegian*: "Seattle Displays Outrageous Lack of Daycare Facilities." In 1970, she became cofounder and chair of the Seattle Central Community College Childcare Coordinating Committee.

The struggle for childcare, like that for Referendum 20, raised important questions about seeking progressive reforms. How can radicals work in coalitions with established political leaders? How can activists create effective cross-class, multiracial coalitions? How can organizations that identify as socialist or radical negotiate with university, municipal, or state bureaucracies? What demands should be nonnegotiable? In the long run, is it better to settle for incremental changes or continue to call for comprehensive solutions? What keeps individuals and organizations from being co-opted? What is the relationship between reform and revolution? Can idealistic radicals maintain their passion as they slog through the daily, often years-long political struggle necessary to effect progressive change? These questions, which were hotly debated in the late 1960s and early 1970s, still matter today.

In the summer of 1968, the newly organized WL-s announced that day care was its highest priority. An early document said that it had

> embarked upon its first project—the establishment of a day care center, free of charge for all U. of W. staff, faculty & students. The need for such facilities exists not only with the "university community" but in society as a whole and we are hoping that this venture will serve as a pilot project for other day care centers for all children and parents. The establishment of day care centers is essential for meaningful equality between the sexes.... However, as long as women are unable to find agencies to care for their children, they cannot escape from their confinement. Hence the establishment of day care centers allows women to be able to participate in productive ventures and become richer socially. In the same vein our society's institutions will become itself richer when the talents of women are fully realized.[42]

This statement makes it clear that day care was integral to radical feminists' vision.

In a November 1968 interview in the UW *Daily*, Bette Nieme announced that the committee was going to organize for day care and send out a questionnaire to ascertain childcare needs. They hoped to begin with a program accommodating five hundred children of staff, faculty, and students and build from there.[43] The first International Women's Day celebration organized by WL-s in March 1969 focused on childcare, as did the next year's activities. The leaflet summed up Left feminist thinking: "Child Care Centers are a necessity for the children of women and student mothers; an essential step toward the emancipation of women from domestic servitude; a plan for children to be treated as human beings, to develop and learn in relationship to others; a basis for a new and gradual relationship between men and women."[44]

Buoyed by the growth of the women's liberation movement, the struggle for day care took off in 1970. Noting that the UW was the second-largest employer of women in the state, the campaign focused on day care for mothers who were employed at the UW, as well as for students with children.[45] In early February WL-s convened a meeting on the issue that drew about sixty people. Lee Mayfield announced they were sending a letter to UW president Charles Odegaard that read in part, "Women workers and students have been performing a necessary service for society while receiving no pay by society for this service—the care and raising of children." Other speakers pointed out that the university was a perfect place to set up childcare, since it had so many resources to offer in its Schools of Education and Medicine and its departments of Home Economics, Physical Education, and Psychology, as well as experts in the arts and foreign languages.

An ad hoc committee on day care was immediately organized. A few men complained that the women's liberation activists didn't do enough to involve them. Mayfield replied, "The men who take care of children have the attitude they are helping women out with the work. It's a rare case when raising children is people's work, not women's work."[46] According to WL-S, this was "the first time a student based political group has ever successfully made contact with staff employees to work on a common project! (This has many political possibilities for the future like organizing women clerical workers around their working conditions and wages.)" Members of WL-S thought they were being realistic by asking for a pilot project to provide day care for three hundred children of staff, students, and faculty, understanding that the number represented only 3 percent of the need. Activists hoped that this program might "start the precedent . . . that all large places of employment provide day care for their female employees. Maybe one day we'll agitate at Boeing."[47]

A day care coalition was formed when WL-S approached Anne Schweisow of the University YWCA and then brought together Radical Women, Campus Women's Liberation, the ASUW Women's Commission, the Graduate and Professional Student Center, the University YWCA, and the Women's Action Forum. The 1968 WL-S survey had shown that more than four thousand married students had children under age eleven. The coalition was committed to setting up a "non-authoritarian, cooperative relationship with the children"; the "non indoctrination of sex roles" would be "especially emphasized since the coalition, as a group is concerned with women's liberation." The staff would be half women, half men, with no gender distinctions in their activities, equal pay, and no rigid dress codes for women.[48]

The struggle for day care got an added boost during the months of tumultuous protests that began in 1970. Most, if not all, of the day care activists were also involved in protests against the war in Vietnam and government repression. The Campus Coalition for University Sponsored Day Care, along with unaffiliated "faculty wives" and graduate and undergraduate students, began organizing for universal, UW-funded, parent- and staff-controlled day care. During the spring student strike, the coalition organized communal, parent cooperative day care at the campus strike headquarters. In July the university closed the facility, claiming sanitation problems. Undaunted, the coalition moved the day care center to the University Methodist Temple, but the UW administration responded by withholding its annual $500 donation. The coalition then moved the center, which was under the direction of Wanda Adams and Phyllis Selinker, to Freeway Hall, the headquarters of Radical Women, less than a mile from campus, where it stayed through August 21.[49] When President Odegaard met with five day care activists in August, he claimed to care about the cause but "urged the women to reconsider their tactics and to take their demands to society at large."[50]

The campaign gained militancy and momentum when fall quarter began. The ASUW Women's Commission, now run by radical feminists, was able to utilize the myriad resources of student government to push for day care. The administration's official rebuff of the coalition's formal letter only galvanized their struggle. When activists heard that at an alumni gathering Odegaard had called the day care proposal "a new kind of fringe benefit," they responded, "Child care is not a fringe benefit to be won by workers ... it is not a special service ... it is not a welfare benefit ... rather it is a basic right of all women."[51]

In October 1970, linking the struggle for day care with opposition to US imperialism, some two hundred antiwar and day care activists marched to Clark Hall, which housed the Naval and Air Force Reserve Officer Training Corps and the Applied Physics Lab, where nuclear weapons for US submarines were made, and suggested turning them into a day care center and an institute for the study of women's liberation. "Money for day care, not for warfare" was a popular slogan.[52] Two weeks later, over 150 students, faculty, and staff marched on Clark Hall to demand childcare. The Weatherman faction of the defunct Students for a Democratic Society had just bombed the building, and day care activists wanted to rebuild it to house services for children. Speakers included Bernadine Garrett, state organizer for the National Welfare Rights Organization; Jill Severn from Radical Women; and Joanne Bailey and Phyllis Selinker from the Campus Coalition for University Sponsored Day Care All spoke about day care as a woman's right and linked the struggle for day care with opposition to the war in Vietnam and racism at home. Demonstrators carried picket signs reading, "Day care is a right and not a fringe benefit" and "Free women with free day care." Many brought their children. Bailey believed day care could help to end racial discrimination: "I would like to see black and white children playing together. Children learn what they live." Severn urged, "Let childcare be a replacement for war."[53]

Throughout 1971, the campus coalition struggled to keep its day care centers alive. But without substantial financial and administrative support from the university, the centers floundered. In 1972, parents organized the Sand Point Community Day Care Center at the graduate student housing complex there. It initially offered fewer than one hundred places. Activists argued that, although it could not meet the needs of all UW parents, it could serve as a prototype of what could and should be done. In 1972, the UW Child Care Coordinating Committee received money from the UW Student Services to study childcare needs again, which seemed like a delaying tactic. The administration made a commitment to providing some childcare, but the cost would come from student fees rather than the university budget. After four postponements, the university sponsored and financed a childcare center open to children from the age of one through kindergarten. But its capacity enrollment was just fifty-eight—a tiny fraction of what was needed.

Instead of expanding its own childcare facilities, the university set up the Child Care Coordinating Office to operate a referral service. It was directed by Douglas Peterson, who had worked for the King County Child Care Coordinating Committee, Model Cities, and Project Head Start, all War on Poverty programs. He and his assistant, Gail Benson, were chosen not by day care activists but by the UW vice president for student affairs. Radical feminists were furious that the struggle for day care had been co-opted. Cindy Gipple of Radical Women and Carol Riddell of the ASUW Women's Commission penned a scathing op-ed calling the office "a step backwards" and a "token response to the needs of students." Peterson defended the UW administration and urged everyone to endorse its decision to study day care needs and quality childcare programs. Then he attacked the feminist analysis linking childcare with women's emancipation, saying that childcare is not "only a part of feminist politics. It is an issue to be considered on its own merits. While childcare may be considered a woman's issue, it is fundamentally a children's issue."[54] The division between the feminist activists and the UW administration split the Campus Coalition for University Sponsored Day Care. Most of the faculty members saw the proposal as a research, demonstration, and training program, rather than a service provider. Activists were furious that Odegaard held private meetings with other administrators. After 1971, the university's childcare policy was controlled by the administration.[55]

This campaign taught activists a great deal about the dynamics of power, as it moved from confrontation and negotiation to institution building and a struggle for control and resources that produced paltry results. It took collective feminist action and creative tactics to make day care a serious concern. Once the activists got the university's attention, they developed their skills at negotiation with campus administrators and city and state legislators. They learned how to deal with divide-and-rule tactics, how current legislation worked for or against childcare, how to prepare a budget, and how to find appropriate space and qualified personnel. Looking back, feminists could see that the demand for free, twenty-four-hour, staff- and parent-controlled child-care that was not racist, sexist, elitist, or homophobic was utopian, given the pervasive misogyny and inequalities of power in American society. Nonetheless, for over thirty years, as a direct result of feminist activism, the UW, King County, and Washington State expanded day care provision. In 1971, feminist voices for day care were heard in Congress. Two outspoken feminists in the House of Representatives, Bella Abzug and Shirley Chisholm, introduced the Comprehensive Child Care Act. Congress passed bipartisan legislation establishing universal childcare, but it was vetoed by President Richard Nixon, who argued that day care would "sovietize" America's children. From then on, it was clear that day care would be left to parents and private corporations.[56]

THE STRUGGLE FOR ABORTION on demand did not end after the passage of Referendum 20. By 1970, California, Hawaii, and New York had also decriminalized abortion. In Washington State, as in these other states, a wide range of restrictions on obtaining an abortion remained, based on age, marital status, the type of facility, and legal residency in the state. Ability to pay was also a factor. Seattle feminists continued to organize around abortion rights, and in so doing were faced with the continued challenges of race, sexuality, and class, as well as White male control of women's reproductive health. In their struggles, feminist health-care activists made the connections between women's full autonomy and their reproductive rights, health, and sexuality.

In 1971, the Socialist Workers Party inaugurated the Women's National Abortion Action Coalition (WONAAC), which called for a campaign to repeal all restrictive state abortion laws with the slogan "Abortion rights now." Seattle health-care advocates and women's liberation activists opposed this single-issue focus. Members of WONAAC believed that this approach would attract the largest number of people. But this position meant that issues of class, race, and sexuality were deemed "extraneous" or "divisive" and could not be raised in the campaign. Seattle's Left feminists convened a meeting to organize an alternative feminist health and abortion coalition. Since WONAAC refused to embrace the label *feminism*, the "Seattle Woman's Position Paper" began, "feminism—the sense of the special oppression we face as entire sex and the determination to win total equality—must be the analytic foundation of a movement to repeal abortion laws, because the *issue of abortion is a feminist issue, and the demand for abortion law repeal is a demand that can only be won by a feminist movement*." This stance spoke to the experience in Washington State, the importance of not separating the demand for abortion rights from opposition to sterilization abuse, and the need for access to safe and effective contraception.[57]

Members of WL-S were particularly outraged that WONAAC objected to the slogan "Free abortion on demand." "The WONAAC leadership has opposed the demand for free abortion on the grounds that it raises the spectre of socialized medicine. To evade this issue when the brutally discriminatory nature of health care is a national scandal" was unacceptable. "We are appalled by a coalition that shows more concern for the prejudices of the ultra-right than for the rights of women."[58]

On September 27, twenty-five women, representing Radical Women, WL-S, the UW YWCA, and the Group Health Cooperative of Puget Sound, as well as a number of women's health clinics, met to form the Feminist Health and Abortion Coalition. Its platform called for free, safe, legal abortion and contraception on demand; an end to all coercive medical practices; repeal of all laws restricting sexual expression between consenting adults; an end to repressive and harmful restrictions on medical care for women receiving welfare; an end to exploitation by medical insurance and drug companies; and the defense of the full civil, human, and medical rights of low-ranking military women and military wives.[59] At the meeting, Lee Mayfield, Kathi Dowd, and Elaine Schroeder presented an open letter stating, "It is imperative that we counterpose our *feminist* abortion campaign to *any* campaign that attempts to separate abortion from feminism." They proposed a number of specific actions and demands for educational campaigns; widespread licensing and training for abortion providers, including paramedics; full insurance coverage for procedures; the invalidation of "conscience" clauses, which allowed physicians to refuse to perform abortions because they believed abortion was immoral; and the elimination of hospital review boards because their purpose was "to decide whether or not we get abortions."[60]

The Feminist Health and Abortion Coalition and WONAAC both ended their campaigns early in 1973, after the US Supreme Court ruled in *Roe v. Wade* that the right to privacy, which had previously been endorsed in a decision regarding contraception, extended to a woman's and her doctor's decision to terminate a pregnancy within the first two trimesters. After *Roe*, the struggle for abortion took both a more expansive and a more defensive posture, in Seattle and nationally.

Antiwar, Antidraft, and Anti-imperialist Feminist Activism

6

THE WOMEN'S LIBERATION MOVEMENT was inextricably interconnected with the global movements opposing the US war in Vietnam and supporting anticolonial and anti-imperialist struggles. Seattle Left feminists looked to women freedom fighters in the Third World as models of revolutionary womanhood as they attempted to create peace and a sense of global sisterhood. They challenged the White and male leadership of the US antiwar and peace movements, questioned the previous maternalistic approaches to women's peace activism, and began to develop a new gendered analysis of war, peace, and imperialism.

Historically, women have been associated with pacifism. A centuries-old essentialist argument used by feminists and antifeminists alike contends that women's reproductive capacities and their experiences in bearing and nurturing sons and taking care of fathers and husbands make them more compassionate than men and therefore naturally opposed to violence and war. In the nineteenth century, most feminists opposed war, at least in theory, although many American women who advocated abolition and equal rights supported the Union in the Civil War. Few late nineteenth- and early twentieth-century European and American feminists were active antiracists and anticolonialists. These White, middle-class women attempted to organize an international sisterhood, but in the context of White European and US domination their efforts often amounted to "women's orientalism" or "imperial feminism."[1]

Seattle has a long history of feminist pacifism. During World War I, Louise Olivereau, a feminist anarchist, served twenty-eight months in prison for distributing antiwar leaflets. Women's peace activism reappeared after World War II with the emergence of the Cold War and the threat of nuclear war. Seattle Women Act for Peace (SWAP), the local affiliate of Women Strike for Peace (WSfP, founded in 1961), played a significant role in the protests against the Trident submarine base at Bangor, Washington. The women were moved to action by the Soviet resumption of atmospheric nuclear tests after a three-year moratorium and by the United States' declaration that it would hold its own tests in retaliation. Members of SWAP were mainly married with children, middle class, and politically left-wing White women.[2] Both WSfP and SWAP articulated a maternalist approach to opposing nuclear testing. Members of SWAP emphasized that radioactive fallout from nuclear testing was found in mothers' milk and commercially sold cows' milk. While many members were internationalists, they hoped that as White middle-class mothers speaking on behalf of children, they would be less vulnerable to the red-baiting that held radical activity in check during the McCarthy era. The organization kept its single-issue focus and did not address women's rights until after 1970.

The generation of Left feminist activists in Seattle who founded the first women's organizations had been active in a range of antiracist and labor struggles, as well as opposition to the US war in Vietnam. The war and the civil rights movement were pivotal events in their lives, and as their feminism developed so did their gender-, class-, and race-based critique of war and imperialism. Only men were subject to the draft and could serve in combat. Women in the military were volunteers, and most worked as nurses, at the time a female profession. Men fought; women cared for the casualties. The racism and socioeconomic inequality of American society was apparent in the military, as the fighting forces in Vietnam included disproportionate numbers of African Americans and Latinos, who were more vulnerable to the draft largely because few were in college, which would have made them eligible for deferments. As in all US wars, working-class men bore the brunt of the fighting.[3] Privileged White men—Donald Trump with his bone spurs, George W. Bush's vacation in the Texas Air National Guard, and Bill Clinton's college deferment—avoided military service and combat.

Organized opposition to the draft began with the Black Freedom struggle.[4] Muhammad Ali refused to fight, sacrificing his title as the world champion heavyweight boxer, and became an inspiration to millions. Student Nonviolent Coordinating Committee (SNCC) activists popularized the slogan "No Vietcong ever called me nigger," and it was seen on placards at countless demonstrations. The draft brought the war home in a very personal way for a generation of young men. In 1967, over ten thousand marched and fought with police at the Military Induction Center in Oakland, California, as part of Stop the Draft Week. By 1969, student body presidents at 253 universities had written to the White House to say that they personally planned to refuse induction, joining the half million others who would do so during the course of the war. Selective Service Centers, the Reserve Officer Training Corps, and campus and school military recruiters became targets for protest. Draft resistance was successful because too many people participated for the authorities to punish them all or send them to prison. So great were the numbers of draft resisters that in 1977 President Jimmy Carter declared a general amnesty to all those who had fled abroad to escape the draft, allowing them to return to the United States. Of 209,517 accused draft offenders, fewer than 9,000 were convicted.[5]

Seattle was one of the centers of draft resistance and GI organizing. In addition, Seattle women brought gender issues front and center into the resistance struggle from the very beginning. Draft Resistance Seattle (DR) was one of the more active chapters in the US, in part because of its strategic location. The Seattle-Tacoma airport was the second-largest disembarkation point to Saigon; US Army Base Fort Lewis and McChord Air Force Base were nine miles south of Tacoma. During the peak years of the Vietnam War, 100,000 military personnel were stationed in Washington State.

When one of DR's founders, the African American Earnest Dudley, refused to be inducted on April 14, 1967, the group organized a protest campaign around his trial. At both Seattle Central Community College and the University of Washington (UW), DR organized graduating seniors and first-year graduate students whose draft status was changing to 1-A, making them immediately available for military service. In 1967, Private First Class Michael Bratcher marched into the Fort Lewis office and quit complying with military orders. He was imprisoned, went on a hunger strike, was defended by the Seattle ACLU, joined DR, and then was arrested, court-martialed, and sentenced to four years at hard labor. Russell Wills, a graduate student and DR activist from Seattle, went to jail. Together with Students for a Democratic Society (SDS), DR organized antiwar groups at area high schools, and in 1968 and 1969 it organized Northwest Draft Resistance conferences. According to its literature, DR was "delaying the induction of from 5 to 10 persons a week" by 1968, and it continued its support campaigns for draft resisters, solidarity protests at the Canadian border, and marches to Selective Service System offices throughout the late 1960s.[6]

Seattle Radical Women members joined DR from its inception (figure 6.1). Opposing Joan Baez's flippant, sexist, but popular slogan "Girls say yes to boys who say no," women in DR sought to integrate feminism into the movement. In a 1968 position paper, "Women and Draft Resistance: Revolution in the Revolution," Jill Severn of Radical Women connected the oppression of women with that of African Americans as well as the people of Vietnam. In arguing for women's leadership in the draft resistance movement, she began by acknowledging, "There are those inside and outside the antidraft movement who would deny women full participation in this movement on the grounds that since we aren't directly confronting 'the man,' we are not entitled to leadership in the antidraft movement." But, she contended, the "exclusion of women from the military is no less and no more than a denial of women's equality at a time when refusal of induction is one of the few potent forms of protest and resistance to American imperialism." Although women did not want to fight against the Vietnamese, "draft exemption means *a denial of full participation in the struggle against the military* at a time when that struggle is one of the most important things happening." She pointed out that exemption was not a privilege: African American men had historically been excluded from the military. Exempting women only perpetuated the idea of women's weakness and dependence on men. She concluded by declaring that solidarity and unity necessitate the full participation of women in draft resistance.[7] In 1968, at Seattle DR's first Fourth of July rally, picnic, and "be-in," a member of Radical Women was a featured speaker.

In the first issue of the feminist journal *Lilith*, Judith Bissel, a member of the Women's Majority Union, declared that "civil rights laws, police brutality, the draft, the war in Vietnam . . . are women's issues. In short, any example of social injustice can and should be seen as a woman's issue."[8]

Along with Seattle DR, the main antiwar organization was the UW Committee to End the War in Vietnam, replaced in 1969 by the Student Mobilization Committee (SMC). The UW Vietnam Committee was led by men, but Stephanie Coontz led the SMC and became the most prominent spokesperson of the antiwar movement in Seattle. The SMC was the largest antiwar group on the UW campus and involved members of the Young Socialist Alliance, the youth wing of the Socialist Workers Party. Coontz believes that the SMC "had a higher percentage of female leaders than most antiwar movements around the county."[9] In addition, a student-soldier antiwar group, the GI-Civilian Alliance for Peace, put out an underground newspaper for soldiers called *Counterpoint*, held citywide antiwar conferences and marches, and even staged a maritime "invasion" of Fort Lewis to "liberate soldiers" from the military. The

Figure 6.1 / Women's Liberation Brigade at an antiwar demonstration in October 1970, with Jody Olvera, member of Women's Liberation–Seattle, in the center, Seattle, Washington. Photograph by Barbara Winslow.

GI-Civilian Alliance for Peace was one of the first organizations in the country to form links between civilians and antiwar soldiers and inspired similar organizing elsewhere in the country. After 1970, GIs and veterans led antiwar demonstrations. Despite the often-repeated canard, the antiwar movement did not hate GIs or spit on them but rather supported soldiers' resistance.

In the fall of 1968, the SMC announced that it was going to send "girls" into GI dances as a way to organize against the war. There was an immediate uproar from Radical Women and the Women's Liberation Committee of the Peace and Freedom Party and SDS. No doubt some of the objections reflected sectarian politics, but the fundamental problem was the plan's sexual objectification of women. For antiwar feminist activists, talking with young male soldiers was a challenge. Should women use their sexuality to attract soldiers to antiwar activities? How could women develop political relationships with young soldiers, mostly draftees, who were isolated from civilians and women, without replicating the gendered notion of woman as sex object? At a packed meeting called to debate the issue, the SMC and the GI-Civilian Alliance for Peace defended the plan, arguing that getting GIs to oppose the war was paramount. Some even asked members of Women's Liberation–Seattle (WL-S) what was wrong with being attractive! The most effective speakers against sending women into GI dances were male veterans, members of SDS, and the Peace and Freedom Party. After an intense debate, the meeting overwhelmingly condemned the proposal. Coontz and other SMC members changed their approach to women and GI organizing: "When people proposed sending women into coffee houses to dance with them . . . I was personally repelled, for reasons that were probably similar to those of women's liberation. But I think I learned a lot from the force of that debate and why I should oppose it for much more deep and much more strong reasons."[10]

In 1968, antiwar activists and veterans organized the Shelter Half, a GI coffeehouse in Tacoma, Washington. A shelter half is a three-by-five-foot piece of sticky canvas issued to every soldier in the field: one shelter half is useless, but when two are joined together it creates a comfortable two-person tent. Tacoma's coffeehouse was conceived to serve the same purpose: getting people together to construct something useful. Most of the personnel at the Shelter Half were men. Megan Cornish was a full-time volunteer and tried to raise feminist politics as part of a larger understanding of war and peace. She distributed antiwar information to Fort Lewis GIs when she could. Cornish later moved to Seattle and joined Radical Women and the Freedom Socialist Party.[11]

In May 1971, the Jane Fonda *FTA* show, which included Donald Sutherland, Ben Vereen, and Holly Near, came to a park on the outskirts of Tacoma.[12] Members of WL-S met Fonda, showed her their writings on behalf of women, and spoke alongside her at a rally defending GIs who were incarcerated in the McNeil federal penitentiary for their antiwar activities. Fonda spoke about GI organizing and Indigenous peoples' rights; WL-S activists spoke about women's liberation, racism, and incarceration. Fonda also met with a number of women working at the Shelter Half and was supportive of their work.

As the women's liberation movement grew and the Vietnam War ground on, feminists began writing about the interconnections among war, racism, peace, and gender. Jill Severn's piece on draft resistance was one of the first. Articles concerning women and war began appearing in the UW *Daily*. An op-ed published both in the *Daily* and in *And Ain't I a Woman* challenged the notion that women are essentially pacifist. In addition, women had the potential power to end the war, not by "crossing their legs as was envisaged in Lysistrata" but through collective action. The single-issue focus of the antiwar movement and its narrow conception of political activism was criticized. "In very few places were demands raised around the problems that women face such as child care, abortion, equal pay. . . . Perhaps [had] there been more meaningful interconnections between the question of American imperialism, the war in Southeast Asia and the role of women in society, and perhaps had the student movement acted upon that interconnection, more tangible results, a stronger women's liberation movement and student movement might have emerged."[13] Members of Radical Women also wrote op-eds connecting sexism, racism, and imperialism for the *Daily*.

By 1970, women's liberation groups had begun to make feminist as well as antiracist and anti-imperialist demands on existing antiwar organizations. For example, during the student strikes over the invasion of Cambodia and the murders of protesters at Kent and Jackson State, Radical Women demanded that a plank on women's rights be included in the strike's manifesto. The group also insisted that women, especially welfare mothers, African American women, and working-class women, be given leadership roles and speaking positions at all antiwar activities.[14] At the October 1970 Moratorium antiwar march, a contingent called the Women's Liberation Brigade brought the various women's groups together for the first time. Members of the Anna Louise Strong Brigade, Radical Women, WL-S, the Women's Caucus of the Seattle Liberation Front, and individual women such as Kathy Naughton and Anne Schweisow signed a statement announcing that the brigade was organized in opposition to the sexism of the march organizers. Originally no women were scheduled to speak, and when the organizers finally relented, the brigade's representative was low on the list of speakers. When the march organizers issued a press release proudly announcing participation by "new sectors of the community," they did not mention any women's organizations.[15]

Finally, the women's liberation groups and activists opposed the march's single-issue politics, demanding that race, class, gender, and anti-imperialist analyses and demands be added. Their leaflet, with the headline "OPPOSE THE WARMAKERS, OPPOSE THE WAR ON WOMEN," read, "We therefore support and solidarize with all our sisters and brothers of the 'third world.' We pledge ourselves to the liberation of third world people because we recognize the common source of our degradation and because as women, we feel it is our duty to work for the most oppressed of our sex: black and brown women of America and the colonial world." The leaflet concluded by connecting oppressions based on class, race, and gender with colonialism and imperialism: "We believe that a movement calling for peace must demand a just peace: for an end to war and violence, not only in Vietnam, but an end to America's war on women—a war which leaves us dead from criminal abortions, that has murdered, raped, jailed and worked to death countless numbers of women, and which doubly brutalizes and exploits our black and brown sisters."[16] Women's contingents marched in subsequent antiwar demonstrations.

AS THE WOMEN'S LIBERATION MOVEMENT began to change the antiwar movement, radical feminists looked to the women of Vietnam as role models. On Memorial Day 1968, members of Radical Women tried to emulate Vietnamese women freedom fighters whom they regarded as their sisters by demonstrating their support at an antiwar veterans' rally in the Seattle Civic Center. Women's Liberation–Seattle produced the first women's liberation button with the image of a Vietnamese woman carrying a gun and a baby. When Nguyen Thi Binh—Central Committee member of the National Liberation Front, vice-chairperson of the South Vietnamese Women's Liberation Association, and in 1969 the foreign minister of the Provisional Revolutionary Government of the Republic of South Vietnam—represented Vietnam at the Paris Peace Treaty negotiations, Left feminists were ecstatic. The contrast could not have been starker. The US delegation was all White and male; a woman led the Vietnamese delegation. Many on the Left believed that the Vietnamese had a greater commitment to women's equality than the US government. A popular song, "Mme Binh Round," sung to the tune of "Hey, Ho, Nobody's Home," at International Women's Day celebrations went, "Live like her, Mme. Binh. Dare to struggle, dare to win. Dien Bien Phu will come again. Live like her, Mme. Binh."[17]

A letter to the *Seattle Times* illustrated the somewhat naïve belief in women's equality in North Vietnam:

The political cartoon that appeared in last Friday's (November 15th) editorial page of the *Times* could only appear in a country that regarded women as second-class citizens. I am referring to the cartoon that depicted Madame Binh, a delegate from the National Liberation Front to the Paris Peace talks, as only interested in the haute couture of Paris. The National Liberation Front does not regard women as merely sexual objects or mass consumers, desiring only hand creams, lipsticks, and better laundry detergents. Unlike the United States of America, there is complete social, political and economic equality for women in the National Liberation Front. Perhaps this is but another reason why the NLF is defeating the United States Army.[18]

Left-wing women, including women's liberation activists, wished to make formal and informal contacts with Vietnamese women. A few women, most famously (or notoriously) Jane Fonda and Angela Davis, traveled to North Vietnam to meet them. It was easier for US women to meet with Vietnamese women in Canada. In 1971, the University of British Columbia in Vancouver hosted a conference organized by the Canadian Voice of Women (VOW) and the US organization WSfP. The conference had to be held in Canada because people from North Vietnam were prohibited from entering the United States. The organizers brought six women from Laos, Cambodia, and Vietnam to "meet and talk in order to set up a better understanding and to strengthen our solidarity so as to give information to Canadian and US friends on the situation in IndoChina."[19] Because of the large numbers of attendees from the US and western Canada with differing agendas and interests, the Indochinese women first met for two days with women from VOW and WSfP. Then Third World women (who today would be described as women of color) met with them for two days. Women's liberation activists met with them on the last two days.

Rather than promoting unity, as the organizers had hoped, the conference was fraught with dissension, infighting, and conflicts between sectarian factions from the moment the planning began. VOW and WSfP wanted to control the North American agenda; the Southeast Asian women had their own agenda. Canadians were appalled at what they believed was the great-power chauvinism of the US delegates and declared themselves colonized. This description did not sit well with the delegates of color, who regarded their own peoples as living under the domination of the US and Canadian White colonial settler states.

Contention raged around almost every question. Should the conference be open or closed? Should those who attended be delegates, and if so, what groups would be invited to send representatives? Should issues of women's oppression be on the agenda? Should lesbian oppression be on the agenda? One Canadian group protested the presence of US women's liberation activists:

Women's Liberation, although somewhat diverse, does not [as] of now speak to many of the important oppressions of women in North America and many therefore cannot work within it. The error comes from an arrogance that what we define as the political and social oppression of women applies to all women similarly. WL, both the anti-imperialist wing and the feminist wing tend to do this—the worst manifestation of this being racist. Having assumed that, we go on to presume that we can make a conference without including women outside of WL in the central planning and policy making decisions.

Further, they pointed out that "the Indochinese had explicitly asked to meet with many women outside of WL—'Third' world women, welfare women, GI wives and women doing GI organizing work. This meant that the conference could not be described as a WL one and that should have been the a priori assumption from the beginning. As it was, other non–WL white women from oppressed groups and 'third' world women were 'added on' rather than being part of the conference decision-making bodies."[20]

Such comments by Canadian feminists were echoed by some of their US counterparts. Washington State was allotted twenty-three delegates, with eight from Seattle. Elaine Schroeder, a member of WL-S, pointed out that "considering the number of Women's Liberation groups (over ten) and independent feminists, a democratic selection of eight delegates was virtually impossible." Women from WL-S felt that the conference organizers downplayed the intersections of class, race, gender, sexuality, and imperialism and did not allow Left feminists to talk with their Southeast Asian sisters about "the connections between male supremacy and imperialism and how the war affects the lives of North American poor and working women."[21] Teresa Williams angrily described the conference leadership as elitists who justified their efforts to prevent poor women, feminists, and lesbians from speaking by claiming they were not anti-imperialist enough. She was appalled at the factionalism, lesbian-baiting, and attacks on Trotskyist groups. In contrast, she found a great deal of sisterhood in the Seattle delegation.

Delegations from Ellensburg and Pullman, cities in eastern Washington, wrote a scathing critique of exclusion and elitism entitled "They're All Fuckin' Trots": "The leadership-dominated agenda was almost entirely lacking in consciousness of sex and class oppression in America. Instead of recognizing that exploitation, racism and sexism are everywhere linked, those in control considered it 'selfish' in the presence of the IndoChinese, for women to give expression to the deep oppression that the vast majority suffer in North America." The pamphlet continued, "We are sure that our Third World sisters at the conference were not told that their struggle was secondary to support for the IndoChinese struggle. In short, we faced the same hostility at this conference that we have faced from the male dominated left since the inception of our movement: the struggle of women for liberation from their sex and class oppression is not legitimate, rather women must subordinate that struggle to the 'more important' struggles of other people."[22]

All participants praised the Vietnamese, Cambodian, and Laotian women; were moved by their presentations and inclusiveness; and, despite the conference's disunity and disorganization, renewed their commitment to fighting US and Western imperialism.

An appraisal of the conference by Liz Briemburg, a British-born activist who had lived both in California and in Vancouver, provides insight into the political problems facing Left feminists then and later. Before the concept of intersectionality was theorized by Kimberlé Crenshaw, bell hooks, and other feminists of color, the women from Vancouver, Seattle, and Ellensburg were struggling with the impact of interlocking systems of power on those who are most marginalized in society. In order to bring about women's liberation, feminists must overcome divisions based on race, class, gender, abilities, age, religion, nationality, and citizenship status. But most of the attendees were new to left-wing politics, and few had any experience with coalitions.

Briemburg's reflections put the divisions that so troubled the conference in perspective. "We are very divided amongst ourselves," she began. "Racism, US chauvinism, sectarianism, and so on all divide us. I am not suggesting we pretend those divisions do not exist. It was the recognition of these divisions which seems the most healthy outcome of the conference in addition, of course, to the inestimable benefits we all received from listening to the lives and steadfast determination of the Indochinese women." Acknowledging differences that arose from women's diverse experiences and differing positions in society, she suggested that "instead of a definition of sisterhood based on one's sexual preference" or any other dimension of identity, "we may be able to strive for a genuine, authentic sisterhood based on understanding and support between us for our respective struggles. The way those divisions were dealt with at the conference was very bad and many women who could not accept the extreme hostility between different groups just left the conference. . . . There was little self-discipline apparent."[23]

Although "we all came out of the conference feeling tired and confused" because "our encounters with women in our own movement left many of us despairing and angry," "two weeks later I feel quite differently. I think the WL movement has to do a lot of hard political thinking and exploring; it has to recognize that a Sisterhood based on gender alone is nonsense; the divisions between women are wide and deep and based on much more fundamental conditions than competitiveness—conditions such as class, race, lesbianism, age, and chauvinism."[24]

The conflicts that arose over organizing feminist and women's support for women in Vietnam, Cambodia, and Laos in 1971 reflected and presaged debates and struggles over the problematic faith in and search for that "universal we." Was it possible to guarantee sisterhood and solidarity among all women across the myriad divisions of unequal power and difference? These debates continue today.

ANTI-IMPERIALIST FEMINISM was profoundly shaped by the US war in Vietnam, but women's liberation groups also supported anti-imperialist struggles in Algeria, Angola, China, Cuba, Mozambique, Palestine, South Africa, and Central and South America. Three of the Left feminist groups in Seattle were named in honor of anti-imperialist struggles. By choosing the name Fanshen, the women who condemned the sexism of the Seattle Liberation Front identified themselves with women in the Chinese Revolution. Another short-lived group named itself the Sisters of Than Hoa, referring to a Vietnamese city that was a stronghold of the Viet Minh and the National Liberation Front. During the Vietnam War, US strategic bombing destroyed much of its buildings and infrastructure. Since then, the city has been totally rebuilt. The Anna Louise Strong Brigade was named for the socialist feminist activist who had become an anti-imperialist and Maoist.

Along with these three groups, all the Left feminist groups spoke publicly, organized open meetings, wrote op-eds for the UW *Daily* or for their newsletters, and had study groups on anti-imperialist issues. They researched and discussed the Russian, Vietnamese, Chinese, and Cuban revolutions; read Vladimir Lenin and Joseph Stalin on imperialism in relation to capitalism; and considered the connections between Third World or colonized people of color in the US and those in regions that were emerging from colonialism and struggling against imperialism and underdevelopment. For some Left women, being anti-imperialist was a central political commitment that they privileged over gender. Members of the Anna Louise Strong Brigade were very critical of Women's Liberation–Seattle for not being an anti-imperialist women's organization.[25] Nevertheless, all the groups celebrating International Women's Day always spoke out against the war in Vietnam and expressed solidarity with women of color and women involved in revolutionary and anticolonial struggles. Seattle's activists laid the groundwork for the theory and action developed by the next generation, which aimed to decenter the West and forge postcolonial, transnational feminism.

Draft Resistance Speech Given by Barbara Winslow on July 4, 1968

These days it is extremely difficult to stress the importance of women's liberation. On the one hand we have the male chauvinists—the Philip Wylies who declare that women have too much freedom already. Women are happiest doing the conventional feminine duties—the idea goes—American women cannot and should not assert themselves in any meaningful social and political sense outside of being baby-making machines or working within the PTA or the League of Women Voters. And on the other hand, there are American women who don't even realize their oppression—women who believe that their fulfillment is found in the pages of *Cosmopolitan* and *Playboy* magazine. But this should not be too surprising. American women live in the same society which brutally exploits and oppresses black people and its own poor—a society which is systematically destroying the people of Vietnam.

But a greater tragedy, in a sense, is that in a movement that is dedicated to liberation and equality women still are not free. We see this when women in an SDS convention are booed down for wishing to chair meetings, when women were asked to be the cooks during the liberation of Columbia University—and women in Seattle saw this when snickers and sneers greeted the first Radical Women's conference. Women in the movement who have been relegated to stamp licking, envelope stuffing, and note taking at meetings can hardly tolerate this discrimination and degradation. Men and women together must reject this hypocrisy and work for a movement which demands the same rights for all minorities.

Women who wish to participate in the movement must do so on an equal basis with men. We refuse to be merely ladies' auxiliaries of an all-male-directed antiwar, antidraft, and antiracist movement. It is not enough for women to say yes to guys who say no!—we demand that men and women fight side by side against American imperialism, whether in Vietnam or in the Central Area. If the women of Cuba and Vietnam achieved equality through common struggle, so must American women.

It's about time for women to begin asserting themselves. Women should make damned sure that [they] join movement organizations, whether Draft Resistance or SDS and especially Radical Women. They should make damned sure that they demand and get equal treatment in these organizations. Women must remember they are radicals first and women second. Men also better be damned sure that they do not play the usual sex discrimination games. It is going to be a hard struggle, but the fight for equality within the movement must be won. Women have two important roles within the movement—we must fight on an equal basis with men to fight the war, the draft, and racism. We also must fight for our own freedom. For without liberation for all—no one is free.

The Multiplicity of Us

7

BY 1970, WOMEN'S LIBERATION ACTIVISTS were mobilizing increasing numbers of people and waging successful campaigns around many issues. Women of color led in connecting class, race, and gender. Women's and gender studies developed as a new intellectual discipline, and programs were set up at both the University of Washington (UW) and Seattle Community College. Staff women at the UW organized a labor union for the first time. The gay liberation movement, closely allied with Left feminism, exploded on the scene. Women's liberation activists established the first rape crisis clinic, women's divorce cooperative, and battered women's shelters. They fought for women's commissions at the UW and in city, county, and state governments. Feminist media expanded with the publication of *Pandora*, *And Ain't I a Woman*, and *Lilith*; Left feminists wrote columns and were interviewed in the UW *Daily* and the Seattle Community College *City Collegian*. Ideas that were identified with women's liberation made it into the mainstream television and print media. Institutions, organizations, academic programs, clinics, and centers founded by activists were premised on a Left feminist belief in nonhierarchical structures, collective democratic processes, and reaching out to empower the most marginalized and dispossessed. Many of these institutions and programs have not only lasted but also expanded.

WOMEN OF COLOR PLAYED FOUNDING ROLES in women's liberation organizations in Seattle. The National Council of Negro Women and the Delta

Sigma Theta Sorority had active chapters in Seattle. Many Black women leaders visited the city in the 1960s and early 1970s to speak to women's and civic groups, including Dorothy Height, president of the National Council of Negro Women; Myrlie Evers, activist and widow of slain civil rights worker Medgar Evers; Jeanne Noble, educator and activist; Shirley Chisholm; Florynce "Flo" Kennedy; Fannie Lou Hamer; Margaret Sloan; Aileen Hernandez, president of NOW in 1970–71; and writer Toni Cade Bambara.

Recently much has been written about radical feminism's origins within the African American, Latinx, Indigenous, and Asian American and Pacific Islander movements. But we must acknowledge the Whiteness and racism of both the mainstream and radical women's liberation movements, ranging from cluelessness and insensitivity to exclusionary viewpoints and practices. Multiracial radical women's liberation organizations did not exist.[1] Michelle Moravec's exhortation in "How Did We Get to Feminism So White?" needs repeating:

> Stop locating the origins of women's liberation with Casey Hayden and Mary King. Instead read, cite, and teach Patricia Robinson or early essays like Black Womanhood by Black Panther Judy Hart from July 1967 or Frances Beal's 1968 draft of the Black Women's Manifesto or her proposal that same year for a SNCC women's caucus. Don't just talk about white feminists at the big moments of 1968; Flo Kennedy was a prominent figure at the Miss America Protest. Cellestine Ware was a co-founder of New York Radical Feminists in 1969 and author of 1970 monograph *Womanpower*. Seek out Mary Ann Weathers's essays that appeared in *No More Fun And Games*, or pieces by Maxine Williams and Myrna Hill members of both Redstockings and the Third World Women's Alliance, who wrote for *The Militant*.[2]

I would add the names of Nina Harding, Jody Olvera, Constance Scott, and Flo Ware to Moravec's list. They were members of Radical Women, Women's Liberation–Seattle (WL-S), and the Women's Majority Union. They wrote for *Lilith*, *And Ain't I a Woman*, and *Pandora*, as well as for the *Helix* and the UW *Daily*, and were interviewed in the mainstream Seattle newspapers. They were active in International Women's Day celebrations, opposition to the war in Vietnam, support for Indigenous struggles, the grape boycott led by the United Farm Workers Organizing Committee, labor organizing, and other antiracist and anti-imperialist campaigns.

Flo Ware exemplifies this pattern of radical activism both in the Black community and in interracial groups of leftists and women (figure 7.1).[3] Born

Figure 7.1 / Flo Ware, member of the Peace and Freedom Party, Seattle, Washington, published in the *Seattle Post-Intelligencer*, August 1976. Courtesy of the Museum of History and Industry.

in Texas in 1912, she spent her childhood moving around the South, where her father worked for the railroad. The family settled in one place when she started high school, and after she graduated, she attended college for a short time. Then Flo married Waymon Ware, and the couple moved to Seattle right after World War II. She and Waymon belonged to the Freedom Socialist Party Menshevik and the Congress of Racial Equality (CORE). Seattle CORE supported the Freedom Rides and Mississippi Freedom Summer nationally and fought for school desegregation, open housing, and equal employment in Seattle through boycotts, picket lines, and demonstrations.[4] In the spring of 1968, Flo was elected vice-chair of Seattle CORE, signed her name to the *Lilith* manifesto, and joined what soon became WL-S. That summer, she served as spokesperson for the Northwest contingent of the Poor People's March on Washington, DC. Known as forthright and persuasive, she hosted a show called *What's Going Down* on KRAB radio from 1968 to 1979.

Women of color also established autonomous organizations. The demography, history, and political development of Seattle affected the trajectory of women of color feminism. Unlike Boston, Chicago, Los Angeles, New York, and Washington, DC, Seattle was overwhelming White. So too was the UW, the locus of much Left feminist organizing. In 1967 there were only 150 Black students out of an undergraduate and graduate student body of thirty-four thousand. There were even fewer Chicanos (estimated at between ten and ninety) and Indigenous people (estimated at between twenty-five and one hundred). The numbers of Filipinos/as, Chinese, Japanese, Koreans, and South Asians are impossible to estimate.[5] It was not until 1968 that the UW, under pressure from the Black Student Union and Students for a Democratic Society, began to actively recruit students of color.

While Black women from Radical Women were active in Seattle community politics and on the UW campus, they did not join the Black Panther Party (BPP). In fact, Radical Women was quite critical of the masculinist postures of male BPP members. In the early years, many Panther women deferred to their male comrades. In a 1969 interview with the UW *Daily*, three women BPP members, Kathy Haley, Verlaine Keith, and Kathey Jones, said they saw their roles as revolutionary Black women as complementary to and supportive of Black men. "People move as people, not as men or women," stated Keith; "a female Black Panther faction would be superfluous."[6] They were not involved in the abortion referendum, and while they were invited to participate in International Women's Day activities, some, such as Alice Spencer, expressed hostility to feminism, especially over acceptance of homosexuality. Jeri Ware, a longtime activist in the Black Freedom struggle, said that Panther women "did not want to be a part of what are perceived to be gay issues."[7] In August 1969, Roberta Alexander from the Oakland, California, Black Panther Party came to Seattle to speak about the role of Black women in the liberation struggle. As early as 1970, women in the local BPP began to challenge male domination in practice, programs, and activities.[8]

Nina Harding wrote a "discussion draft" for a February 1970 Radical Women conference held at the UW, "Interrelationship of the Black Struggle and the Woman Question . . . It Is a New Day." This paper was clearly written from a Marxist perspective, but, unlike orthodox Leninism, it recognized the intersection of feminism and Black liberation. "The history of the question for women's rights has always been inseparable from the quest for the liberation of all Blacks from institutional racism," she asserted. Harding emphasized the leadership of Black women, who "by nature have been radical women concerned about their children, environment and community and strong enough to help execute change in that system for all humanity." She was critical of Black men who believed that Black women should play a subordinate role in the struggle. "Male leadership is frequently insensitive to the drive of Black women for acknowledged equality within the movement," she charged. "Like racism, male supremacy pervades our society and male chauvinism pervades our thinking. Race and sex discrimination are synonymous." Harding concluded by underlining the centrality of the "Black struggle for liberation," which "therefore becomes the training ground for the movement of women's emancipation and each strengthens the other for emancipation are indivisible."[9] This document was in accord with the contemporaneous intersectional writings of Fran Beal from the Third World Women's Alliance and anticipated the development of Black feminist theory, such as the 1977 Combahee River Collective Statement.[10]

Because of activism and pressure, more Chicanos/as came to the UW in 1968. Until that time, the majority of Chicanos/as in the state were agricultural workers living east of the Cascade Mountains, and many were involved with the United Farm Workers Organizing Committee. In 1968, the Brown Berets, an organization of young revolutionary Chicanos/as was formed, most likely in Granger, Washington. The Brown Berets celebrated Chicano/a culture, supported and worked with the United Farm Workers Organizing Committee, opposed the war in Vietnam, and combatted racism toward Brown people. The group's members moved from the Yakima Valley to Seattle as students and were recruited to the UW in the late 1960s and early 1970s. The Seattle Brown Berets chapter worked at the community level fighting discrimination, poverty, and police brutality, and it initiated or participated in a number of programs, including a drive that collected food, clothing, money, and Christmas baskets and distributed them to those in need in the Yakima Valley. In 1970, Las Chicanas, composed primarily of women students and staff at the UW, was formed to address issues pertinent to women who struggled against both sexism and racism.[11]

In 1970 Wanda Davis and Nina Harding announced the advent of the Black Woman's Coalition. "Our program emphasizes the correlation of the Black struggle for liberation with women's struggle for liberation." The coalition demanded courses on the "true history of Black women and the Black family." The next year, Chicanas and Black women organized a coalition of Third World Women. Leonor Barrientes, its cochair, stated, "We are a new organizing force representing the ethnic bloodlines of Chicano, Asian, Indian and black women. We are about liberation."[12] Harding, who was also its cochair, emphasized that "one of the basic concepts that has united the Third World

Women's Coalition at the University of Washington is the fact that as women we are together a people of color who, as a race, are colonized globally. Our common bond, identity and ideology is that of liberation and revolution."[13] That year they unsuccessfully ran candidates for offices of the Associated Students of the University of Washington (ASUW). The coalition broke up the next year as a result of conflicts spawned by gender and racial politics at the UW. In these early years of the women's liberation movement, the small number of women of color in Seattle were the first to connect gender, race, and class, and they took on both the sexism of men of color and the Whiteness of the existing Left feminist organizations.

THE LESBIAN AND GAY LIBERATION MOVEMENT in Seattle, which was overwhelmingly White, was originally connected to the Left and Left feminism. Relationships between socialist, Marxist, and anarchist beliefs and LGBTQIA identities and struggles have had a long and mixed history. Prominent leftists involved in early struggles for LGBT rights include Edward Carpenter, Oscar Wilde, Harry Hay, Marie Equi, Bayard Rustin, and Emma Goldman. While many homosexuals were able to participate freely in left-wing organizations, the post–World War II political climate was aggressively anticommunist and antihomosexual. At the end of the war, after serving with distinction in the armed forces, thousands of lesbians and gay men were purged without honorable discharges. Hundreds of homosexuals working in the US State Department were denied due process rights and summarily fired, ostensibly because they might be subject to blackmail by foreign agents and reveal state secrets. Joseph McCarthy, right-wing senator from Wisconsin, went further, equating homosexuality with communism, demanding that homosexuality be criminalized, and seeking to purge gay men and lesbians from public life. J. Edgar Hoover, the head of the FBI, joined with McCarthy in an attempt to criminalize homosexuality.[14] In order to protect themselves from McCarthyite attacks, Marxist organizations, such as the Communist Party and the Socialist Workers Party, took homophobic stands, forbidding membership to homosexuals or outlawing homosexual relationships outright. These Leninists believed that homosexuality was a perversion symptomatic of bourgeois decadence and a by-product of capitalism and fascism. Ironically, orthodox Marxists, like anticommunists in the US government, also viewed homosexuality as a security risk that would undermine their organizations or lead to exposure that would discredit their politics.

Even in the repressive, misogynist, and homophobic 1950s and early 1960s, there were early stirrings for lesbian and gay liberation in Seattle, as in other cities.[15] The Hub, the first Seattle bar catering to lesbians, opened in 1950. Located on Capitol Hill, it was operated by Marjory Taylor and Anne Thompson until it closed in 1966. In 1967, the Dorian Society, founded by UW professor Nick Heer, was the first group in the city to support lesbian and gay rights. It published a newsletter about current issues and events in the gay community and sought to create a more respectable image of lesbian and gay Seattleites. The group advocated the reform of the state's antisodomy laws and provided counseling and employment assistance for homosexual men and women who suffered from discrimination—the first institution of its kind in the United States.[16] Dr. Robert Deisher, head of the UW Division of Child Health, who was also in charge of Dorian House counseling, estimated that there were between thirty thousand and forty thousand lesbians and gay men in the Seattle area.[17] In May 1967 the UW *Daily* did a series on the gay community that for the first time presented lesbians and gay men in a more positive light. In March 1968, Ernie Freitas opened a gay bar, the Centurian, in downtown Seattle. He explained the bar was "a service to the gay world that's both clean and pleasing," offering alcohol, food and drink, and magazines and postcards. According to Freitas, the Centurian was not hassled by the police.[18]

Writers for the magazine *Lilith* and at least three members of WL-S began addressing lesbian and gay issues before Stonewall. A small number of women of color who were active in *Lilith*, Radical Women, and WL-S were early members of lesbian feminist organizations. In addition, the membership of the University Young Women's Christian Association (YWCA) included a number of out lesbians, and the organization played a central role as a meeting place for lesbian activities and organizations.[19] Unlike in some other cities, where feminist groups were involved in bitter splits over support for lesbian and gay liberation, in Seattle Left feminists—whether lesbian, straight, or bisexual—remained united and supportive.[20] Mary Rothschild attributed this unity primarily to the work of the YWCA. Jody Olvera, Shelly Crites, and Theresa Nighthawk credited the strong bonds of sisterhood in WL-S.[21]

From its inception, the Seattle Gay Liberation Front (GLF) worked closely with antiwar, antiracist, and women's liberation organizations. Writing anonymously in *And Ain't I a Woman*, an activist rejoiced, "At the October 31 ant[i]-war march in Seattle, ... people from the Women's Liberation movement and the Gay Liberation movement found themselves marching together and sharing chants aimed at sexism, male chauvinism and the institution of the nuclear family. The gay liberation movement in Seattle is just beginning to exert its influence within the rest of the left movement and to state its demands."[22] At that 1970 march, the GLF and feminists confronted the organized Left, in particular the antihomosexual policies of the Young Socialist Alliance and the Socialist Workers Party, which excluded open and practicing homosexuals. On behalf of the GLF, Harlan Kerr Jr. wrote to WL-S in October expressing a need to "establish contact and communication with the Women of WL-S to further our understanding of each other. The sisters of GLF no doubt have much to discuss with the women of WLS."[23]

Radical Women, which was usually willing to denounce the Young Socialist Alliance and the Socialist Workers Party, was silent on this issue, for the Freedom Socialist Party also had an antihomosexual policy at that time. The Freedom Socialist Party and Radical Women formally supported lesbian and gay liberation after 1972 but offered no reflections on their earlier positions.[24] Attitudes toward homosexuality on the Maoist feminist left were not particularly supportive. According to Grey Osterud,

> It may seem strange in retrospect, but the Anna Louise Strong Brigade did not acknowledge that lesbianism was a political question. We opposed the CP, SWP, FSP, and PL [Progressive Labor] position that homosexuality was a form of capitalist degeneration (which was also held by the Cuban revolutionary leadership) as well as the establishment position that it was a psychiatric disorder, and we saw the predominantly male GLF as a coalition ally. But we treated sexuality as a personal matter that people might choose to keep private. There were several almost-out lesbians in ALSB, but their partners were not members. I suspect that this approach was the result of defining our goal as synthesizing Marxism and feminism, as distinct from a consciousness-raising group.[25]

The support of Left feminists and lesbian and gay liberation activists, many of whom were one and the same, forced many organizations to rethink and later change their positions.

The unity of straight and lesbian Left feminists and radical lesbian feminists was demonstrated in 1973 when Betty Friedan came to Seattle. The author of the *Feminine Mystique*, founder of NOW, and major mover for passage of the ERA was a very outspoken opponent of lesbian participation in NOW and other women's rights organizations. In 1970, Friedan infamously described lesbians in NOW as a "lavender menace," believing their visible presence in the movement would tarnish the group's respectability, make feminist activists look like manhaters, and hinder progress toward women's rights.[26] Friedan, once close to or a member of the Communist Party, had no doubt absorbed some of the party's homophobia, as well as its fear that communism would be equated with homosexuality. She made herself especially unpopular with

Left feminists and lesbians not just for her outspoken opposition to lesbian activism but also for her imperious appearance and demeanor. She arrived in Seattle wearing a mink coat, demanded a scandalously high honorarium, and was quite rude to many of the people who organized and attended various parties and receptions for her. Students in Mary Rothschild's Introduction to Women's Studies course organized a coalition of lesbian and straight feminist activists to stage a public demonstration protesting Friedan's position. Taking over the stage with banners condemning Friedan, they issued a statement that reflected their understanding of intersectional politics: "We strongly protest Friedan's racism, classism and anti-lesbianism. She has continually ignored, degraded and insulted poor women, third world women and lesbians." Friedan's speech proved her critics' case. She asserted "that lesbianism shouldn't be an issue in women's struggle for independence from a patriarchal power" and then denounced lesbians as "disruptive" elements in the women's movement. Most outrageously, Friedan charged that the protesters were paid agents who intended to hurt the women's movement. Rothschild, self-defined as a straight woman, stood up and defended the protesters: "I was so angry. I saw red for the first time in my life." Friedan refused to answer questions and left the meeting, only to be met by other protesters leafleting and chanting.[27] This event cemented alliances between lesbian, straight, and bisexual activists, leading to a proliferation of LGBTQ organizations and activism in Seattle.

In the early 1970s, UW students organized the Gay Student Association and the more radical GLF. Working with the Seattle Gay Alliance, the GLF opened the first Gay Community Center in Seattle on September 15, 1971, in Pioneer Square. Feminists, many of whom were active in the radical women's liberation movement, were highly critical of the masculinist attitudes of the GLF and organized the Gay Women's Alliance. Later came the Gay Women's Resource Center (later the Lesbian Resource Center), the Union of Sexual Minorities, the Stonewall Recovery Center, the Lesbian Mothers National Defense Fund, the Metropolitan Community Church, the Seattle Counseling Center for Sexual Minorities, and Parents, Families, Friends of Lesbians and Gays (PFLAG). As awareness of gay and lesbian civil rights spread, groups articulated numerous political objectives, focused on various special interests, and began to uncover for the first time the diversity among themselves. At that time, however, LGBTQ activism in Seattle was overwhelmingly White, in contrast to movements in other cities with more non-White residents.

ANOTHER LONG-LASTING ACHIEVEMENT of the radical women's liberation movement was the development and creation of a whole new body of knowledge around gender and sexuality. The emergence of women's (now gender and sexuality) studies and Black and Chicano/a studies as respected academic disciplines did not begin with tenured professors discussing curriculum reform. These radical movements brought theory learned from activism into the academy.[28] In Seattle, feminist theory was developed in the streets, demonstrations, rap groups, union meetings, political coalitions, jails, PTA meetings, religious gatherings, the YWCA, and storefronts, as well as in women's kitchens and bedrooms. The first class about women in society, which was offered by socialists, took place in 1967 at the Free University in the University District. A year later, Seattle Radical Women hosted a ten-part series on women in US society. This course touched on Black women, in part because Eleanor Flexner's *Century of Struggle* (1959), which everyone read, included material on their activism. Many of the women involved in these early years were students at the UW or Seattle Central Community College; they had access to libraries and used their training to discover and uncover feminist history, politics, and theory. Radical feminist publications such as *Lilith*, *And Ain't I a Woman*, and *Pandora*, along with the endless stream of leaflets and position papers, helped to develop feminist ideas. Judith Bissell, writing in *Lilith*, brought a gendered perspective to war, peace, and the draft. In two lengthy articles in *And Ain't I a Woman*, Jody Olvera wrote in depth about the intersection of race and gender from the perspective of Latinas. Members of the Anna Louise Strong Brigade produced position papers on gender, socialism, and race. After 1970 lesbian and gay liberation was included in discussions on race and gender. Seattle feminists were voracious readers and researchers. All the women's groups hosted educational discussions that upended the taken-for-granted sexist assumptions in almost every imaginable subject. Out of this activism came the drive for women's studies courses, programs, and departments in Seattle's colleges and universities.

As early as 1969, women's liberation activists began to successfully pressure academic departments at the UW to create credit-bearing courses on women. Aldon Bell, an associate dean of the College of Arts and Sciences who headed General and Interdisciplinary Studies, was a great supporter of women's studies. In the fall of 1970, he appointed Mary Rothschild, then a graduate student in history, to be the graduate student representative on the dean's Blue-Ribbon Committee on Women's Studies, whose responsibility was to recommend whether the UW should develop a program. Rothschild remembered that "at the same time, he asked me if I would like to teach a Women's History course of my own design in the Spring Quarter, which would be the first Women's History course taught at the UW."[29] Two activists from the University YWCA,

Julie Coryell and Anne Schweisow, had previously taught courses, but their classes were not connected to any department and did not count toward a degree. Many of the earliest women's studies professors came from the YWCA or WL-S.

Women students at Seattle Central Community College (SCCC) who were members of WL-S also demanded a course on women in US society, and after six months of agitation, the president of the college agreed. But he was concerned that the Department of Social and Behavioral Sciences did not know of any scholar who could teach the course. The WL-S at SCCC found one of its own members, who taught an introductory course for two years.

By 1972, women's studies was established at the UW, first as a program and later a department. Its first tenure-track director was Sue-Ellen Jacobs, an anthropologist, who was hired in 1974. She was not the students' first choice. Writing about the origins of the women's studies program, Jacobs remembered that "a contingent headed by radical women activists in Seattle were concerned with other candidates."[30] The earliest courses included Introduction to Women's Studies, with readings of classic White women such as Mary Wollstonecraft, Virginia Woolf, and Betty Friedan. There were courses offered on women and the novel, the psychology of women, women in US history, and women in the educational system. None of the courses that were offered from 1970 to 1974 dealt specifically with race or included writings by women of color. There were no Black, Latina, Indigenous, or Asian women faculty.[31] Many of the UW Women's Studies founders had been in women's liberation groups and participated in numerous discussions on race and the intersection of race and gender. They were familiar with African American feminist writings from organizations such as the Third World Women's Alliance, the Mount Vernon Women's Group, and the Black Panther Party, and they had discussed the writings of Black women, such as Maya Angelou's *I Know Why the Caged Bird Sings* (1969), Frances Beal's *Double Jeopardy: To Be Black and Female* (1969), Cellestine Ware's *Womanpower: The Movement for Women's Liberation* (1970), and Toni Cade Bambara's *The Black Woman* (1970). Rothschild, whose PhD dissertation was about Black women in the civil rights movement, remembers including Black women in her courses. According to Antonia Castañeda, one of the founders of the Chicana/Chicano Studies program at the UW, her 1972 course on Chicanas was the only course that focused on women of color; Jody Olvera remembers teaching one of the courses in the Chicana/Chicano Studies program.[32] The absence of women of color from the curriculum was in part a reflection of the state of the field at the time, but

Left feminists should—and could—have known better. White feminist activists and founders of women's studies must acknowledge this serious failing.

MEMBERS OF THE WL-S WORKING WOMEN'S COMMITTEE joined with other Left feminist activists who worked at the UW to organize clerical workers. These women had worked together in the Coalition for University Sponsored Day Care, the United Farm Workers Organizing Committee, and Black and White Concern, as well as in the struggle for abortion rights. According to two of its founders, the Staff Women's Forum was organized immediately after the 1970 student strike. "The staff felt excluded; they felt they had no part in the strike. As a result of this feeling of alienation and impatience, several working women decided to form an organization that was broad enough to appeal to all women." Staff Women's Forum was not opposed to forming a union, but its leaders preferred to wait until they were sure of majority support.[33] Initially they spoke out against wage and salary discrimination. They demanded that more women be chosen for senior administrative posts and that the university provide support for childcare. The logo of the *Staff Forum Newsletter* was a woman chained to a typewriter with the iconic Pablo Picasso antiwar painting *Guernica* in the background. It reported on activities at the UW that were relevant to the staff and the nascent organization, such as involving staff women from Harborview Hospital, which was located downtown, and working with the ASUW Women's Commission to ensure that a woman be appointed as one of the UW's seven vice presidents. The newsletter also publicized women's liberation activities in the city. Members who worked in the library began organizing literature deemed relevant to women and the women's movement and requested that the library accelerate the acquisition and cataloging of feminist books. Staff Women's Forum held monthly meetings on a wide range of topics such as female sexuality, abortion, the war in Vietnam, and workplace and union issues.

In 1972, Staff Women's Forum renamed itself Concerned Staff Workers. The newsletter stated, "We are not militant. The fist we raise will open with reason." This was a small group of organizers; its membership ranged between ten and twenty, with a "minority" caucus.[34] Like most unions, it demanded that the university give staff members two hours a month, with pay, to attend its meetings, because "if you are like most women who work you cannot afford time or money to attend meetings outside working hours." Urging staff workers to stand up for themselves, they asked, "Or are you afraid of alienating you supervisor by asking too many questions about your rights?"[35]

Throughout the 1970s, Concerned Staff Workers organized staff throughout the UW and worked with the ASUW Women's Commission, UW faculty, and the existing American Federation of State, County and Municipal Employees (AFSCME) local to win greater rights. Concerned Staff Workers affiliated with the working women's organization, 9 to 5, and in the 1980s it formally affiliated with the Service Employees International Union (SEIU) and became UW Local 925.[36] Because of opposition from university administrators as well as indifference and hostility on the part of AFSCME officials, it took decades to organize clerical workers at the UW and throughout the state. This union movement began with feminists extending their newly learned women's liberation politics, skills, and energy to workplaces that employed many women.

AFTER THE LEGALIZATION OF ABORTION IN 1973, Left feminists, especially from the Anna Louise Strong Brigade, Fanshen, and the Red Mountain Collective, worked to expand health care. The Open Door Clinic was among the first, most innovative endeavors started by people active in the city's gender-mixed Left. Doug Southend came up with the idea while drinking with friends at the Blue Moon, the fabled tavern in the University District. The clinic initially served young people on bad LSD trips. By 1971, it offered medical services seven nights a week and staffed a twenty-four-hour telephone hotline. It provided minor surgery and venereal disease screenings, and a sympathetic dentist gave the clinic an X-ray machine. The staff provided information about social services including housing, foster child placements, suicide prevention, and crisis interventions. After receiving a federal grant as well as an anonymous $30,000 donation, by 1971 it had four full-time paid staff. Volunteers remained essential; 260 volunteers worked long hours. A number of its medics, such as Nancy Stokely, of the Let H̶I̶M̶/HER Live graffiti, also worked for the Aradia clinic when it was organized.

Other New Left activists, one of whom was a Vietnam veteran with training as a medic, founded Country Doctor in 1971. A number of the founders had collaborated with members of the Black Panther Party who had worked in the party's Sidney Miller Clinic in the Central District. According to Aaron Dixon, chair of the Seattle Black Panther Party, the Sidney Miller Clinic was the first free medical clinic in the Pacific Northwest. Country Doctor was located on Capital Hill, a district with a diverse mix of working-class, African American, LGBTQ, and student residents.[37]

The Abortion–Birth Control Referral Service and the Aradia Women's Health Center grew out of the University YWCA. Left feminist activists there saw a need for feminist health care, began by writing a grant, raised other monies, and organized other women to work on the project. Many of its first staffers and paramedics came from Open Door and Country Doctor, and their experiences helped to shape Aradia's feminist politics. Elaine Schroeder, a member of WL-S who was a reproductive rights counselor and later a therapist, remembers the debate over the clinic's name. Because they were applying for federal grant monies, they avoided an "inflammatory" name. "We were going to name it something like the Radical Women's Health Collective, or Witches' Coven.... We toned it down to something like the Feminist Women's Collective.... But then somebody... found the name Aradia, which was the Greek goddess of women's health and of healing. And they liked that because it was innocuous, and they weren't going to get in trouble."[38] The clinic was launched in April 1972. At first it was open three days and two evenings a week. The architect, construction workers, and volunteers were all women. The all-women staff included one doctor, two nurses, and one licensed physical therapist. Everyone who worked at Aradia met monthly. Women from the YWCA, the Lesbian Women's Resource Center, Rape Relief, the Abortion–Birth Control Referral Service, Mechanica (an organization of women in the trades), and the Ad Hoc Committee were all represented.

Aradia provided caring, nonhierarchical health care and education in a feminist setting. It offered contraceptive information and devices, taught women how to perform breast self-examinations, did screening and treatment for venereal disease, and provided referrals for tubal ligation, vasectomy, and abortion. The clinic held meetings and offered resources on abortion, birth control, conception, fertility, health law, infertility, lesbianism, masturbation, menopause, menstruation, pregnancy, reproductive health, sexuality, and tubal ligations. The women who designed Aradia did not want it to look like an austere and alienating doctor's office. The walls were gaily painted; posters and children's drawings were everywhere. Women were encouraged to watch health-care procedures. They could observe their own pelvic examination and examine their slides under a microscope. Women could walk around the clinic to see how it operated. Never separating sexuality from women's reproductive health, clinic staffers brought in vibrators to help patients who had difficulty achieving orgasm. The vibrators became so popular that the clinic had to order them in batches of twenty-five from adult bookstores. The clinic not only demystified sex, it opened up nonjudgmental discussions on all aspects of sexuality. The guiding principle was that women should control their bodies, their sexuality, and their medical care.

In order to live up to its commitment to nonhierarchical feminist health care, Aradia encouraged women to observe and learn about their bodies. At self-help groups dubbed "pelvic parties," women examined their own and others' cervixes, which helped them to overcome shyness about their "private parts," and learned how to treat minor gynecological problems, such as vaginal infections. They also taught other health-care professionals. Elaine Schroeder remembered, "We were right on the cutting edge. We went into the medical school with the medical students and showed them how to do pelvic exams. They didn't show us how to do them, we showed them how to do them." Schroeder and other paramedics witnessed autopsies at local hospitals, "so we could see the reproductive organs as part of our medical training." Aradia and other feminist health clinics gave women the confidence that they understood their own bodies and could make their own decisions, and even impart their knowledge to the elitist, White, and male medical establishment. For feminist health-care providers like Schroeder, Aradia was "one of the best times of my life." Making "decision[s] by consensus was obviously the mode of operating. And it worked. I do not remember fighting. I remember harmony."[39]

Other health clinics soon followed Aradia's example. The Hall Health Center at the UW had long failed to serve women's needs, especially for reproductive health information; in 1969, it did not even provide contraception for women. But by 1971, Hall Health was a center of feminist organizing. The Family Planning Unit opened that year and distributed and fitted over 1,500 contraceptive devices for women. It also provided testing and treatment for sexually transmitted diseases. While the clinic's patients were overwhelmingly female, a few men came in for vasectomies. Schroeder was a Hall Health clinic counselor and led weekly discussions on women's sexuality, health, and reproduction. All medical records were confidential, "so that a student shouldn't worry that her parents would be told about her visit."[40]

The Fremont Women's Clinic, founded in 1971 and located in the working-class and student neighborhoods of Ballard, Fremont, and Wallingford, provided low-cost health care to women and also served men. It offered gynecological, prenatal, pediatric, and gerontological care and provided transportation and babysitting to make clinic visits more accessible. By the mid-1970s, because of pressure from state and federal funders, the clinic no longer specialized in women's health.

Feminist cross-pollination occurred among the clinics. Every Sunday night was Women's Liberation Night at the Open Door Clinic. According to two volunteers, "We are a medical clinic dealing with problems most prevalent with women, the gamut of gynecological treatment, pregnancy detection, birth control counseling, abortion and prenatal referral." Lorne Sone and Kathryn Karjala explained that the clinic was designed to educate women about their bodies as well as to demystify medicine.[41] As did their sisters at Aradia, they emphasized that gynecology was closely related to sexuality and hosted educational sessions on orgasm, "frigidity," heterosexual intercourse, and lesbianism as well as prostitution. They hosted pelvic parties and encouraged women to train as paramedics and community health-care activists.

One night a week, Country Doctor had an open meeting on women's reproductive health and sexuality. Many of the women working with Country Doctor had been involved in the Referendum 20 campaign and advocated for the clinic to perform abortions. Others in the collective, which was overwhelmingly male, argued that the issue was too divisive, and the clinic would lose community support if it offered this service. The vote to oppose providing abortions fell along gender lines. In order to maintain feminist support, the clinic trained midwives to attend home births. By not providing abortions, Country Doctor remained eligible for federal funding.[42]

Acutely aware of racism, feminist activists in the Seattle YWCA created the Third World Women's Resource Center in 1972. Theresa Sakudo, Sarah Sakuma, Shelly Yapp, and Janet Krause founded the center and secured its funding. The center was intended to extend the YWCA's outreach to women of color, sponsor rap groups for women of color, and "increase understanding and knowledge between Black, Spanish American, Asian and Native American Women."[43] The YWCA was able to get funding from the federal Health, Education, and Welfare Department to create a women's clinic serving the "Third World" community. The women deliberately did not announce the clinic's feminist perspective. The Third World Women's Preventative Medicine and Health Education Center was located in El Centro de la Raza on Beacon Hill, a neighborhood with significant African American, Latinx, and Filipino populations. The center offered both contraception and treatment for infertility.

The 1973 revelation of the involuntary sterilization of the Relf sisters, two African American teenagers, by a federally funded clinic in Alabama fueled the belief that birth control, sterilization, and abortion were part of the federal government's genocidal policies toward people of color. Feminists at the YWCA knew that their programs must be led by women of color and attuned to their needs. Along with health-care services, the center sponsored rap groups on feminism and racism. It organized a major conference, Solidarity through Sisterhood, with panels on the law, prisons, the media, education, and organizing. The keynote speaker was Frances Beal, founding member of SNCC's Black Women's Liberation Committee, which later evolved into the Third World Women's Alliance. She is most widely known for *Double Jeopardy: To Be Black and Female*, which theorized the intersection of oppression based on race, class, and gender.[44] This conference was part of a growing feminist movement of women of color in Seattle and throughout the US.

Radical women's liberation activists created a new body of knowledge. The Left feminist health, reproductive rights, and sexuality movements produced a wide range of literature that educated feminists and, over time, reached a large portion of the US population. Much of the early research and writing was circulated in the form of mimeographed or printed leaflets and pamphlets. During the abortion referendum campaign, WL-S published *One Out of Four*, a booklet about feminism and abortion rights. All of these writings drew directly on women's own experiences. Women went into libraries seeking information, only to discover misogynist literature about women's bodies, women's health, and women's sexualities. The most long-lasting and influential feminist work was *Our Bodies, Ourselves*.[45] It has spawned women's health education projects around the world and remains the touchstone for feminist, women-controlled perspectives on women's health, sexuality, and reproductive rights.

At the same time that the feminist collective in Boston was meeting, researching, and writing their self-help manual, so too were members of the ASUW Women's Commission. In 1972, they published *How to Have Intercourse without Getting Screwed*. The first eight thousand copies sold out immediately and fifty thousand more were printed. It was dedicated to Dr. A. Frans Koome, the courageous abortion provider. The contributors were activists in the Referendum 20 campaign and members of WL-S, as well as Planned Parenthood and the Abortion–Birth Control Referral Service. The booklet discussed female anatomy, contraception, sterilization, pregnancy, abortion, sexually transmitted diseases, and sexual counseling from a feminist perspective. It argued "that women have the right to know about the kinds of assistance that are available for controlling conception and birth." Anne Schweisow ended the book with these words: "The challenge to the *sexual status quo* must come from women. To ensure physical and psychic survival, we must demand new definitions of masculine or feminine that do not require dominance of one sex over the other, or better yet, do away with such antiquated notions completely. We as women must first get at the roots of our own oppression." She expressed an optimism that, in retrospect, appears somewhat naïve: "As we develop self-determining healthy self-concepts and sexual expectations, men will change in response."[46]

The Aradia clinic separated from the University YWCA in 1973 and continued to serve women. In spite of the growing antifeminist and antiabortion movement, Aradia remained committed to connecting feminism to women's health and sexuality. By the time the clinic closed in 2006, the majority of the women it had served were women of color or immigrants; 70 percent of its clientele were Medicaid or Medicare recipients, reflecting Aradia's founding promise of providing accessible services to diverse communities. Feminist health organizing in Seattle grew out of the commitment of women's liberation activists to challenge the racial, gendered, and class hierarchies of the medical health-care establishment. Most of these activists were and remain committed to the idea that public health care is a right and not a privilege.

LEFT FEMINISTS IN SEATTLE organized some of the first clinics dealing with divorce, rape, self-defense, and battered women. The impetus behind the Feminist Karate Union, Mechanica, and the Divorce Cooperative came from an Anna Louise Strong Brigade retreat called the Survival Revival.[47]

The Divorce Cooperative was organized by seven Left feminists, including members of Seattle Radical Women. None was a lawyer; a number were divorced, and others worked as legal secretaries. They brought a Marxist analysis to the classed and gendered institution of heterosexual marriage. In Washington State, until the 1970s the spouse seeking a legal separation had to prove cruelty, adultery, or abandonment. Many women were unable to get a divorce because it was too complicated and lawyers were too expensive. The Washington State Bar Association had set a $350 minimum fee for an uncontested divorce, which was almost as high as the average monthly earnings of employed women. It was clear to the founders of the Divorce Cooperative that most women, especially those with children, could not afford even the simplest divorce.[48] One explained, "A lot of us had just married young, knew we weren't going to make it, but didn't want to have to blame our spouses of some activity they had not engaged in. The no-fault divorce law, which was one of my favorite things that came out of the 1970s, was a wonderful piece of legislation that was supported by many people in the Radical Women organization who lobbied for it heavily. Many women who were attorneys were able to guide this piece of legislation." Another co-op member said, "I actually waited until this passed to get a divorce." Over fifty women used the services of the co-op, which met once a week. "As feminists we wanted to talk to women, who because they are getting a divorce, are in the position to question their training only to be wives and mothers." The co-op believed that "the attendant pain" of divorce "was not an indication of individual failure in a marital relationship, but as a natural reaction to an oppressive relationship." Their discussion topics—female sexuality, the war in Vietnam, rape, women in prison—reflected the overarching positions and priorities of Left feminism. The Divorce Cooperative had a short life-span.[49] By the mid-1970s, as women entered the paid labor force and higher-paying professions, issues of equitable distribution of resources and custody battles made self-help divorces problematic and legal representation a necessity.

One of the many contributions and achievements of Left feminism was bringing the issue of rape, sexual harassment, and other forms of violence against women to the fore. Seattle's Left feminist activists organized the first rape crisis center in the US as well as the first feminist self-defense group. The clinic, called Rape Relief, was founded in 1972 following a speak-out. It was a grassroots, volunteer-driven agency for survivors of sexual assault. Its twenty-four-hour hotline began with eight women taking over 150 calls a month from their homes. More than one-third of their fifty-six hours of training was devoted to confronting racism, sexism, homophobia, and other forms of oppression that fostered violence. The staff, volunteers, and those who came to the clinic received education and counseling premised on the understanding that women were not responsible for rape; rather, rape was about male power over women. Seattle Rape Relief was also unique because it reached out to veterans; gay, lesbian, and transgender people; prostitutes; homeless youths; and people of color. Its reputation grew, and for decades it survived on volunteer contributions and government funding. The clinic closed in 1999, when both sources of financial support had declined. But during its life-span it changed "the blame-the-woman-for-getting-raped" attitude and influenced legislation, treatment, and police responses to rape and other forms of sexual violence.

At the same time, Left feminists organized women to learn how to defend themselves. In January 1971, a small group of women wanting to learn karate met in a wrestling room in the UW gymnasium for a class taught by Py Bateman, a member of the Anna Louise Strong Brigade who had just earned a brown belt. *And Ain't I a Woman*, which supported feminist self-defense, reprinted an article from another Left feminist publication, *It Aint Me Babe*, which argued that American culture "does not allow women to develop strength. Girls are not supposed to do physical things. The result is that women are pitifully weak. Women feel . . . that they need a man to protect them. Only when we have gained the self-confidence which comes through developing our physical potential and exercising it, will we be able to gain any individual mobility."[50] At the end of the first ten-week course, the students wanted to continue in an all-women environment. Out of that class came Alternatives to Fear and the Feminist Karate Union. Bateman remembered that until the formation of Rape Relief, there was little understanding about sexual assault. Rape Relief and the Feminist Karate Union worked closely together. Over time, both groups took up child sexual abuse, date rape, teen rape, and disabilities. Ted Bundy's killing spree in the 1970s and the Green River Killer's murders in the 1980s and 1990s created an urgent need for greater awareness and self-defense training for women. The Feminist Karate Union is still operating.

Flow and Ebb

8

IN 1970, Seattle had six women's liberation organizations that were organized openly by socialists, and all defined themselves as socialist feminist, anti-imperialist, antiracist, and internationalist. With a total membership numbering in the thousands, these groups' activism led to a sea change in laws, institutions, and thinking about women and gender: the passage of Referendum 20, liberalizing restrictive abortion laws; the creation of women's commissions, feminist health-care centers, antiviolence, and other clinics to empower women; and the establishment of women's and gender and sexuality studies programs at the major colleges and universities. In addition, socialist feminist women fought for legislative changes, beginning with support for the Equal Rights Amendment (ERA), action against sexual harassment, and agitation for day care and equal pay. Many engaged in union organizing, raising feminist issues in the workplace and in their unions. K–12 teachers and their students challenged and changed the public school curriculum, which had celebrated White men's achievements and ideas and erased those of women and people of color. In sum, radical feminists began to turn the world upside down.

By 1973, only one of these radical women's liberation groups remained: Radical Women, with a membership of twenty-eight.[1] Radical Women claims that it owes its longevity to its organizational affiliation and agreement with the program of the Freedom Socialist Party, a claim that, given the longevity of

Trotskyist sects, seems an accurate assessment.[2] The reasons for the disappearance of the other groups are more complicated. The Anna Louise Strong Brigade, Fanshen, and the Women's Majority Union agreed to disband; Campus Women's Liberation died as a result of sectarianism. A number of women moved out of Seattle, exhausted by what seemed to be endless faction fights not just in their women's groups but in the larger left-wing movement. Others found employment in fields where they could continue their socialist, feminist, antiracist, antiwar, and union organizing. Some became involved in non-feminist educational organizations and institutions. Others who had children and full-time jobs found it impossible to go to meetings three or four times a week, whether or not they had partners. Seattle's socialist feminist journals ended publication: *Lilith* in 1970, *And Ain't I a Woman* in 1972. *Pandora* lasted until 1979 but became much less radical.

Beginning in 1970, branches of more mainstream feminist organizations, such as the National Organization for Women (NOW), the National Abortion Rights Action League (NARAL), the National Women's Political Caucus (NWPC), and the Coalition of Labor Union Women (CLUW), were organized in Seattle. The major focus of NOW was on passing the ERA; NARAL lobbied legislators to protect abortion rights; the NWPC tried to persuade more women to run for political office. CLUW promoted bringing more trade union women into the leadership of the American Federation of Labor and Congress of Industrial Organizations (AFL–CIO). Once shunned by Left feminists, the Democratic Party began to draw in more activists. Left feminists joined these organizations because they wished to stay involved in women's struggles, but with the overall decline and defeat of the Left, the influence of Left feminism was minimal.

WOMEN'S LIBERATION–SEATTLE (WL-S), the largest of the socialist feminist groups, disbanded in 1972. The immediate cause was a dispute over the proposal to set up an office of women's affairs within the Associated Students of the University of Washington (ASUW), which turned on racial and gender discrimination, as well as factional maneuvering over what groups would exercise control. This struggle led to bitter recriminations, name-calling, broken friendships, and severed alliances, which left the WL-S membership so demoralized and exhausted that they decided they could no longer continue.

This two-year ordeal is worthy of discussion because it conveys a sense of the day-to-day involvement of Left feminists in concerted efforts to change a powerful institution. Socialist feminists at the University of Washington (UW) had founded Black, Chicano/a, and women's studies programs; gained control over ASUW administrative posts; transformed the Hall Health Center; reinvigorated the ASUW Women's Commission (WC); and organized the Staff Women's Forum. Students who won ASUW posts had budgets that enabled them to travel and to hire people to staff their offices. They gained greater access to UW administrators, local and state officials, and business and cultural leaders, and they had a bully pulpit for their political viewpoints. No wonder there was competition for these leadership positions.

Feminists and other radicals became involved in the electoral politics of ASUW. Members of WL-S who were UW students, faculty, or staff paid very little attention to student government or sororities. The organization never had a formal or informal discussion about how to relate to student government politics. Members of WL-S believed that grassroots organizing, demonstrating, writing and distributing leaflets, and campaigning on specific issues were more effective ways of advancing radical feminist politics and building institutions than seeking office in ASUW. It never formally endorsed women or feminist candidates, although some individual members did. In 1972, when Ann Johnson ran for ASUW president with a progressive feminist platform, she won overwhelmingly, becoming the first woman to hold that office since 1945. Cassandra (no last name), another outspoken feminist and UW *Daily* columnist, was elected ASUW secretary by a landslide, although the two men elected to ASUW offices that year won by very narrow margins.[3] Members of WL-S worked closely with the ASUW Women's Commission.

In 1969 feminists took leadership in the WC and expanded its scope to include staff and faculty women.[4] Throughout the 1970s, the WC worked closely with both Left feminists and more mainstream women activists. In October 1970, it produced a bombshell report that conclusively documented massive sex and race discrimination at the UW on both the individual and structural levels. The specific facts in the report were so damning that the WC expected the administration to act on its recommendations regarding hiring, retaining, and promoting women and people of color in faculty, staff, and administrative positions; recruiting more women and students of color into graduate programs; reviewing the undergraduate and graduate curriculum; and reconsidering the racial and gendered character of financial decision making.[5] Instead, the administration ignored the report, and when the executive vice president, Philip Cartwright, finally met with members of the WC, he taunted them that only militant action would get results.[6]

Undaunted, the WC filed a class action complaint with the Office of Federal Contract Compliance for violating federal laws that prohibited institutions receiving federal funds from discriminating against women. Academic department after academic department, including Library Services, voiced their support for the changes proposed in the report. Only when faced with opposition from the majority of the faculty and much of the staff, combined with the potential loss of federal money, did uw president Charles Odegaard begin to address the women's concerns, mostly by organizing committees and making promises. The wc asked that an office of women's affairs be created at the vice-presidential level with staff, money, and authority to carry out its mission of ending discrimination. Cartwright refused, explaining that no new post was needed and leaving it up to each academic department to address racial and gender discrimination.

Immediately the wc called a demonstration to support its proposals. But the administration outflanked the wc. Ernesta Barnes, the staff assistant in the Equal Opportunities Program's Office for Women, announced the formation of the Coalition of University Organizations for Women's Rights (cuowr) and persuaded a number of women to accept Cartwright's offer. Furious, the wc mobilized its supporters, repeated the demand for an office with clout, and won over a number of women in cuowr. The administration, not wanting to cede control to the wc, then proposed that it would create a new women's office under the leadership of Carver Gayton, an African American uw alumnus from a legendary abolitionist and civil rights family. The predominantly White women's coalition turned down this proposal, arguing that Gayton and Barnes were not committed enough to either the Black Freedom struggle or feminist activism.[7] Gayton did not accept the post. Barnes, who admitted coming from a privileged background, was quoted in a local newspaper suggesting that if housework interfered with a woman's activities, she should hire a woman housecleaner. When asked if she would resign her position if Cartwright did not support her efforts, Barnes said, "I do not know whether I would have the strength."[8] Negotiations continued but made little progress.

All this time, Third World Women, other socialist feminists from the Freedom Socialist Party, Radical Women, and wl-s were heavily invested in researching and writing the *Report on the Status of Women at the University of Washington*. Theresa Shapiro, a Latina member of Third World Women, introduced a resolution to cuowr demanding that "minorities be given preference (even men) over white women in the hiring at the uw," threatening a walkout by women of color if the resolution was not approved.[9] On March 23, Leonor Barrientes, the representative of Third World Women, resigned as the chair of the uw Women's Coalition. In a scathing "exit statement," the group denounced the uw administration, Barnes, and cuowr: "The Woman's Affairs Office and along with the Women's Coalition DOES NOT

REPRESENT the survival needs of Third World Women." The WC and CUOWR, it charged, are on a "revisionist, guilt ridden white woman missionary trip, and we refuse to play this game." According to the statement, CUOWR "hopelessly prioritized" the needs of White women over the needs of Chicana, Indian, Asian, and Black women.[10] Finally, the organization stated that it had been deceived by the coalition and would never again listen to the "inane rhetoric of women's liberation claiming that sex discrimination is more basic than race discrimination."[11]

The White socialist feminists who had been involved in writing the report and in the negotiations with the administration were devastated by the walk-out, bitter at the success of the UW administration's racial divide-and-conquer tactics, and mortified at their inability to maintain a multiracial coalition. Members of WL-S were distraught but did not agree on whether or how to respond. They issued a statement clearly condemning the UW administration, calling the proposed office of equal opportunities for women "a sham which is being used to avoid any action against sexual discrimination at the University," and advocating the creation of a new coalition that recognizes the needs of all women to "oppose both sexual and racial discrimination."[12] But nothing more was resolved. Apparently ignoring the serious charges of racism by Third World Women, WL-S then published a platitudinous, tone-deaf statement: "We believe the only way we can aid our black sisters in this struggle is by developing a dynamic, independent movement for the emancipation of our sex."[13]

Even after the women of color walked out, some members of WL-S and Radical Women stayed in CUOWR, fighting within the coalition and against the UW administration. Half the members of the coalition, however, wanted to work with Barnes and accept the structure offered by the UW. Barnes quit her position shortly thereafter. As a result of the WC's lawsuit, the administration was forced to set up an equal opportunities office for women to monitor hiring practices, which was headed by Kathy Thom, a member of NOW, and to establish a women's studies program. The WC continued its work and advocated for reforms, but in a less militant and radical way.

This struggle ended in a very painful defeat for feminists at the UW. As in the struggle with the administration over day care, the women equated feminist commitment with real political power. White women failed to or refused to understand the centrality of opposing racism in any progressive struggle. Cartwright cynically pitted women of color against White women, White women against Black men, and radicals and militants against more mainstream and conservative women, the tried and true strategy of divide and conquer. Lee Mayfield of WL-S lamented, "Here was a case of the university's racism and sexism combined and our group was split on whether to respond. Old friendships broke up, bitter words were spoken, and tears were shed. As a result, the IS [International Socialist] women left. New women joined, but the left movement was so fragmented, each section isolated from each other, that we could not feel we were part of a movement."[14]

Members of WL-S agreed that they were too politically and emotionally exhausted to try to rebuild the organization. Its swan song was a Sisterhood Is Powerful teach-in on May Day 1972. The event was well attended, with a wide variety of participants including organizations of women of color, and it featured plenaries and workshops dealing with the state of the women's liberation movement. Even though the event was upbeat, Mayfield explained, "we were just unwilling to go back and start again." She believed that the organization had strayed too far from the anti-imperialist movement. "With the end of the war in Vietnam, the left completed its fragmentation and polarization process.... We could not radicalize the newer women because we lacked connections with the radical movements ourselves."[15] Mayfield's comments about the important connections between Left feminist organizations and the mixed-gender anti-imperialist organizations have merit. At the time of the debacle, however, WL-S had only about a dozen members, so the defection of six International Socialist members was a serious blow. Two non–International Socialist women found jobs in other states. Members of WL-S continued to pursue Left politics in other arenas.

THE HISTORY OF THE FEMINIST COORDINATING COUNCIL provides another useful example of the challenges, difficulties, and obstacles facing Left feminist groups after 1970. Founded in 1972, it brought together a wide range of socialist, trade union, lesbian, health, and community organizations in a coalition to fight for women's rights. What appeared as a promising alliance of feminist and progressive organizations collapsed in factionalism. First NOW left after a national directive forbade local chapters to join coalitions, which it may have seen as potential rivals. A faction fight between the Socialist Workers Party and the Freedom Socialist Party soon arose within the council, and as a result other individuals and organizations left, including the Women's Rights Committee of the American Civil Liberties Union, Marjorie Stern from the American Federation of Teachers, the ASUW Women's Commission, the Divorce Cooperative, the Gay Women's Resource Center, Mechanica, and *Pandora*. Lesbian separatist organizations withdrew because they objected to socialist political perspectives. Other groups had folded. Kathi Dowd and

Jody Olvera, former members of WL-S, argued that the lack of substantive political discussions over the role, purpose, and structure of the Feminist Coordinating Council led people and groups to drop out: "Instead of fighting out differences, everyone picked up their marbles and went home." After the Socialist Workers Party left, Radical Women and the Freedom Socialist Party were in charge of the Feminist Coordinating Council. Olvera, Dowd, Mayfield, and others tried to organize another coalition of Left feminists: "We need a Council that is not just a mouthpiece for Radical Women and a women's center that is more than a city-wide skill and crafts collective."[16] But reviving a broader coalition proved impossible, and the Feminist Coordinating Council ceased operating in 1977.[17]

Feminist organizations such as Rape Relief, the Feminist Karate Union, the Divorce Cooperative, Mechanica, and Aradia and the other feminist health clinics provided essential services for underserved populations. An unintended consequence of the creation of these groups, however, was a decline in grassroots organizing. Py Bateman ruefully admitted that members of the Anna Louise Strong Brigade gave up the struggle for revolutionary change as they focused on founding organizations inspired by the "survival revival." "We turned to reform," but "if you worked for reform, you put off revolution."[18] While Bateman founded the Feminist Karate Union, other members of the Anna Louise Strong Brigade went to law school, served in the UW administration, or took jobs in other organizations they helped to create. As they moved on, they did not necessarily abandon their Left feminist politics. But they learned that they had to work, collaborate, and even compromise with the racist, sexist, homophobic state and with private individuals and institutions whose policies and practices they sought to change. For example, in order for Rape Relief to be successful, its staff had to develop a working relationship with the Seattle Police Department. Feminists could not demonstrate in front of a police station chanting antipolice slogans if they wanted the police to listen to and work with them to transform their responses to complaints of rape or to enlist them in addressing rape culture.

Feminist organizations had to maintain a level of what radicals had ridiculed as "bourgeois respectability." These women had to raise money, hire and pay staff, keep records, and pay rent and utility bills on time; the offices had to be clean and inviting to workers and clients, many of whom did not share the revolutionary, hippie, or alternative ethos of their founders. The women had to know and abide by federal regulations regarding hiring, as well as workplace health and safety. They had to negotiate with city, county, state, and federal authorities. They learned how to write grant proposals and find donors, which demanded a different set of social skills from those learned in rap groups or on picket lines. Institution building took precedence over grassroots organizing. Anne Enke's *Finding the Movement: Sexuality, Contested Space, and Feminist Activism* shares this assessment but suggests that the creation of feminist spaces—bars, bookstores, baseball fields, cafés, and clinics—shaped future feminist activism.[19] She might agree with Py Bateman's remark (albeit using different language) that "as they took on this work, they did not make politicization an explicit goal."[20]

Similar forces contributed to the decline of the radical impulses that led to the creation of women's studies. Despite its undeserved reputation as a bastion of left-wing thought and action, academia is quite conservative. It took more than militancy and lawsuits to develop a credentialed women's studies program at the UW. Older, more mainstream, tenured academics, who were overwhelmingly White and male, had to approve the hiring, tenure, and promotion of the women's studies faculty. White men chaired the committees that governed the institution, approved curriculum, allocated money, made committee assignments, and approved services for departments and programs. Finally, the Washington State legislature, a very White, male, and conservative body, had the final say in approving all the programs at its flagship university. The tiny number of women faculty, and the minuscule number of faculty of color, had to toe a very fine line just to be ensured a place at the table. With the decline of the radical women's liberation movement, fewer activists were hired; over time, the curriculum focused on theory abstracted from political activism. Women's studies was no longer the academic arm of the women's liberation movement but a respected and credentialed component of a liberal arts education.

THE EMERGENCE OF BOTH THE NEW RIGHT AND NEOLIBERALISM had major consequences for radicalism. While 1968 is often considered a potentially revolutionary year, Richard Nixon was elected president by a narrow margin as he appealed to disaffected White racists in the South. In 1972, at the high point of the women's movement, massive opposition to the war in Vietnam, the emergence of an antiwar veterans' movement, and the peak of the Black Freedom struggle, Nixon won the largest landslide of any Republican president, winning every state save Massachusetts and the District of Columbia. Today, compared with Ronald Reagan, both Bushes, and Donald Trump, Nixon almost seems liberal: he supported the ERA, created the Occupational Safety and Health Administration, and enforced Title IX. But at the same time, he championed the FBI's murderous attacks on the Black Panther Party and other Black revolutionary organizations and expanded the war in Vietnam by invading Cambodia. Nixon's resignation in 1974, when he was about to be impeached for obstruction of justice, abuse of power, and contempt of Congress, did not result in the advance of a liberal, feminist, or civil rights agenda. Instead, it ushered in a fifty-year bipartisan, racist, and neoliberal era in US politics.[21]

In Seattle the move to the right was not as acute or violent as it was in other parts of the country. The Black Freedom struggle, the backbone of all social justice struggles in the United States, had become demoralized. The Seattle Congress of Racial Equality, which had been at the forefront of militant racial social justice struggles, disbanded in 1968, in part because it had been surpassed by the militancy of the Black Panther Party. But by 1972, the Black Panther Party was in serious disarray. Aaron Dixon, the Seattle chairman, had moved away; many of its members were dead, in prison, or in hiding. What remained of the organization was filled with informants and agents provocateurs. Its offices were constantly raided and destroyed by the police.[22] Racial justice militancy continued at the UW, led by the Black Student Union as well as by Tyree Scott of the Central Contractors Association, which organized massive demonstrations that shut down construction sites until the UW agreed to hire a significant number of African Americans and other people of color on building projects.[23] Radical Women and other Left feminists went to all their demonstrations. The National Association for the Advancement of Colored People (NAACP), long derided as too timid, stepped in as the major organization in Seattle that promoted racial justice.

The radical White student movement led by Students for a Democratic Society (SDS) and then by the Seattle Liberation Front (SLF) fractured in 1969, leaving in its wake numerous tiny anarchist, Maoist, Stalinist, Trotskyist, and other revolutionary sects warring with each other or engaging in destructive public activities. For the most part, feminism was not on their agenda. On January 27, 1973, just as the US war in Vietnam was drawing to a close with the military and diplomatic victory of the National Liberation Front, President Nixon announced that no more men would be drafted as of July 1. Ending conscription was an effective political weapon against the antiwar and student movements. Nixon understood that middle-class youths would lose interest in protesting the war once it became clear that men would not have to fight and die in Vietnam. The antiwar movement and GI organizing all but disappeared. Student protests at the UW and Seattle Central Community College declined markedly. Only Vietnam Veterans against the War continued its activism, since returning soldiers were disillusioned, traumatized, and suffering from injuries and illnesses with lifelong consequences.

The move to the political right was also misogynist, as successive presidential administrations were indifferent or hostile to feminism and women's rights. The ERA was defeated, led by a right-wing, White women's movement organized by Phyllis Schlafly. Nixon vetoed the Abzug-Chisholm federal childcare bill. The success of Referendum 20 and the 1973 Supreme Court decision in *Roe v. Wade* did not lead to greater grassroots organizing for women's reproductive health. Instead, the leading feminist organizations, such as NOW, NARAL, and NWPC, abandoned the Left's popular from-the-ground-up organizing strategies, increasingly relying on lobbying state and federal lawmakers and hoping that the courts would protect reproductive rights. Almost immediately after the *Roe* decision, conservative Protestant and Catholic denominations organized a right-wing campaign to overturn *Roe*, oppose birth control, stop the ERA, and block other women's rights legislation. After 1973, with the exception of the short-lived Reproductive Rights National Network, there were no active socialist feminist organizations advocating an intersectional approach to reproductive freedom as they had in 1969–70.[24] The movement for reproductive rights was on the defensive, struggling to prevent the continued erosion of women's health care.

The rightward move in the US and the assault on women's rights took a toll on Left feminist organizations as well as individual women in Seattle. The exhilaration, even joy, of the exciting days of the women's liberation movement was replaced by the troubles generated by factional splits, the end of personal friendships, and the collapse of alliances. The protracted struggles ending in political defeats and the wearisome day-to-day grind of finding and keeping a job during the difficult economic climate of the 1970s contributed to discouragement and the decline of activism. Shelly Reddick believed that 1972 marked the beginning of "what we now call the women's community." The belief that sexism was the root of women's oppression was a "politics dealing with that one facet of our lives. We were starting to burn out a little bit." Reddick, a White Left lesbian feminist, thought that the early women's liberation groups had "outlived their purposes, but in their places the hordes were coming." The hordes Reddick described included the It's About Time bookstore, the MadWoman Feminist Center, the Coffee Coven, the Rape Crisis Clinic, the Gay Mothers' Union, and all the "incredible groups coming out of specific needs rather than general consciousness." In other words, it wasn't necessarily Left feminism that led women to organize but rather a particular experience of rape, lesbian motherhood, or friendship. Reddick, who was struggling with poverty, left Seattle in 1973 when "there was no large unifying lesbian organization. There were mostly project oriented things. We'd almost completely lost touch with the straight woman's movement. . . . It was an isolated, polarized time."[25]

Left feminist organizing did not disappear and new groups emerged, although not the "hordes" Reddick hoped for. Many of the founders of socialist feminist groups continued their activism, often around new issues and in new forms: women's prison projects; organizing sex workers in COYOTE (Call Off Your Tired Old Ethics); MAMMA, a single mothers' organization; Leftist Lezzies; and Women in the Trades. Members of the Third World Women's Alliance moved to Seattle in 1972, and in 1975 formed a campus group at the UW that worked with *Casa de la Raza* in the Latinx community. The women never formed an official part of the TTWA, but continued to meet to do political education and activism.[26] Seattle feminists defended Yvonne Wanrow, the Indigenous woman who was convicted of murder in 1972 for killing the man who tried to molest her son, in a campaign that linked issues facing Indigenous women and other women of color with women's right to defend themselves and their children from abuse. In 1977 the Washington State Supreme Court overturned her conviction and established a new standard for evaluating women's acts of self-defense.[27]

The conservative backlash and Seattle's economic troubles in the 1970s contributed to the persistence of racial and gender injustice. In 1977, the Washington State Conference for Women, held in Ellensburg, attempted to bring women together to discuss common issues and develop problem-solving strategies. Instead, it became a catalyst for conflict. Conservative women mobilized by Schlafly defeated the Washington State ERA. Their feminist opponents managed to elect a pro-ERA slate of delegates to represent the state at a national women's conference in Houston. Conservatives responded by organizing a campaign that led to the dismantling of the Washington State Women's Council a year later.

DESPITE DECADES OF BACKLASH, some gains were maintained, and some progress has continued. By 1976, the state had protected abortion rights, liberalized divorce, enacted laws giving women equal access to credit, and added an ERA to the state's constitution. Seattle is considered one of the most LGBTQ-friendly cities in the United States, and support for LGBTQ rights extends statewide. Much progress was at the top. Dixie Lee Ray, a conservative Democrat and successful environmental scientist in a male-dominated field, was the first woman elected governor in 1976. In 1993 Patti Murray, a Democrat, became the first woman elected to the US Senate from Washington State. In 2019 Laurie Jenkins, an out lesbian, was the second woman elected speaker of the state legislature. More women of color have been elected or appointed to city, county, and state agencies. In 2015 Ana Mari Cauce, a Latina, became the first permanent woman president of the uw. The Women's Gender and Sexuality Studies Department offers undergraduate and graduate degrees, including a PhD. It has a diverse faculty and curriculum dedicated to social justice feminism. The struggle for intersectional feminist studies had always been on the early pathbreakers' agenda. In 1999, an Indigenous woman was admitted to the Women's, Gender, and Sexuality Studies PhD program. "The amazing thing," Sue-Ellen Jacobs enthused, "is that she was part of the community of local radical women who fought to establish women's studies at the University of Washington."[28]

Much of this progress came about because in the mid-1960s Black women, women of color, White straight women, lesbians of color, and White lesbians, most of whom were socialists, built radical women's liberation organizations. They took on racism, red-baiting, and lesbian-baiting; they confronted their fathers, husbands, lovers, professors, school principals, university deans, union officials, and employers to fight for dignity and liberation. In so doing, they learned how to build grassroots movements and to deal with the challenges and complications of being a revolutionary who must work for reform. As many of today's Black feminists argue, several elements of these earlier struggles and political perspectives have been incorporated into contemporary coalitions and movements, such as Black Lives Matter, reproductive justice, voting rights, and climate crisis groups. In Seattle, they changed the social, cultural, political, racial, and gendered landscape, and most of these women have continued their social justice activism. Socialist women were not the only ones to do so. But for the most part, Seattle's revolutionary sisters have been written out of the women's liberation movement. This book restores them to their rightful place in history.

Epilogue

ON JANUARY 21, 2017, the day after Donald Trump was inaugurated as the forty-fifth president of the United States, more than 100,000 people marched through the streets of Seattle in what was perhaps the largest demonstration in the city's history. Initially, the organizers expected 50,000 people; twice that number showed up. Participants carried banners and signs connecting racism, sexism, homophobia, transphobia, xenophobia, and all forms of hate to issues such as economic inequality, the climate crisis, and immigration. They wore the signature hot-pink pussy hats as they marched from Judkins Park in Seattle's Central District to the downtown Seattle Center. In Seattle, as in the thousands of other cities in the US and on every continent around the globe, many of the marchers were progressives. The founders of the Anna Louise Strong Brigade, Campus Women's Liberation, Fanshen, Radical Women, and Women's Liberation–Seattle marched with their children, their grandchildren, their partners, other members of their immediate and extended families, and longtime and new friends. After fifty years, women of color and revolutionary feminists continued to be at the forefront of the critique of hetero White supremacy and the ongoing struggle for social justice and liberation.

THERE IS NO CONCLUSION to this story of women's liberation in Seattle, or anywhere else for that matter, for the struggle is ongoing. As I reflect on my activism in the women's liberation movement, I am brought back to the words of William Morris, a White English socialist, who was summing up the struggles of revolutionaries in nineteenth-century England. His assessment is applicable to us today, provided we substitute "women" for his "men": "I pondered all these things, and how women fight and lose the battle, and the thing that they fought for comes about in spite of their defeat, and when it comes turns out not to be what they meant, and other women have to fight for what they meant under another name."[1] In the radical women's movement, we organized, won and lost, compromised, and fought with each other as well as against the powers that be. Our cause faced many setbacks, and the present-day problems that are blamed on feminism do not represent our goals or result from our actions. New generations continue to rise and take up the unfinished struggle.

This epilogue reflects on my role in the women's liberation movement. Since I cannot possibly encompass everything, I focus on four aspects of the movement that span the range of theoretical and political questions: White supremacy, abortion rights, standards of beauty, and what we got right, got wrong, and did not anticipate. To demonstrate that those who participated in the radical women's liberation movement between 1965 and 1975 continued this work throughout their lives, this chapter is followed by appendix 1, Seattle Activists: Where Are They Now?

I BEGIN WITH SELF-REFLECTIONS on race and White supremacy. W. E. B Du Bois, a leading African American revolutionary, scholar, and activist, wrote in 1903 that "the problem of the Twentieth Century is the problem of the color line."[2] This problem has metastasized since he made this prescient pronouncement. This photograph and story, which appeared in the UW *Daily* on April 11, 1969, has haunted, perplexed, and rankled me for over fifty years (figure E.1).[3]

The *Daily*'s description disturbs me because the storyline is about a confrontation "as emotional as any seen at the University this year" between an unnamed Black man and me, a named White woman. The writer identifies me as "Barb," a diminutive for "Barbara" I have always resisted. As I see it, this picture captures a dangerous, ongoing gendered and racist narrative that pits White women against Black men. The image and storyline are upsetting for what they say about me, the Black man in the picture, and the biases of the editorial staff of the UW *Daily*. Although the name of the photographer, Jan Shaw, is given, we don't know who wrote the copy, chose this illustration, or designed the page. Every other person in the room is shaded out except me and the unnamed Black man. Whoever wrote the caption claimed that I was "met with fierce opposition from an angered black man" and that "tempers flared." But what was I saying that the Black man opposed? Who lost their temper? Me? Him? Members of the crowd? Am I attacking this person because he is Black or because he is a man? Is he attacking me for being White,

UNIVERSITY OF WASHINGTON **DAILY**

Inside:
Volunteers . 16
Meditation . 16
Honors . . . 17

C25   SEATTLE, WASHINGTON, FRIDAY, APRIL 11, 1969   No. 88

—photo by jan shaw

The atmosphere was right yesterday for a confrontation small in numbers but as emotional as any seen at the University this year. Open Forum was dominated by talk of women, or more precisely, their exploitation and oppression. One woman, Barb Winslow, met with fierce opposition from an angered black man, but though their tempers flared, the marathon session lasted three hours, long enough for the assembled group to condemn the socialization process for propagation of false values.

Figure E.1 / Barbara Winslow speaking at a University of Washington Open Forum. Winslow and an unidentified African American man are highlighted in the version published in the University of Washington *Daily*, April 11, 1969.

being a woman, or being a feminist? Had I said something racially offensive? We don't know, and the *Daily* writer never explains. Looking carefully at the shaded characters in the photograph, all of whom are White men, we see that some were listening, others lounging around rolling joints or cigarettes, hardly caught up in this confrontation. I do not remember this incident, and I think I would recall it if it had been a three-hour, emotionally fraught confrontation. What I do know is that in every issue of the UW *Daily* from 1965 to 1975, no other photograph pits White women against Black men, or vice versa. Yet for the fifty-some years I have looked at this picture, it reminds me to constantly evaluate and reflect on my own role in White patriarchal supremacy as it relates to my political Left feminist activism.

I grew up in an affluent White suburb, an inquiring, rebellious daughter of the White upper-middle class. There was one Black student in my elementary and middle school and one Black student at my public high school. I was such an alienated mess of contradictions—a bleached-blond cheerleader and wannabe beatnik getting terrible grades—that my parents sent me to a progressive private school where there were Black students. Most families in my hometown, including mine, employed Black domestic workers; some even lived in their employers' homes. I do not remember ever being taught by a Black teacher, although in my public high school one Black teacher taught French. The only Black person I learned about in my classes until the explosion of the civil rights movement was botanist George Washington Carver. By the time I was in middle school I was aware of racism. The town in which I lived had restrictive real estate covenants based on religion and race. Jews could live only in certain districts; African Americans were not allowed. The town refused to change these restrictions to allow Harry Belafonte to buy a house—and he would have lived on the end of my street!

Even before my women's liberation activism, I became an ally of the Black Freedom struggle. I write this not to praise my participation but to remind readers that some White people actively supported civil rights struggles, just as many White people today have joined the mass demonstrations, rallies, and pickets called by Black Lives Matter to oppose the police murders of Black people. In high school I cut classes to picket Woolworth's Five and Dime because it refused to serve food to African Americans or allow them to sit at its lunch counter.

I chose to attend Antioch College mainly because I was impressed by its commitment to racial justice. In the "Welcome to Antioch College" packet was a membership form for the campus chapter of the Congress of Racial Equality. The packet urged incoming students not to get their hair cut at Gegner's Barbershop because the owner refused to cut Black people's hair. Antiochians joined with students from the nearby Black institutions, Central State College and Wilberforce University, to hold demonstrations, one of which landed a cover on *Life* magazine.[4]

I wanted to participate in the Mississippi Freedom Summer Project, which brought hundreds of White and Black students from outside the South to register Black voters in Mississippi. Volunteers had to be twenty-one years of age or have parental permission. I was under twenty-one, and my parents refused to give me permission even though I begged, pleaded, and fought to go. The project organizers were very strict about the age limits. The people who were going to Mississippi had two weeks of training at the nearby Western College for Women (now a part of Miami University) in Oxford, Ohio, in early June. We Antiochians who were not going visited to show our support for our comrades who were. When we heard the horrific news about the disappearance of James Chaney, Andrew Goodman, and Michael Schwerner, we knew they were dead. For many people of my generation, the 1963 assassination of John F. Kennedy was their defining moment. For me, it was the KKK murders of civil rights workers.

I studied history in college, and in 1969 we went to England to study with E. P. Thompson, the internationally renowned activist scholar whose book *The Making of the English Working Class* inspired a generation of activist historians to investigate the past from the bottom up.[5] In 1970, not only did I earn an MA in US and British labor history at the University of Warwick, but I became friends with Sheila Rowbotham, the equally renowned historian and activist who was the foremother of the new women's history. I was involved in England's emerging women's liberation movement and helped to found Coventry Women's Liberation. Germaine Greer, the author of *The Female Eunuch*, taught at the University of Warwick and was a neighbor and friend. I participated in the 1969 protest at the Miss World pageant. I was invited to speak about women's liberation to the Dagenham women workers later made famous by the movie *Made in Dagenham*; was one of the organizers of the Ruskin College Women's Liberation Conference in March 1970, the first feminist conference in the UK since the suffrage movement; and began my research on Sylvia Pankhurst, the socialist, antiracist, and anti-imperialist suffragette. That year in England combined everything I loved: educating myself politically, organizing with others, and agitating for change.

The Left in Britain at that time was even more segregated than the Left in the United States. In Britain the orthodox Leninist organizations opposed racism and demonstrated against Enoch Powell, the racist anti-immigrant member of the House of Commons. They supported the Indian Workers Association and Black Britons in the emerging Black Power movement. But, with very few exceptions, these Leninist organizations held to the position that Black nationalism and feminism were bourgeois movements that "divided the working class." I found myself in constant arguments about race with my English comrades. Coming back to the US, I continued my activism in socialist feminist and revolutionary politics. I earned an MA and later a PhD in British and US women's history and taught women's studies at Seattle Central Community College.

In 1973, I moved from Seattle, a predominantly White city with a Black enclave, to Cleveland, Ohio, which had a much more diverse population: approximately 35 percent African American with a much smaller number of Puerto Rican and other Latinx residents.[6] I taught women's studies, Black studies, and labor studies at Cuyahoga Community College. I was active in my American Federation of Teachers union local and belonged to the Cleveland

Council of Union Women and the Cleveland chapter of the Coalition of Labor Union Women. I spoke about women's liberation at the United Auto Workers local headquarters in Lordstown, Ohio, and worked with women in trade unions in male-dominated industries, including steel workers in Youngstown, Ohio; coal miners and the Harlan County Women's Club in Kentucky and West Virginia; and postal workers in Cincinnati. Ohio was a national center of abortion and antiabortion activism; I belonged to the Cleveland Pro-Choice Action Committee and served on the board of the Reproductive Rights National Network. I can't count the number of reproductive justice rallies, meetings, and demonstrations I attended throughout the state. In 1981, I helped to organize and joyously participated in a Ladies against Women demonstration against Phyllis Schlafly, which made national headlines.[7]

In February 1979 I became involved with a strike at a large poultry-processing plant in Laurel, Mississippi, most of whose workers were Black women.[8] This experience forever changed how I looked at the South and its history, as well as how I made alliances and worked with Black women. I met three of the strikers at a Cleveland National Lawyers Guild event where union leaders spoke. My husband and I invited them back to our place to meet other activists who wanted to support the strike. The moment they walked into our house, I could tell that this was the first time they had been in a White person's house as a guest, not as a domestic. As I got to know the women, they confirmed their unease with White people. Gloria Jordan, the president of Local 882 of the International Chemical Workers Union, told me that the Sanderson company treated its workers like "slaves on a plantation." The two hundred workers were demanding changes in policies toward absences from work, an end to sexual harassment, more overtime pay, and toilet breaks. They were allowed only three bathroom breaks *a week*, and the workers had to explain their request for a bathroom break to a supervisor. One plant supervisor was an open Klansmen who was indicted but acquitted by an all-White jury for murdering an NAACP leader. Another supervisor, Sam Bowers, was one of the organizers of the murder of civil rights workers Chaney, Goodman, and Schwerner.

With two White friends from England, I went to the May 17, 1980, International Chemical Workers Union March for Dignity and Justice in Laurel. As we drove through rural Mississippi, we saw Klan signs openly displayed. At the Laurel Historical Society, we discovered the story of the Jones County Rebellion, led by a White farmer, Newton Knight, which waged a guerilla war against the Confederacy in 1864. Knight later lived in an interracial community, married a formerly enslaved woman, and served in Mississippi's

Reconstruction government. We were blown away by this knowledge, as we had never heard anything about such rebellions in history courses.[9] The night before the march, we went to the union fund-raising party held in the segregated African American part of Laurel. There were no paved roads, sidewalks, or streetlights, and some of the homes did not have indoor plumbing. I had read about this part of the US but had never seen it for myself. As I walked into the party, I noticed two pictures on the wall: one of Marcus Garvey, founder of the Universal Negro Improvement Association, and the other of John F. Kennedy, Garvey's opposite in almost every respect. We were astonished that, in the heart of rural Mississippi, the local Black social club honored the leader of the largest Black internationalist movement in the diaspora, who personified Black power and pride, alongside the White and privileged president of the United States who did very little to defend or advance the rights of African Americans.

The 2,500-strong march the next day was overwhelmingly made up of African Americans. I was told to march with the teachers, most of whom were White women—a telling sign of school segregation in Mississippi. A young Black man was in charge of our contingent, and we could tell he was having a ball telling White teachers to yell louder, sing louder, keep in line, and stay with the chants. The spirited and defiant march was led by Black women, which I had never experienced before. After two years of sacrifice and struggle, the strikers were abandoned by their White union leadership and went back to work. I went to visit Gloria Jordan twice after the strike. One visit was memorable and terrifying. As she put me up in her daughters' bedroom, she asked if I knew how to shoot a rifle, explaining that Klansmen were driving past her house. Jordan's leadership, strength, and humanity live on in union leaders like the late Karen Lewis of the Chicago Teachers Union.

In 1984, when my marriage ended, along with my membership in the International Socialist Organization, I moved to Brooklyn, where I raised two daughters; was active in union, reproductive rights, and social justice campaigns; played on a women's tennis team; finished my PhD; wrote books and articles; and worked as an adjunct faculty member at three City University of New York campuses, the New York University extension program, and Barnard College. I even taught women's studies at the Rikers Island jail for two years. Then I finally landed a tenure-track position at Medgar Evers College, City University of New York. Four years later, I was asked to coordinate the Women's Studies Program at Brooklyn College. I got tenure, was promoted to full (of it) professor, taught secondary social studies educators, and worked with students in the Brooklyn public schools. In addition to coordinating the

Women's (now Women and Gender) Studies Program, I founded the Shirley Chisholm Project of Brooklyn Women's Activism. I still find ways to continue my socialist feminist and antiracist work. My two daughters follow in the footsteps of our generation. One teaches social studies in a public school; the other is a union organizer. Because of my daughters and my two grandchildren, I have hope for our future.

As a White woman active in radical feminist politics, I believed that I was as good an antiracist ally as most. After all, I attended the early Black and White Concern classes at the University of Washington (UW) and supported the Black Panther Party by attending rallies and demonstrations and donating money. I supported the demands of the Black Student Union and the Movimiento Estudiantil Chicano de Aztlán (Chicano Student Movement) to create Black and Chicano studies programs and to hire Black and Latino studies faculty and administrators. In Seattle, my husband and I lived two blocks from the Black Panther Party headquarters. We had a "Free Huey" bumper sticker on our car. I taught mainly Black working-class students at Seattle Central Community College. In Cleveland and in New York, my students were mainly working class, immigrants, and people of color. I thought I always included Black history, but I now admit that I did not center studies of African Americans or other people of color. When I wrote or spoke, I always included "and Black women" or "and Black people." Yet as I write this, I cringe. When I spoke publicly about women's liberation, I believed in my heart and soul that I meant ALL women, the universal we. I have come to realize that, even though I imagined that my talks were about all women, Black, Latina, Indigenous, Asian American and Pacific Islander, lesbian, queer, young, older, differently abled, citizens, and immigrants, as well as native-born White women, many, if not most, of the women in the audience did not see them— or me—as representing all women. Until I read Lorraine Bethel's powerful "What Chou Mean We, White Girl? Or, the Cullud Lesbian Feminist Declaration of Independence (Dedicated to the Proposition That All Women Are Not Equal, i.e. Identical/ly Oppressed),"[10] I did not realize how my own Whiteness contributed to my incomprehension of the full extent and depth of White supremacy.

Researching this book pushed me to reflect on White supremacy, race, and racism—personal, institutional, and structural—within the Seattle women's liberation movement as well as in my subsequent scholarship and activism. I learned to recognize the presence and power of White supremacy in the movements in which I was involved. As I reviewed the statements and educational materials we produced, I was genuinely shocked at how little we considered race. The first classes held by Radical Women in the spring of 1968 did not have a single session on race or any material about or by Black women. The first three years of women's studies at the UW did not include a course on Black women or any readings by Black women. Why were we so unaware? Were we clueless? Racist? Indifferent? Or just White?

My formal education was a perfect example of the biases and erasures created by patriarchal White supremacy. I never had an African American, Latinx, Indigenous, or Asian teacher. All my graduate school professors were White men, and my interest in Black and women's history was ignored or put down by almost all of them. Whatever I learned about the history of the working class, people of color, women, and people with lesbian, gay, bisexual, or queer identities, I learned outside and despite the academy.

When I taught the only Black studies course at Cuyahoga Community College in Cleveland, I will never forget the expression on the students' faces, most of whom were African American, the first time I walked into the classroom. They asked me why I was teaching it, rather than a Black professor. I did not have a good answer. How could I? Over time, likely because of the writings by radical Black Americans I assigned, including C. L. R. James, Martin Delany, Zora Neale Hurston, W. E. B. Du Bois, Angela Davis, and Richard Wright, some of the students came to act as if I could be respected or trusted. One student told me he couldn't believe that a White professor would let students read such materials. Several Black women belonged to the local chapter of the Coalition of Labor Union Women, and two women of color belonged to the Cleveland Pro-Choice Action Committee. I worked in coalitions with the farmworkers, the Domestic Workers of America, and the Attica Defense. But for the most part, the Cleveland Left was segregated, and I worked mainly with the White Left.

When I moved to New York City, I was finishing my PhD, writing a book on Sylvia Pankhurst, and becoming involved with other feminist scholars and teachers. Attending my first Berkshire Conference on the History of Women in 1973, which was held at Rutgers University in New Jersey, I was finally forced to confront feminist White supremacy, racism, and racial indifference. The sponsoring organization was founded in 1930 by White women historians who were marginalized by the overwhelmingly White and male profession. It brought women historians together to support each other's scholarship, mentoring and teaching. In the late 1960s a generation of women's liberation activists who were studying or teaching history joined the Berkshire Conference and hosted the first major women's history gathering, called the Big Berks. The edited collection that emerged from the conference did not include any historians of color or essays about women of color.[11] The problem was not that no one was writing the history of women of color and that all women historians were White. Black women historians were simply not invited to submit their presentations for publication, and no one except those who were excluded noticed this absence. The Berkshire conferences on women's history, which met every three years, remained overwhelmingly White in their programs and participants, despite the collective efforts of Black women historians and historians of Black women to gain representation.

At Baruch College, I team-taught a course with art historian Mary Gibbons called The Female Nude in the Western Tradition. One three-week module dealt with race and representation. I met artists of color such as Emma Amos, Benny Andrews, Camille Billops, Josely Carvalho, Elizabeth Catlett, Marina Gutierrez, and Faith Ringgold. Gibbons and I presented with these artists at conferences of the Women's Caucus for Art and the College Art Association. We organized a panel for the 1990 Berks titled "Influence of Race, Gender on the Representation of the Female Nude in Twentieth Century America" with Amos, Billops, Carvalho, and Gutierrez as presenters. We were scheduled for the session at eight o'clock on Friday evening alongside Juanita Ramos (Juanita Diaz-Cotto), currently a professor of sociology, Latin American and Caribbean studies, and women, and gender, and sexuality studies at Binghamton University. Ramos was a cofounder of both the Comité Homosexual Latinoamericano and the first Latina lesbian group, Buenas Amigas, in New York City. She and I met while adjunct teaching at Hunter College, City University of New York, and she had just published an anthology about Latina lesbians.[12] Her copanelist was June Chan, cofounder of Asian Lesbians of the East Coast, who was presenting the first slideshow on Asian lesbian history in the United States. Their panel was entitled "Documenting Our Communities: Third World/Lesbians of Color." We had been assured by the conference organizers that having our panels on Friday night, when there were only two other panels, as well as a dance performance, meant that we were guaranteed a large audience. Ramos told me later that she thought that "scheduling our panel as the last event on Friday at 8 P.M. was racist."[13]

The keynote speaker for the 1990 Berks was Bernice Johnson Reagon, former member of the Student Non-Violent Coordinating Committee (SNCC), who founded the Albany Freedom Singers and the all-women a cappella group Sweet Honey in the Rock. She had been awarded a MacArthur fellowship and served as a cultural historian of music at the Smithsonian. Of all the extraordinary plenary speakers at the Big Berks over the years, her keynote was the most unforgettable because of her exhortation to White women.

For White women to struggle against racism, she said, we had to do it every waking minute, every day and every week. White women had to think about racism not just in our teaching but in our families, our communities, and our day-to-day activities, from the most mundane to the most important. Reagon received a wildly enthusiastic standing ovation. Then everyone went to their sessions, met friends for lunch, or perused the book exhibit.

That Friday night, Amos, Carvalho, Billops, Gutierrez, Gibbons, and I went to our session. Ramos and Chan's session was across the hall. To our astonishment no one—repeat, no one—showed up. What had happened? It turned out that at the very last minute Catharine Stimpson, an eminent feminist literary critic, had brought famous women's liberation activists, scholars, and writers Alix Kates Shulman, who wrote *Memoirs of an Ex-Prom Queen*, and Kate Millett, author of *Sexual Politics* and *The Loony-Bin Trap*, to speak at the same time as our panels. Every White woman disregarded the words of Reagon and decided not to attend the only sessions at that time—which were led by women of color and addressed issues of gender, sexuality, race, and racism—but to hear two famous White women speak.

Gibbons and I were beside ourselves with rage and embarrassment. I apologized to our presenters. Amos replied, "It's not your fault. We're used to this." Her words only made me angrier at the conference. Ramos was furious as well, and we talked about what we should do. Ramos told me she was tired of always having to fight with White women about their racism. If anything was to be done, I would have to do it. And so I did. Looking back, I was a total unknown, a mere adjunct lecturer without a PhD, confronting the eminent Stimpson and every women's historian who might be in a position to hire me. Ramos's and Reagon's words gave me courage. I went into that huge auditorium, reminded the audience of Reagon's challenge, and asked them why they chose not to attend one of the only two sessions on women of color that night. Ramos recently reminded me that once I came out of the meeting, I yelled at the White women who were in the hallway and unable to enter the overfilled auditorium. I told them that they should support the two panels that had presenters who were women of color instead of just standing there! Eventually about ninety women went to Ramos and Chan's panel, and about twenty to ours, but not initially of their own choice.[14]

A number of colleagues and friends came up to me later to apologize, make lame excuses, or claim with embarrassment that they intended to go to our sessions after they heard Millett speak. At the next day's business meeting, the conference organizers seemed pathetically defensive. In all fairness, the conference planners struggled to advocate for scholars of color; to ensure that the panels at the conferences reflected the intersectionality of race, class, and gender; and to elect women of color to leadership positions.[15] Today the Berks is led by women of color and centers women of color and LGBTQIA people in our understanding of historical events. In retrospect, I wonder if my fury about this debacle was more about the humiliation of no one showing up at a session we organized. Several colleagues I contacted who were at that Berks do not remember my interruption of the meeting with Millett. Lyn Weiner did not mention the disturbance in her report on the conference; her "impression was that more women of color were in attendance than previously."[16] After two conversations with Ramos, I still maintain that what happened was an example of both personal and structural White supremacy, which I believe the Berks is now addressing.

The National Women's Studies Association (NWSA), of which I was a founding member, had many reckonings with White supremacy, although I was not involved in the struggles to transform the organization. Until recently, I had not felt the same close connection to NWSA that I did to the Berkshire Conference. NWSA was founded in 1977, and its roots were deeply embedded in the radical women's liberation movement. Its goal was to bring together activism, the academy, and the full range of women's experiences and to be as inclusive as possible. The earliest practitioners determined to incorporate women's voices and viewpoints, not only in universities and K–12 schools but also in women's centers and even prisons, into the curriculum. Confronting White supremacy, as well as anti-Semitism, homophobia, ableism, and elitism, has marked its history. In 1990 I was presenting at the Akron NWSA conference when a group of women of color walked out to protest the firing of Ruby Sales, the only woman of color working at NWSA. The entire staff subsequently resigned, and NWSA suffered a dramatic loss in membership. Disgusted and discouraged, I did not attend a conference until Beverly Guy-Sheftall, the founding director of the Women's Research and Resource Center and professor of women's studies at Spelman College, which educates Black women, became president of NWSA and began its transformation. Guy-Sheftall urged the organization to "commit ourselves to the big fights but not fight ourselves." She was followed by leading activist feminist scholars of color: Bonnie Thornton Dill, Vivian May, Yi-Chun Tricia Lin, Barbara Ransby, Premilla Nadasen, and now Karsonya (Kaye) Wise Whitehead.[17] Today NWSA is probably one of the best US models of global intersectional feminism, and for the first time I feel connected and committed to its future. At the 2019 annual conference, keynote speaker Angela Davis welcomed ALL of us. She confessed, "In 1968,

I thought feminism was white and bourgeois. It has taken many years to recognize that feminism encompasses the various struggles of women."[18]

MY SECOND SELF-REFLECTION concerns our early critiques of beauty, which created the impression that we were attacking women. We focused our initial protests on models and beauty pageant contestants, none of whom wielded power, rather than on the men who controlled these institutions. We didn't attack *Vogue, Seventeen*, or other fashion magazines that infantilized and sexualized White women and excluded women of color. Looking back, it took shocking, even outrageous acts to attract women to our groups and to get media attention.

The first two public and publicized women's liberation demonstrations in 1968—the disruption of a meeting with a Playboy Playmate in Seattle and the Miss America protest in Atlantic City, New Jersey—targeted the dominant culture's standards of beauty. Female attractiveness was defined as White, young, thin, tall, busty, preferably unmarried, and childless; whatever a woman's professional aspirations, they were secondary to pleasing White men. In the spring of 1968, when we confronted the Playmate, we honestly believed we were not attacking Reagan Wilson but rather the ethos of *Playboy*. Hugh Hefner was promoting his magazine on college campuses to recruit women to become models and to persuade men to subscribe. In retrospect, it is clear that we did single out the Playmate herself. In fact, we were objectifying Wilson at the same time we were protesting the objectification of women. While on the stage we chanted, "Reagan Wilson, you are an empty vessel," and afterward we wrote leaflets and letters to the UW *Daily* demeaning Playmates.

A few years ago, I managed to get in contact with Wilson, and for a while we had terrific email conversations. I could tell from her Facebook page that she was a liberal Democrat, and we appeared to agree on many things—except Hefner and *Playboy*. When she read my remembrance of the Playboy protest in *The Feminist Memoir Project*, she was furious and hurt, and wrote on her Facebook page that I had praised personal attacks on *Playboy* models. For a few years after 1968 there were protests against beauty contests and *Playboy*, but by 1970 the women's liberation movement and mainstream feminism were organizing around issues such as reproductive justice and the Equal Rights Amendment.

In the late 1970s and 1980s, disagreements regarding sexuality, pornography, erotica, prostitution, and other issues of sexuality and gender deeply divided the feminist movement, taking it away from the objectification of women in popular culture. Beauty contests, Hefner, and *Playboy* and other so-called girlie or nudie magazines no longer played a major role in defining female sexuality, as online pornography replaced print media. Yet very little is known and written about how women of color critiqued the racism of beauty contests. At the same time that women protested the 1968 Miss America contest in Atlantic City, across the boardwalk an organization of Black activists and entrepreneurs was holding a beauty contest celebrating Black women's beauty as well as highlighting the racist exclusion of women of color from the official Miss America contests.[19] Carol Hanisch critiqued the Miss America protest in an essay entitled "What Can Be Learned": "One of the biggest mistakes of the whole pageant was our anti-womanism. . . . Posters which read 'Up Against the Wall, Miss America,' 'Miss America Sells it,' and 'Miss America is a Big Falsie' hardly raised any woman's consciousness and really harmed the cause of sisterhood. Miss America and all beautiful women came off as our enemy instead of as our sisters who suffer with us. . . . Crowning a live sheep Miss America sort of said beautiful women *are* sheep." Hanisch reflected, "We didn't say clearly enough that we women are all FORCED to play the Miss America role—not by beautiful women but by men who we have to act that way for and by a system that has . . . institutionalized male supremacy for its own ends." She concluded, "Unfortunately the best slogan for the action came up about a month after when Roz Baxandall came out on the David Susskind show with 'Every day in a woman's life is a walking Miss America contest.'"[20]

Feminists began to critique other powerful institutions that had greater power to define female beauty—the media, the fashion and food industries, and the art world. Black feminists critiqued and challenged the dominant image that feminine beauty was White. Black women in the civil rights movement, the Black Panther Party, and other Black Freedom struggles rebelled against the pressure to conform to White standards, for example by not straightening their hair and wearing it in a "natural" or Afro. By 1972, Angela Davis was an international symbol of revolution and, for many feminists, a positive symbol of womanhood. A revolutionary activist academic, she was one of the first to analyze the gendered racism of beauty in her pathbreaking article "Reflections on the Black Woman's Role in the Community of Slaves."[21] Other women of color, feminist, and LGBTQ organizations followed suit, condemning the gendered, classist, and White supremacist portrayal of Indigenous, Latina, Asian American and Pacific Islander, and LGBTQ women. Since 1968, the Miss America pageant has been dramatically reconfigured:

the contestants no longer have to parade in skimpy swimsuits and five-inch heels; the sponsors promote the professional achievements and aspirations of the competitors and advertise it as a scholarship contest. Miss America and *Playboy* no longer set the standard for womanly beauty, largely thanks to the women in the civil rights, Black Freedom, LGBTQIA, and women's liberation movements.[22]

THE RECENT OVERTURNING of constitutionally protected abortion rights by the US Supreme Court, as well as the possibility of a congressional ban on abortion and the prospect of a Supreme Court ruling or federal legislation forbidding contraception, prompted me to consider what we can learn from our experience in Washington State. After our successful referendum campaign and the founding of feminist health clinics, we believed that our continuing struggle would be mainly to expand accessible feminist health care. We did not anticipate the depth and breadth of the racialized misogyny that soon demonized and punished poor women and women of color. Given the profound changes that took place in women's lives in the 1960s, how could we imagine that even contraception for women would come under attack? Having won abortion and contraception rights without much pushback, we could not imagine how quickly the right wing would silence feminists' advocacy of abortion on demand. Upon reflection, as well as research, I realize that in our struggle to make women's health care feminist and accessible, we inadvertently isolated clinics, making them targets for antiabortion violence. Carole Joffe singles out the medical establishment for not embedding reproductive health care in hospitals, claiming that this resulted in the medical and political marginalization of reproductive care. Furthermore, pregnancy termination was seldom taught in medical schools, so fewer doctors could perform such procedures.[23]

In Seattle, feminist health-care activists played a role in detaching clinics from hospitals. They distrusted and disliked hospitals, believing that the medical establishment mirrored capitalist White and male supremacy in every facet of hospital operations from the administration to the care of patients and the treatment of staff: for-profit medicine; nonunion and wretched working conditions for nonmedical, nonadministrative personnel; poor medical care for the working class and patients of color. The people involved in Aradia, the Fremont Women's Clinic, Country Doctor, and the Sidney Miller Clinic wanted their institutions to be controlled by the constituency they served. With that in mind, they set up freestanding clinics in working-class, Black, and student neighborhoods. To our incredulity and shock, the clinics and their health providers, unlike hospitals, became targets for violent attacks and eventually suffered from their isolation.

The Trump election in 2016 and Senate majority leader Mitch McConnell's success in placing three antiabortion jurists on the Supreme Court encouraged states to enact even more draconian restrictions. In 2021, according to the Guttmacher Institute, individual states introduced some 566 antiabortion laws. The Texas, Mississippi, and Florida antiabortion laws are forcing feminist activists to rethink how we struggle for reproductive justice.[24] Although 2022 is not 1969, there are lessons to be learned from our experience, especially from grassroots radical activism. First and foremost, we did not look to the leadership of the two political parties, the governor, state and federal legislators, or the courts. We were glad that we had mainstream support, and we worked in coalitions with people whom we distrusted and with whom we had political disagreements. We relied primarily on popular activism, which ranged from door-to-door canvasing to confrontations. We wrote letters to the newspapers, and we appeared on television and radio shows. What we need now is more of what we did in Seattle. We need tens of thousands of people like A. Frans Koome, the courageous doctor who openly flouted Washington State's antiabortion laws. Koome stood alone, and many other doctors who supported a woman's right to abortion remained silent. But now the medical profession should not just sign petitions and speak out in the media; practitioners at all levels should publicly defy the restrictions and challenge the laws. Koome was protected by thousands of women who supported his work. We will protect those who stand up for women's rights.

Tens of thousands of us should be like Lee Mayfield, who drove women to Vancouver, Canada, where a trusted nurse performed abortions. We must organize people to take women to states where safe, legal abortions remain available, as well as to Mexico and Canada. We need to shout our support for reproductive justice from as many rooftops as possible: social and print media, talk radio, podcasts, places of worship, schools, unions, workplaces, and community meetings. We need to demand that elected representatives in the local, state, and national arenas make reproductive health a priority. More people should follow the example of the activists who courageously graffitied antiabortion billboards. We could use more people like Bree Newsome, the militant performance artist who was arrested for removing the Confederate flag from the South Carolina State House grounds in the aftermath of the Charleston church massacre by a White supremacist. Women in Washington State won a well-organized grassroots campaign for abortion rights over fifty years ago. It took fifty years to all but destroy what we did in Seattle, but we must begin again, relying on our strength in numbers.

FINALLY, WHAT HAVE I LEARNED from my experiences in the Seattle women's liberation movement and from researching and writing about it? Writing about this movement has been challenging. White women who write about "our" movement have profound, passionate, visceral feelings about our involvement. We are deeply invested in this history because our movement fused the personal and political. We ourselves made history; we discovered another world, forged a new language, upended gender norms, created feminist institutions, and transformed social and sexual relations. Yet every step of the way was a massive struggle, because public officials, politicians, media pundits, entrenched academics, and even our romantic partners demeaned and dismissed us. Our former allies on the Left denounced us for promoting divisive identity politics. Some women, understandably defensive, accepted these misogynist attacks and turned on the movement we had built. Others attacked anyone who wrote or made films about the women's liberation movement that did not reflect their own personal experiences. It took me years to get those demon voices out of my consciousness. I think that one of the reasons we have been so self-reflective, as well as vilified, is that we challenged reigning patterns of gender. Women have always been active and welcome in social and political struggles—but only in other social movements. It is perfectly acceptable for women to organize for peace, civil rights, welfare rights, the environment, and tenants' rights and to form women's auxiliaries in the labor movement. But when women begin to organize for their own rights, they are subverting the idea that women are selfless and self-sacrificing.

I look back at the Seattle women's liberation movement as the most important and transformative experience of my life, as do many other Seattle activists. We changed our lives, the lives of other women, and the lives of women in the generations that followed us. What we did not anticipate was the success of the backlash that arose in response to the challenges our movement posed to prevailing power relations. For the first few years, the media in Seattle and elsewhere highlighted feminist activism. Our radical demands—free day care, abortion on demand, equal pay, sexual freedom, and liberation—were seriously considered. For many of us 1968 was a revolutionary year, and we believed that our successes would only increase exponentially. We were wrong. We did not anticipate fifty years of misogynist neoliberal austerity politics. We underestimated the power and violence of patriarchal racial capitalism. Many White women's liberation activists came late to recognizing and addressing

White supremacy. Others were initially too confident about feminism's potential appeal to liberate men from gendered constraints.

The years since the enormous pink pussy hat demonstrations by global and intersectional feminist activists have only highlighted the imperatives of radical visions of women's liberation. We experienced a global pandemic, a racial crisis over state violence, a breakdown in political norms from the grass roots to the US presidency, and a war in Europe that may engulf the world. Yet many of the strategies and tactics we employed in Seattle in the late 1960s and 1970s give us a glimmer of hope. Women of color now lead interracial, mixed-gender, and cross-class coalitions. They are calling for massive mobilizations to protect the planet; to fight for the right to vote, to get an education, to migrate or find refuge from violence, to health care and day care; to promote gun safety; and to call for a living wage, peace, and an end to murderous policing. The struggle continues.

Appendix

Seattle Activists:
Where Are They Now?

These brief biographies focus on the lives of activists after the period discussed in this book. Some veteran activists stayed in Seattle, and others moved away but stayed in touch with their friends in the city. Many of the older generation of radicals who mentored younger women have died, but I honor them here. Regrettably, it proved impossible to locate some people; they might have moved or changed their names, or they simply could not be found on the internet. I apologize to anyone who was inadvertently omitted, but the search had to end when this book went to press.

Barbara Arnold (SDS, Radical Women): A native of Baltimore, Arnold transferred from Wellesley College to the UW in January 1968. After changing her last name to Herbert, she became involved in healthcare at the St. Mark's Free Clinic in New York City, which treated people who were lesbian or gay, uninsured, or homeless. She earned an MD at Stony Brook University in 1984 and specialized in surgery and emergency medicine. At Boston City Hospital, which treats mainly low-income people, immigrants, and people of color, she developed a program to screen women in the ER for domestic violence. Herbert has held fellowships to study and write about the identification, treatment, and prevention of domestic violence and drug addiction. She now practices at St. Elizabeth's Medical Center in Boston and at the community hospital in Lawrence and works with the Commonwealth Care Alliance, which serves Medicaid and Medicare recipients.

Py Bateman (SDS, ALSB): In 1971, Bateman founded the Feminist Karate Union, one of the first all-women karate schools in the nation. After a few years, she added a simplified program for self-defense, which later spun off to form Alternatives to Fear. Then she added education about date and acquaintance rape. Next, Bateman developed programs to address the needs of specific groups. The Self-Defense Sleepover brought together high school girls and their mothers, who sometimes met separately and at other times jointly. A play, *Truth or Consequences*, focused on four characters as they struggled with an attempted acquaintance rape. A program of self-defense for blind and visually impaired women was adopted by organizations in other states. Other programs, such as one for mothers of infants and toddlers, addressed specific issues. Recently, Bateman cooperated in the production of the documentary series *Ted Bundy: Falling for a Killer* (disclosure: so did I) and was a featured guest on *Empowerment Podcast*.

Joan Bird (WL-S): After graduating from the UW in 1972, Bird earned a PhD in zoology at the University of Montana, where she continued to organize women and advocate for gender equity. She pursued a career in conservation and eventually filed a gender discrimination grievance against the Nature Conservancy. In addition, Bird taught classes in women's studies at Great Falls College in Montana.

Stephanie Coontz (SMC, SWP): After leaving Seattle, Coontz served as the national coordinator of the National Peace Action Coalition based in New York City. From 1975 to 2012, she taught history and women's studies at Evergreen State College in Olympia, Washington. Coontz's seven books include *The Way We Never Were: American Families and the Nostalgia Trap*; *A Strange Stirring: "The Feminine Mystique" and American Women at the Dawn of the 1960s*; *American Families: A Multicultural Reader*; and *Marriage, a History: How Love Conquered Marriage*, which was cited in the US Supreme Court decision on same-sex marriage. Her op-eds have appeared in the *New York Times*, the *Washington Post*, and the *London Times* and on CNN. Coontz currently serves as director of research and public education at the Council on Contemporary Families.

Megan Cornish (Radical Women, FSP): Cornish was hired along with nine other women in the first—and only—class of female electrical trades trainees. The women struggled with Seattle City Light management and sometimes with the union, the International Brotherhood of Electrical Workers Local 77, to hire more women and address workplace sexism. Cornish and her Radical Women colleagues Heidi Durham and Teri Bach pushed the hardest and were targeted for some of the worst reprisals. Through this struggle, she became the second female operator and the first female power dispatcher at Seattle City Light. Cornish helped found the Committee for Equal Rights at City Light, and in 1991 she and Durham were named Active Advocate of the Year by Washington Women in the Trades. Cornish retired in 2004. She remains a committed member of Radical Women and the FSP, as well as an antiwar activist and environmental advocate.

Shelley Crites (WL-S, SDS, International Socialists): Crites continued her activism in Indian Fishing Rights, Leftist Lezzies, and the Yvonne Wanrow Defense. She worked in print shops for twenty years. In the 1980s she organized a walkout of female print workers who were protesting management's posting photographs of nude women throughout the workplace. Charging a hostile work environment, they won their antidiscrimination suit, and Crites won an award for her organizing. The women got their jobs back but refused to work in a shop that continued to post sexist images of women. Crites also participated in martial arts performances. Now retired, she proudly wears her "Capitalism makes me barf" button.

Dotty DeCoster (WL-S, Women's Majority Union): DeCoster was a lifelong community activist, researcher, and writer. In the 1970s she continued her child-care advocacy with the Washington State Office of Community Development, and then as an administrator at Seattle Central Community College's Early Childhood Education Program. After a brief stay in California, she returned to Seattle, where she worked in the Health and Welfare Department of the Seattle Urban League and then with the Seattle Children's Museum, as well as advocating around a wide range of environmental issues. She was a researcher and writer for HistoryLink.org, the online encyclopedia of Washington State history. DeCoster died in 2015.

Diane Eggleston (WL-S, International Socialists): Eggleston went from driving a Seattle Metro bus to attending acupuncture school, doing an internship in China, and going into private practice. In 1988, she moved to a small farm on Bainbridge Island, Washington, playing cello and raising chickens. She participated in grassroots organizing against antigay and pro-gun statewide referendums, which built effective coalitions and support in local communities. In 2003 she moved to Ajo, Arizona, a tiny town near the Mexican border. For two years, she commuted 130 miles to Tucson to teach in an acupuncture school; then she relocated to Apache Junction, east of Phoenix. Now semiretired, she continues her activism via the internet and does property care for her women's community.

Karen Foreit (WL-S): After finishing her PhD at the UW, Foreit went to Brown University for a postdoctoral fellowship and then a teaching position. There she helped students establish a day care center. Next, she taught at Brooklyn College and the University of Texas at Arlington, including a pioneering course on the psychology of sex and gender. In 1978, Foreit and her husband began working in international public health, first in Korea, where she taught a course on sex and gender for the US Army, followed by Brazil, Honduras, and Peru. They now live in Washington, DC. She has published widely on family planning, reproductive health, and HIV/AIDS. Foreit continues to consult in reproductive health and serves on a research ethics review board.

Clara Fraser (Radical Women, FSP): In 1973, Fraser was hired by Seattle City Light, a publicly owned utility, to create a program to hire and train female electrical workers. Fired in 1974, Fraser immediately filed a discrimination complaint that documented pervasive political bias and sexism. After a seven-year battle, Fraser won a ruling that affirmed the right of workers to speak out against management and to organize on their own behalf. She returned to her former job at City Light just as a new furor broke out over discrimination against women in traditionally male trades. Fraser joined with women in the field and the offices and with sympathetic men to form the Employee Committee for Equal Rights at City Light, which combatted discrimination by sex and race. She retired in 1986 and continued her activism in Radical Women and the FSP until her death in 1998.

Erika Gottfried (Women's Majority Union, WL-S): The daughter of progressive political activists, Gottfried helped to found an antiwar group for high school students. She was fifteen when she joined WL-S in 1969. She also worked on *Lilith*. At the UW, she took some of the first courses offered on women's history and did original research on Pacific Northwest women. After a decade as a freelance researcher and associate producer for leftist documentary films, she joined the Tamiment Library, a special collection at New York University preserving the history of labor and the Left, as its photograph archivist. Since her retirement in 2015, Gottfried has freelanced as an archival consultant and returned to researching, writing, and publishing articles about women's history.

Nina Harding (Radical Women): Born Euphemia Correy in Boston in 1938, this African American activist moved to Seattle in 1960 and joined Radical Women. Harding graduated with honors from the UW in 1974. In the 1980s she earned a JD and an MA in public administration from the University of Indiana at Bloomington. Returning to Seattle, she passed the Washington State Bar exam in 1990 and then practiced and taught law at community colleges and universities. She was active in the African Methodist Episcopal Church, focusing on Black women's health, especially breast cancer research and mammograms. In addition, she launched a successful GED program for youth incarcerated in King County jails. Harding earned over one hundred awards and commendations from national, regional, state, and local organizations. She died in 2010.

Anci Kopple (WSfP, SWAP): Kopple, an Austrian-born peace and antinuclear activist, moved to Seattle in 1931. A founder of SWAP in 1963, she was arrested in 1978 for scaling the fence at the Bangor Naval Base to protest the building of nuclear-armed submarines in Washington State. In 1981, the YMCA of Greater Seattle gave her its Milnor Roberts International Understanding Award. Before her death in 2007, Kopple received a United Nations Association Human Rights Day Award.

Gloria Martin (Radical Women, FSP): Born in 1916, Martin was a major organizer of Seize the Time for Oppressed People, known as STOP, a coalition against police brutality. During the 1970s, STOP fought for an independent, elected, civilian review board in order to bring the police under the control of the community. Later in life she managed the bookstore Shakespeare and Company at the Pike Place Market. From 1973 to 1978, she was the organizer for the FSP, and in 1990 she was an organizer for Radical Women. Martin died in 1995.

Lee Mayfield (FSP, WL-S): Born in 1937 as Cecilie Scott, a name she resumed using in later life, Mayfield moved to Duvall, Washington, in 1980 and received her MA in whole systems design from Antioch University in 1993. She worked as a development editor for Microsoft and supervised a team of more than forty volunteers for its Survivors Community, moderating discussions among survivors of cancer, abuse, bereavement, chronic illness, divorce, and addiction. After being diagnosed with breast cancer at age fifty-four, she spoke and wrote about the environmental causes of cancer. Eschewing the societal expectation that she would replace the excised breast with an implant, she decorated the area with a beautiful tattoo of waves as a reminder of Bali, an island and people she loved. In 2004 she and her husband moved to Portland, Oregon, where she did her own creative writing while continuing her employment with Microsoft. Her memoir, *Knowing Bodies*, was published in 2012, and she died in 2013.

Jody Olvera (WL-S): A lifelong Left feminist and Latina activist, Olvera was the first female journeyman electrical worker hired by Seattle City Light, where she worked from 1973 until 2003. For seventeen years she served as the electrical safety and health specialist, and she was a leader in transforming ideas of safety from concerns about electricity into environmental issues. Her contributions were recognized when she was named Employee of the Year. After retirement, Olvera continues to be involved in environmental and safety activism and is researching the history of women fighters during the Spanish Civil War.

Grey Osterud (SDS, Radical Women, ALSB): Osterud, who grew up on the Left, was on leave from college in 1968 when she became active in the women's liberation movement in Seattle; she returned in the summer of 1969. A socialist feminist, she studied the history of American women, worked in community history museums, and conducted oral histories with farm women. Then she edited an international feminist journal and became a freelance editor for Black, feminist, and left-wing historians and sociologists. Osterud continues to work for peace and justice globally and locally.

Mary Logan Rothschild (Women's Studies): After finishing her PhD at the UW, Rothschild directed Women's Studies at the University of Puget Sound and then moved to Arizona State University, where she developed the women's studies program and taught women's history. She was active in progressive Democratic Party politics and in feminist groups. Her work on behalf of curriculum reform, teacher training, and local women's history projects, as well as her public talks around the state, led to her being named Humanities Scholar of the Year. Rothschild chaired the Women's Committee of the Organization of American Historians and wrote its sexual harassment policy. Now retired, she remains active in local and national Democratic politics.

Elaine Schroeder (WL-S, WC): Schroeder has been active in social justice and environmental issues for most of her adult life. After completing her PhD at the UW in 1983, she and her husband moved to Alaska, where she taught at the University of Alaska Southeast and opened a psychotherapy practice. She is the recipient of several awards, including Distinguished Alumnus, UW; Woman of Achievement, Anchorage YWCA; and Woman of Distinction, Juneau. Schroeder cofounded Juneau People for Peace and Justice and, more recently, 350Juneau–Climate Action for Alaska. Currently her activism focuses on the climate emergency and a campaign to divest the state's public funds from fossil fuels. Her greatest joys are hiking and cross-country skiing in the Alaskan wilderness and enjoying the arts and culture of Paris.

Anne Schweisow (YWCA): Born Anne Elizabeth Harvey in Vancouver, Washington, Schweisow majored in English at the University of Puget Sound. After earning a master's degree in psychology from Stanford, she worked for five years as the director of the UW YWCA. Then she decided to study law, believing it would help in her work on women's issues, but "on the first day of law school I knew it was not for me." Schweisow took pottery classes at the Factory of Visual Arts in Seattle and enrolled in the ceramics program at the UW, studying under Robert Sperry and earning a BFA in 1976. In keeping with her feminist beliefs, she adopted an artist name, Hirondelle, the French word for "swallow," and has pursued her career as a studio artist for over thirty years.

Jill Severn (Radical Women, FSP): The 1960s ended for Severn when she was expelled from the FSP for "bourgeois individualism." She had joined the party because it was the first place she encountered feminism and because socialism seemed like a good idea. She has spent a lifetime thinking about cults, political ideology, and the opposing human instincts of generosity and greed. Now, she says, she would settle for a social democratic party that reined in greed and leaned into generosity. Severn has been a journalist; served as a speechwriter for two Washington governors; done policy analysis; authored two civic education books for schools on state, tribal, and local governments; and is now an editorial writer for a local newspaper. She said that none of that would have been possible without the women's movement of the 1960s, because of both the way it changed the world and the way it changed her.

Judith Shapiro (Radical Women, WL-S, International Socialists): After leaving Seattle in 1971, Shapiro returned to academia in 1976, moving to London, where she had been to graduate school. Slowly abandoning revolutionary Marxism, she took up Soviet studies and health economics in the 1980s. She held a Fulbright professorship in Soviet Ukraine and was the national secretary of the British Association for Soviet, Slavonic, and Eastern European Studies. Joining the "Sachs team of advisers" in the chaos of 1993 Moscow, Shapiro made headlines with her pathbreaking work on Russia's mortality crisis and analyses of women's paradoxical situation in the USSR. In 1998 she became chief of the transition economies section of the UN Economic Commission for Europe, moved on to a professorship in health economics at Moscow's independent new graduate school of economics, and in 2005 returned to the London School of Economics to take charge of work with undergraduates. Shapiro initiated a course in the economics of gender at the London School of Economics / Beijing University Summer School in 2016.

Susan Stern (SDS, Radical Women): Stern was a founding member of Radical Women, but soon left the organization; she continued to be active in SDS and then joined the Seattle Liberation Front. She was convicted in the Seattle Seven conspiracy trial and served three months in prison. Stern moved to Berkeley, where she was involved in radical politics but not women's liberation. Her 1975 memoir, *With the Weathermen: The Personal Journey of a Revolutionary Woman*, met with a hostile reception from her former friends and comrades. In 2007, it was reprinted with an introduction by Laura Browder in Rutgers University Press's series Subterranean Lives. She died in 1976.

Nancy Stokely (ALSB): After seeing Aradia well established as a fully funded feminist health-care clinic, Stokely worked in acute care hospitals, became involved in labor unions and worker-patient alliances, and kept trying to improve the health-care system. Her focus has remained on the reproductive work of women. "At every age, we are impacted by our biological burdens, and by the patriarchal system which seeks to take advantage of our bodies and our labor, but keeps us subject to men in the home, public spaces, and at work." In her thirties, she became an RN, married, and had two children. Later she worked in public health and community clinics, and provided mental health services to women, children, and immigrants as an ARNP. Stokely has now retired.

Erin Van Bronkhorst (WL-S): Van Bronkhorst, who served as an editor of *Pandora*, retired in 2014 after a forty-five-year career in journalism as a copyeditor, reporter, and editor for the Associated Press and newspapers in the Pacific Northwest and Alaska. In the 1970s, she started a class-action sex discrimination lawsuit against Safeco Insurance that was settled for $1 million. Later, she wrote and self-published a booklet with Cara Peters titled *How to Stop Sexual Harassment: Strategies for Women on the Job*. She has also edited books, including *Gifts from the Prairies* by Margaret Auld. Van Bronkhorst is researching the life of a religious leader who opposed nuclear weapons.

Flo Ware (PFP): Born in 1912, Ware moved to Seattle in 1947 and soon became a key activist in the Black community and in interracial coalitions of women. She participated in the struggle for better schools in Seattle's Central District, organizing parents and community members to demand and create change. A foster parent of over twenty children, Ware chaired the Washington State Foster Parent Association. Her concern for the elderly led her to help establish Meals on Wheels, and her commitment to equal employment was expressed in her service on the Seattle King County Economic Opportunity Board. Always a public educator, from 1968 to 1979 Ware hosted a show on KRAB radio. She died in 1981, and in 1982 the city named a public park in the Central District in her honor.

Notes

Introduction

1. Winslow, "Primary and Secondary Contradictions in Seattle," 225.

2. Gordon, "Women's Liberation Movement," 71–73; Shulman and Moore, introduction to *Women's Liberation!*, xxi.

3. Angelou, *I Know Why the Caged Bird Sings*, 228.

4. Ezekiel, *Feminism in the Heartland*, focuses on Dayton, Ohio; Giardina, *Freedom for Women*, focuses on Gainesville, Florida; and Gilmore, *Groundswell*, analyzes the relationship between local chapters of the National Organization for Women and women's liberation organizations.

5. Evans, *Personal Politics*.

6. Horowitz, *Betty Friedan*, 5. See also Rosen, "Female Generation Gap"; and Swerdlow, "Congress of American Women."

7. Baxandall, "Re-visioning the Women's Liberation Movement's Narrative."

8. Baxandall and Gordon, *Dear Sisters*; Rosen, "Female Generation Gap"; Swerdlow, "Congress of American Women."

9. Kelley, *Freedom Dreams*, chapter 7, 45–60.

10. Rowbotham, *Century of Women*, 370. This list is by no means exhaustive. In the past twenty years, over a hundred books have been written that expand our knowledge of women's feminist activism and bring in or center the stories of women of color, LGBTQIA activists, and labor and welfare rights movements.

11. See Jesse DeLauder, "The Seattle Seven: The Smith Act Trials in Seattle (1952–1958)," Civil Rights and Labor History Consortium, University of Washington, 2008, https://depts.washington.edu/labhist/cpproject/SmithAct.shtml.

12. See Cobbins, "Black Emeralds"; Taylor, *Forging of a Black Community*.

13. See Holsaert et al., *Hands on the Freedom Plow*.

14. As quoted in Hewitt, introduction to *No Permanent Waves*, 4.

15. Naomi Weisstein used these words in conversation with the author and others. For example, she said she wanted the movement "to be both passionate and reasonable, ecstatic and utopian, hostile to hierarchy and to unequal power in every form." See Jesse Lemisch and Naomi Weisstein, "Remarks on Naomi Weisstein," https://www.cwluherstory.org/text-memoirs-articles/remarks-on -naomi-weisstein. She also coupled these two words when describing the Chicago Women's Liberation Rock Band, which "summoned up the ecstasy of a utopian vision of a world without hierarchy and domination." See https://web.archive.org /web/20130410213605/http://www.uic.edu/orgs/cwluherstory/CWLUGallery/rock .html. Both websites accessed Sept. 10, 2022.

16. Stern, *With the Weathermen*; Walter Crowley, *Rites of Passage*.

17. See HistoryLink.org, homepage, accessed Aug. 30, 2022, http://www .historylink.org; and Seattle Civil Rights and Labor History Project, University of Washington, homepage, accessed Aug. 30, 2022, http://depts.washington.edu /civilr/index.htm. I am interviewed on the Civil Rights and Labor History Project website.

18. The FBI and state and local police collect information about activists for the purposes of control and intimidation. Progressive social activists need to create our own set of resources for the future so that people can learn history from below as well as from past struggles. Until recently most archives contained the materials of White men. But in the past three decades local historians and activist academics have collected archival materials as well as oral histories from ordinary people in order to enrich our understanding of change over time. Many of these archives include those who have been ignored and marginalized. For example, I created the Shirley Chisholm Project of Women's Activism (http://chisholmproject.com), a community-based project that now holds the largest body of materials about Chisholm and grassroots Brooklyn women's politics and conducts public programs. As I developed the project, I was influenced by the work of Manning Marable's Malcolm X Project (http://www.columbia .edu/cu/ccbh/mxp/); Sarah Schulman's Act Up Oral History Project (https:// actuporalhistory.org/); and Candace Falk's Emma Goldman Project, (https://www .lib.berkeley.edu/goldman/AbouttheProject/index.html). I also relied on White, *Telling Histories*, which discusses African American women's archival collections, and on Chaudhuri, Katz, and Perry, *Contesting Archives*, which focuses on finding women in archival sources.

19. Winslow, "Primary and Secondary Contradictions in Seattle"; Winslow, "Activism and the Academy."

20. For insightful reflections on the challenges facing participant-observer historians, see Frazier, preface to *Harambee City*, ix–xv.

21. I thank Alix Kates Shulman for this insight.

22. Grey Osterud provided me with this insight in an email message, Feb. 3, 2021.

23. Nell Irvin Painter, "Why 'White' Should Be Capitalized, Too," *Washington Post*, July 22, 2020, https://www.washingtonpost.com/opinions/2020/07/22/why -white-should-be-capitalized/.

Chapter One. It's Reigning Men

1. Dixon, *My People Are Rising*, 24–25, 51.

2. See MEChA Program, "Proposal for Program in Seattle's Chicano Community (1970)," http://depts.washington.edu/civilr/images/mecha/docs/pdfs /ProjectForChicanoYouth.pdf.

3. See John Calbick, "1960 Census: First Census to Show Full Effects of Post– World War II Baby Boom in Washington State; Urban Areas Grow in Population, Rural Areas Contract," HistoryLink.org, Mar. 18, 2010, https://www.historylink.org /File/9341. See also Santos and Iwamoto, *Gang of Four*, which discusses the multiracial composition of Seattle's population and the building of multiracial coalitions.

4. Kathy George, "Japantown," *Seattle Post-Intelligencer*, Nov. 21, 2004.

5. See "Segregated Seattle," Seattle Civil Rights and Labor History Project, University of Washington, accessed Aug. 30, 2022, http://depts.washington.edu/civilr /segregated.htm.

6. Nancy Vanderlip, "Commission Avoids 'Tea-Party' Hangup," uw *Daily*, April 22, 1969.

7. Walter Crowley, *Forever Blue Moon*, frontispiece.

8. See Walt Crowley, "Blue Moon Tavern: An Unofficial Cultural Landmark," HistoryLink.org, Apr. 1, 1999, https://www.historylink.org/File/1001.

9. By 1970, redevelopment was changing the nature of the Pike Place Market. The first Starbucks opened that year. There was a huge campaign in the 1970s and 1980s to save the market, but gentrification, the expansion of the waterfront, and the arrival of cruise ships made foot traffic all but impossible, and the high cost of food placed it out of the range of working-class Seattleites.

10. The Moore Theater is now on the list of historic sites. Recent scholarship has exposed its shameful history; at its founding, it had separate entrances and seating for White and Black customers. See Richard Frishman, "Hidden in Plain Sight: The Ghosts of Segregation," *New York Times*, Nov. 30, 2020, https://www .nytimes.com/2020/11/30/travel/ghosts-of-segregation.html. Also see George Arthur, "Ask Any Fringe," Arthur Papers, uw, and in possession of author; and *Seattle Times*, Apr. 25, 1971.

11. Hanson, *World Almanac*.

12. Washington State Legislature, Directory of the 39th Session, 1965, https://leg .wa.gov/History/Legislative/Documents/Pictorial_Phone/39thSession1965opt.pdf.

13. Rosellini, *Report of the Governor's Commission*, 29.

14. See Jones, *Vanguard*.

15. Rosellini, *Report of the Governor's Commission on the Status of Women*, 28.

16. *Tacoma News Tribune*, Mar. 6, 1963.

17. *Seattle Times*, Apr. 10, 1963.

18. Rosellini, *Report of the Governor's Commission*, 33.

19. Rosellini, *Report of the Governor's Commission*, 1–2. Latinas were considered White by the 1960 census.

20. Rosellini, *Report of the Governor's Commission*, 19.

21. Rosellini, *Report of the Governor's Commission*, 8.

22. "The Place for Women," *Columns*, Spring 1966.

23. Rosellini, *Report of the Governor's Commission*, 30.

24. The broad term *progressive*, which I use in lower case, includes a wide range of reformers. Today, *progressive* refers to left-of-center political activists who call for greater redistribution of wealth and power. The Progressive movement of the early twentieth century, with a capital *P*, was led by a White educated elite. It called for greater regulation of corporations and employers to protect the public and the welfare of women and children and advocated democratizing measures such as the initiative, referendum, and recall, but it split over contentious questions regarding immigration, race, and the growing power of ethnic Americans in urban politics.

25. "Mrs. Nettie Craig Asberry," *Crisis* 50, no. 2 (Feb. 1943), 30.

26. Haarsager, *Bertha Knight Landes*.

27. O'Connor, *Revolution in Seattle*, 227.

28. Cobble, "Labor Feminists."

29. Freeman, *Politics of Women's Liberation*, 52.

30. In the 1960s, liberal Democrats were those Democrats, usually from outside the South, who supported New Deal, New Frontier, and War on Poverty programs as well as racial integration. After the escalation of the war in Vietnam, the phrase also referred to Democrats who opposed the interventionist foreign policy of the United States.

31. Rosellini, *Report of the Governor's Commission*, 1–34.

32. *Bremerton Sun*, Jan. 27, 1964.

33. *Seattle Post-Intelligencer*, Mar. 2, 1963.

34. Liberal Republicans were the wing of the Republican Party led by Nelson Rockefeller, which did not oppose all civil rights legislation and supported many government programs to remedy poverty and discrimination.

35. Freeman, *Politics of Women's Liberation*, 227.

36. Walter Crowley, *Rites of Passage*, 201.

37. Walter Crowley, *Rites of Passage*, 11.

38. Walter Crowley, *Rites of Passage*, 14.

39. Jeri Ware, interview by author, Seattle, WA, June 26, 1992.

40. See Taylor, *Forging of a Black Community*; and Singler et al., *Seattle in Black and White*.

41. In 1966, Governor Dan Evans named Charles Z. Smith to the King County Superior Court, and in 1973 Smith joined the faculty of the University of

Washington Law School. See "Charles Z. Smith: Trailblazer," Legacy Washington, Washington Secretary of State, accessed Aug. 30, 2022, https://www.sos.wa.gov /legacy/stories/charles-z-smith/#:~:text=Smith's%20life%20has%20been%20 punctuated,and%20in%201966%2C%20when%20Gov.

42. Jack Straw was one of three leaders of the 1381 Peasants' Revolt in England.

43. Dorothy Strawn Papers, UW #4550-001, Box 3.

44. In Washington State the salmon in the rivers, such as the Columbia, Skagit, and Nisqually, had long been the mainstay of the Indigenous peoples' way of life, and they had the knowledge, structures, and technologies to catch salmon sustainably. In the twentieth century, the damming of rivers for the sake of power generation and large-scale agricultural development decimated the fish population, and the falls where Native Americans had been granted the right to fish in perpetuity had been flooded. By the 1960s the rivers were being commercially exploited and Native Americans were prohibited by law from fishing. See Gabriel Chrisman, "The Fish-In Protests at Franks Landing," Seattle Civil Rights and Labor History Project, University of Washington, 2007, https://depts .washington.edu/civilr/fish-ins.htm#:~:text=Historically%2C%20the%20most%20 important%20civil,States%20between%201854%20and%201855.

45. Walter Crowley, *Rites of Passage,* 45.

Chapter Two. From the Woman Question to Women's Liberation

1. See Buhle, Buhle, and Georgakas, *Encyclopedia of the American Left.*

2. For specific definitions of terms and descriptions of organizations, see the glossary.

3. The first split within the SWP took place in 1940 when a minority opposed the unconditional defense of the Soviet Union during World War II. Led by Max Shachtman, the youth group, the Young People's Socialist League, rejected Leninism, arguing for a more inclusive organization of socialists. In 1949, the youth group split, and the Independent Socialist League was formed. The Left wing, which was active in the radical student movement in Berkeley, California, gave birth to the Independent Socialist Clubs, which in 1969 became the International Socialists. Until 1975, both tendencies rejected Leninist forms of organization and supported the movements of women, Blacks, and antiwar and labor activists, even if they were unconnected to a revolutionary party. Many women members of the Seattle International Socialists were active in WL-S. As I write in the introduction, I joined the International Socialists in 1969 and was expelled in 1976. (IS itself disbanded in 1986.) Along with other expelled members, I helped to found the International Socialist Organization in 1976. I left that group in 1983, and it imploded in 2019. See Milt Fisk, *Socialism from Below: The Origins of the International Socialist Organization,* http://www.marxists.de/trotism/fisk/index.htm.

4. Walter Crowley, *Rites of Passage,* 59.

5. Freedom Socialist Party newsletter, Nov. 1966, in possession of author.

6. Walter Crowley, *Rites of Passage*,177.

7. Walter Crowley, *Rites of Passage*, 75. See also Slonecker, "'It's with Tokens.'"

8. Anci Koppel, interview with author, July 6, 1991.

9. Clara Fraser, "A Half Century of Struggle at Boeing," *Freedom Socialist*, Feb. 1990, https://www.marxists.org/archive/fraser/1990/struggleatboeing.html. Dave Beck rose from West Coast president to international president of the Teamsters Union. He was convicted of embezzlement, racketeering, and income tax evasion and spent three years in a federal penitentiary. After being pardoned, he received a pension of $50,000, and he died a millionaire from investments in parking lots in 1993.

10. Clara Fraser, interview by author, Seattle, WA, May 8, 1991.

11. Clara Fraser, interview by author, Seattle, WA, May 8, 1991.

12. Gloria Martin, interview by author, Seattle, WA, June 8, 1991.

13. Stern, *With the Weathermen*, 2–3.

14. Stern, *With the Weathermen*, 8.

15. Quoted in Evans, *Personal Politics*, 198–99.

16. Students for a Democratic Society (SDS) was founded in 1961 as the youth organization of the social democratic League for Industrial Democracy. In 1962 SDS wrote the Port Huron Statement, which advocated "participatory democracy."

17. Arthur, "Ask Any Fringe," 2–3.

18. Ed Morman, interview by author via email, Feb. 7, 1998. He responded to a question about his commitment to women's liberation by saying, "I think I was also curious and innovative, and even though I didn't quite see how women were oppressed—I felt more oppressed as man, because I faced the draft—I wanted to understand why the 'Woman Question' existed in the Left, and why some people (mainly women, but some men as well) saw this as a significant issue. . . . In retrospect, I wonder also if I didn't have some motivation related to sexual dealings with women—i.e., if I didn't think being an advocate . . . wouldn't make me more attractive." As I wrote in "Primary and Secondary Contradictions in Seattle" (227), "One night at a party, friends told me they were going to call me *Mrs.* Vietnam Committee because they didn't know my name. Ed Morman was so bothered by my passive role at meetings that he gave me a lecture: 'You must speak up, you have a contribution to make.'"

19. People on the Left often used an alias or "party name" when they spoke or wrote for the public, in order to protect themselves against government repression or personal right-wing attacks. When I was a member of the International Socialists, I often used the name Celie Emerson. My first book was on Sylvia Pankhurst, the English suffragette, whose best friend and possible lover was Zelie Emerson, a US socialist feminist.

20. The United Farm Workers Organizing Committee, led by Cesar Chavez and Dolores Huerta, was organizing farmworkers in California, Oregon, and Washington State. The committee asked its supporters to boycott table grapes and Gallo wine, which was made with grapes picked by nonunion labor. In addition,

it called for a boycott of supermarket chains like Safeway that sold Gallo wine and nonunion grapes. See Oscar Rosales Castañeda, "The Fusion of El Movimiento and Farm Worker Organizing in the 1960s," Seattle Civil Rights and Labor History Project, University of Washington, 2009, https://depts.washington.edu/civilr/farmwk _ch6.htm; and "The UFW and Farm Worker Actions in Washington, Oregon, Idaho 1965–1976," Civil Rights and Labor History Consortium, University of Washington, accessed Aug. 31, 2022, https://depts.washington.edu/labhist/maps-ufw.shtml.

21. In doing the research for this book, I discovered that the Men's Commission announced that money raised at the Phil Ochs concert was going to a fund for scholarships for Black students at the UW.

22. Winslow, "Primary and Secondary Contradictions in Seattle," 232.

23. Winslow, "Primary and Secondary Contradictions in Seattle," 232–33.

24. Draft Resistance leaflet, July 4, 1968, in possession of author.

25. Stern, *With the Weathermen*, 10.

26. Martin, *Socialist Feminism*, 125, 88.

27. Fraser, "Which Road Towards Women's Liberation," 11.

28. Fraser, "Which Road Towards Women's Liberation."

29. *Lilith's Manifesto*, n.d., in possession of author.

30. *Lilith*, n.d.

31. Mayfield, "Opening Talk," 3.

32. Martin, *Socialist Feminism*, 126.

33. Lee Mayfield, interview by author, Seattle, WA, June 30, 1992.

34. Peace and Freedom Party Presidential Ticket and Candidates Platform, 1968, in possession of author.

35. In *Soul on Ice*, Cleaver wrote that he raped White women as a way to express his rage about racist injustice. He also admitted to practicing first by raping Black women. At the end of the book, he claimed he regretted the rapes and said that they were not an effective way to challenge White supremacy. In 1968, the Black Panther Party (BPP) leadership dismissed the idea of women's liberation; by 1969, women in the BPP began to change the organization's position.

36. Full disclosure: the Washington State PFP vice-presidential candidate was Cal Winslow, who was my husband at the time.

37. Winslow, "Primary and Secondary Contradictions in Seattle," 238–39.

38. For more on Fannie Lou Hamer, see Clifford, *Walk with Me*; and Blain, *Until I Am Free*.

39. See Kaplan, "On the Socialist Origins of International Women's Day."

40. WL-S/PFP/SDS leaflet, n.d. [probably Mar. 1968], in possession of author and in the George Arthur Papers, UW #1619, CO960a Box 2.

41. Trotsky, *History of the Russian Revolution*, 110.

42. HistoryNet Staff, "*Salt of the Earth*: The Movie Hollywood Could Not Stop," HistoryNet, June 12, 2006, https://www.historynet.com/salt-of-the-earth -the-movie-hollywood-could-not-stop.htm. Also see Winslow, "Activism and the Academy."

43. Karen Daenzer and Judith Bissell, SDS position paper, n.d., in possession of author.

44. Making an analogy between the position of women and that of African Americans was common among women's liberation activists across the US. See Mayer, *Reasoning from Race*; and Randolph, *Florynce "Flo" Kennedy*, 42–45.

45. *Sabot*, June 1969; Morgan, "Goodbye to All That"; Piercy, "Grand Coolie Dam."

Chapter Three. Let ~~Him~~ Her Live

1. Kenneth Vanderhoef, quoted in Morrison, "Choice in Washington," 126.

2. See Petchesky, *Abortion and Woman's Choice*.

3. On Nina Harding, see "Nina Harding Obituary," *Seattle Times*, Nov. 21, 2010, https://www.legacy.com/obituaries/seattletimes/obituary.aspx?n=nina -harding&pid=146716573; and Nina Harding, "How We Won Abortion Rights," interview by Linda Averill, Freedom Socialist Party, Apr. 2004, https://socialism .com/fs-article/how-we-won-abortion-rights/.

4. Nina Harding, interview by author, Seattle, WA, June 30, 1992.

5. To induce a miscarriage, a catheter was inserted through the vagina and the cervix into the uterus, which accounts for the pain Harding described.

6. Doctors were supposed to report a woman who had a nonmedical abortion to state authorities.

7. Nina Harding, interview by author, Seattle, WA, June 30, 1992.

8. Petchesky, *Abortion and Woman's Choice*, 125.

9. Lee Mayfield, interview by author, Seattle, WA, June 25, 1992.

10. Lee Minto, interview by author, Seattle, WA, June 9, 1992.

11. Lee Mayfield, interview by author, Seattle, WA, June 25, 1992. For more, see Lindsay Pyfer, "Abortion: Another Underground Railroad," *Medium*, Oct. 7, 2021, https://medium.com/@lpyfer/abortion-another-underground-railroad -dc2fc47598bd. Cecilie Scott, the older friend Pyfer interviewed, was known as Lee Mayfield in Seattle during the 1960s and 1970s.

12. Lee Minto, interview by author, Seattle, WA, June 9, 1992.

13. Quoted in Morrison, "Choice in Washington," 93.

14. Jill Severn, "Women at Work," *Washington State Service Employee*, Aug. 1969. Severn wrote a series of columns in conjunction with an organizing drive she led among women nursing home workers.

15. "Raisa Trytiak Slain," *Seattle Post-Intelligencer*, Feb. 10, 1967, 16.

16. *Seattle Post-Intelligencer*, Aug. 12, 1969.

17. Lee Minto, interview by author, Seattle, WA, June 9, 1992.

18. In 1909 the state legislature passed its first antiabortion statute, which read, "Every woman quick with child who shall take or use, submit to the use of any drug, medicine or substance, or any instrument or any means, with intent to pro- cure her own miscarriage, unless the same is necessary to preserve her own life

or the life of the child whereof she is pregnant, and thereby causes the death of such child, shall be guilty of manslaughter." The statute never clarified whether the fetus was a legal entity deserving state protection. State of Washington Session Laws, 1909, Sec. 144, Chap. 249.

19. House Bill 312, 41st Regular Session, State of Washington.

20. Clara Fraser, interview by author, Seattle, WA, July 5, 1991.

21. Saying that Harding looked like a "prim and proper Bostonian" meant that she looked like a church lady.

22. Nina Harding, interview by author, Seattle, WA, June 30, 1992.

23. Clara Fraser, interview by author, Seattle, WA, July 5, 1991.

24. Severn, "Women at Work."

25. *Seattle Times*, Feb. 11, 1969.

26. *Seattle Times*, Feb. 12, 1969.

27. Severn, "Women at Work."

28. Barbara Winslow, "Abortion Hearings," *Western Front*, March 1969.

29. *Seattle Times*, Mar. 13, 1969.

30. Herb Robinson, *Seattle Times*, Mar. 21, 1969.

31. *Seattle Post-Intelligencer*, Mar. 29, 1969. When Susan Payntor wrote under her own byline, she treated the women and the issue of abortion more seriously and professionally.

32. Severn, "Women at Work."

33. Quoted in Lader, *Abortion II*, 171.

34. *Daily Olympian*, Mar. 29, 1969.

35. Clara Fraser, interview by author, Seattle, WA, July 5, 1991.

36. Lee Mayfield, *I Came into the World Crying and Each Following Day Teaches Me Why*, 12–14, in author's possession, reprinted from *Revolutionary Age* 2, no. 1 (n.d.), in *The Liberated Rat*, Jan. 1970. Dotty DeCoster inscribed it with a note: "This is Lee's contribution to a piece of herstory you won't have to face. Praise to our former feminists for solving this one!" At that time, Margaret Sanger's racist and eugenicist positions were not well known among reproductive rights activists.

37. Karen Foreit, interview by author, email, July 1, 1999.

38. Frans Koome to Governor Dan Evans, Nov. 23, 1969, Governor Dan Evans Papers, WSA.

39. "Renton MD Risks Career in Protest of Abortion Laws," *Seattle Post-Intelligencer*, Nov. 29, 1969.

40. Lee Mayfield, "What Did We Win?," *And Ain't I a Woman* 1, no. 6, n.d. (probably Dec. 1970 or Jan. 1971): 5.

41. Marilyn Ward interviewed in Cassandra Tate, "Abortion Reform in Washington State," HistoryLink.org, Feb. 26, 2003, http://www.historylink.org /File/5313.

42. Mayfield, "What Did We Win?," 5.

43. Wagner, quoted in Mayfield, "What did We Win?," 5.

44. In the US, a referendum allows citizens to vote directly on particular pieces of legislation. This process allows legislators to refer a statute to voters so they can enact or repeal the measure. It is available to legislators in some, but not all, states.

45. WL-S, "One Out of Every Four of Us Has Had or Will Have an Abortion," leaflet, n.d. [probably Jan. 1970], in possession of author.

46. Ward interviewed in Tate, "Abortion Reform."

47. Bernice Piety, *And Ain't I a Woman* 1, no. 1 (March 1970), 5.

48. Mayfield, "What Did We Win?," 5.

49. Jan Knudsen Krause, interview by author, Seattle, WA, Jan. 19, 1993.

50. "A Place of Our Own," Young Women's Christian Association Papers, UW #1930, Box 2, n.d.

51. *Western Front*, Feb. 10, 1969, 8.

52. WL-S, *One Out of Every Four.*

53. WL-S, "Abortion Is a Woman's Right," leaflet, n.d. (probably Sept. 1970), in possession of author.

54. Theresa Ivy Williams, interview by author, Seattle, WA, July 9, 1991; Lee Mayfield, interview by author, Seattle, WA, June 25, 1992.

55. Nina Harding, interview by author, Seattle, WA, June 30, 1992.

56. Jeri Ware, interview by author, Seattle, WA, June 29, 1992.

57. Linda Corr, interview by author, Seattle, WA, June 2, 1992.

58. Johnetta Cole, interview by author, Wellesley, MA, May 28, 1993.

59. *Seattle Post-Intelligencer*, Mar. 21, 1969.

60. Young Women's Christian Association Papers, UW #1930, Box 2.

61. *Fact*, Oct. 23, 1970. The police murdered Black protesters at Jackson State, a predominantly Black university, but the White students who were shot by the National Guard at Kent State in Ohio received much more public attention.

62. Angie Weiss, "Washington's 1970 Abortion Reform Victory: The Referendum 20 Campaign," Seattle Civil Rights and Labor History Project, 2012, https://depts.washington.edu/civilr/referendum20.htm; Tate, "Abortion Reform." As discussed in the introduction, Seattle's population was not binary, Black/White, but Black/White/Latinx/Indigenous/Asian American and Pacific Islander, but the reporting only referenced Black and White voting patterns. More representative reporting came in the late 1970s.

63. *Seattle Times*, Oct. 30, 1970, B1.

64. Karen Foreit, interview by author, email, July 1, 1999. For more information about the VfU, see Weiss, "Washington's 1970 Abortion Reform."

65. WL-S Planning Committee Proposal for Counter Demonstration, n.d., in possession of author.

66. Lee Mayfield, interview by author, Seattle, WA, June 25, 1992.

67. *And Ain't I a Woman* 1, no. 5, n.d. (probably Oct. 1970): 5.

Chapter Four. Freed Up and Fired Up

1. See Rosen, *World Split Open*.

2. Gordon and Baxandall, "Second-Wave Soundings"; Gordon, "Intersectionality."

3. Rufus "Chaka" Walls, quoted in Walter Crowley, *Rites of Passage*, 141.

4. The International Socialists were among several groups that dissented from the varieties of communism represented by the Soviet Union, China, Cuba, North Korea, North Vietnam, and the Eastern European countries in the Warsaw Pact. Their slogan was "Neither Washington nor Moscow but International Socialism."

5. Walter Crowley, *Rites of Passage*, 167.

6. Py Bateman, interview with author, Seattle, WA, Oct. 8, 1991.

7. Seattle Liberation Front Program for Action, https://digitalcollections.lib .washington.edu/digital/collection/imlsmohai/id/16181.

8. *Seattle Times*, Feb. 22, 1970.

9. Quoted in *Discover America*, 1970, in possession of author.

10. Former SLF member Paul Wick, quoted in Bakke, *Protest on Trial*, 40.

11. Quoted in "Letter to the Movement," Letter No. 1, 77, which was reprinted in *Liberation*, Autumn 1970, and, with rebuttals and critiques, in *Socialist Revolution* 2, no. 7 (Jan.–Feb. 1971).

12. "Letter to the Movement."

13. *Sabot*, Oct. 1, 1970.

14. Stephanie Coontz, interview by author, Seattle, WA, June 2, 1992.

15. "Fanshen Statement," typed copy in possession of the author. It was published in *Lilith*, no. 3 (Sept. 19, 1970); *And Ain't I a Woman*, Oct. 9, 1970; and *Liberation*, Fall 1970.

16. *And Ain't I a Woman*, Oct. 9, 1970.

17. *Sabot*, Sept. 11, 1970.

18. *Lilith*, no. 3 (Sept. 19, 1970). Louise Crowley was also highly critical of William Kunstler's dismissal of the women's charges: "William Kunstler, attorney for the Chicago conspiracy defendants, spoke on the University of Washington campus on behalf of the people indicted here on similar charges and though he had been informed of the women's position and had read their statement, his only (and slightly veiled) comment on the whole thing was to condemn people who would raise disruptive issues when unity is so imperative."

19. Some contemporary documents refer to the Seattle Eight rather than the Seattle Seven because one person was indicted on the same charge but fled before he was apprehended and was not tried with the rest. All were men except for Susan Stern.

20. Editorial, *Pandora*, Nov. 16, 1970, 1.

21. There were a number of references to the Sisters of Than Hoa. This group is mentioned in *Sabot* and listed on leaflets, but I could not find the names of any members or descriptions of activities in which they were engaged.

22. UW *Daily*, Mar. 4, 1971.

23. "Letter to the Movement."

24. Morgan, "Goodbye to All That."

25. Lisa DiCaprio, interview by author, Brooklyn, NY, May 14, 2014. DiCaprio belonged to the Red Mountain Collective.

26. Py Bateman, interview with author, Seattle, WA, Oct. 8, 1991.

27. ALSB, "Women and Imperialism," n.d., in possession of author.

28. Grey Osterud, email to author, Aug. 22, 2019.

29. ALSB, "Women and Imperialism," 1.

30. *And Ain't I a Woman* 1, no. 1 (March 1970), 6.

31. Martin, *Socialist Feminism*, 126.

32. In 1979, after a seven-year fight against eviction, Freeway Hall was demolished to make way for parking lots. The FSP set up a new Freeway Hall in the Rainier Business District in South Seattle.

33. On the history of women's organizing for equality within their labor unions and the Coalition of Labor Union Women, which was founded in 1974, see Cobble, *Other Women's Movement*.

34. Left feminist critiques of the SWP's politics and tactics that were neither red-baiting nor anti-Trotskyist are documented in periodicals and in Baxandall and Gordon, *Dear Sisters*, 61–62.

35. Campus Women's Liberation, informational leaflet, n.d., in possession of author.

36. UW *Daily*, Nov. 19, 1971.

37. *Pandora* 1, no. 9 (Feb. 7, 1971).

38. See Kaplan, "On the Socialist Origins of International Women's Day."

39. *Survival News* is a compendium of articles, now online, that gives information about how to organize in difficult or dangerous periods.

40. Steinem had been a Shirley Chisholm delegate from New York State and wrote one of her campaign speeches. When McGovern won the nomination, she actively campaigned for him.

41. UW *Daily*, Oct. 17, 1972.

42. Rosen, "When Women Spied on Women."

43. Although I was only a minor player, my FBI file was over nine hundred pages, but the government only released three hundred of them. FD-306 (Rev. 9-30-69) SAC Seattle (100-29331). According to Trevor Griffey, scholar of the Freedom of Information Act and one of the originators of the Seattle Civil Rights and Labor History Project, the file "does indicate FBI informant infiltration of New Left and FSP/RW," but "I don't see evidence of informant infiltration of other women's liberation groups." The left-wing groups that COINTELPRO targeted included the CP, the SWP, the Black Freedom movement, and the New Left, all of which had members who were active in women's liberation. Most FBI investigations of women's activism, however, were not counterintelligence operations. Some collected published documents, while others involved covert surveillance.

Informants who infiltrated these groups had the most disruptive effects. Cril Payne, in *Deep Cover*, states that he gathered information mainly on Weatherman, while looking for women as sexual partners.

Chapter Five. The Rising of the Women

1. See Boggs, *Two Revolutions*; Davidson, *Antonio Gramsci*; Femia, *Gramsci's Political Thought*; Gramsci, *Selections from the Prison Notebooks*; and McNally, *Antonio Gramsci*.

2. See, for example, Winslow, "Impact of Title IX"; Meier, Konjer, and Krieger, "Women in International Elite Athletics," https://www.ncbi.nlm.nih.gov/pmc /articles/PMC8429847/; and Bell, "History of Women," https://thesportjournal .org/article/a-history-of-women-in-sport-prior-to-title-ix/.

3. Rik Sortun, "The Revolt of the Athlete," *Workers' Power* 33 (Mar. 26–Apr. 15, 1971), 8.

4. May, *Homeward Bound*.

5. "UW Branded 'Most Racist' in Athletics," UW *Daily*, Apr. 13, 1971, 13.

6. "Whatever Happens to Tomboys?," *Seattle Post-Intelligencer*, May 23, 1971.

7. Amiri Davis, *"Watch What We Do."*

8. *Seattle Times*, Apr. 10, 1971.

9. King, *All In*, 263.

10. "Jim Owens, College Football Coach, Dies at 82," *New York Times*, June 9, 2009, http://www.nytimes.com/2009/06/10/sports/ncaafootball/10owens.html ?mcubz=3; David Wilma, "Huskies Coach Jim Owens Suspends Four African American Football Players on October 30, 1969," HistoryLink.org, Nov. 27, 2001, http://www.historylink.org/File/3645.

11. On Sortun's later life and continued activism, see David Zirin, "Rest in Power, Rick Sortun: NFL Player, International Socialist," *Nation*, Jan. 25, 2016, https://www.thenation.com/article/rest-in-power-rick-sortun-nfl-player -internationalsocialist.

12. Harry Edwards, who taught at the University of California, Berkeley, wrote *The Revolt of the Black Athlete*. After leaving the St. Louis Cardinals, Dave Meggyesy wrote about his experiences in *Out of Their League*; he later became a union representative for the National Football League Players Association. Jack Scott served as athletic director at Oberlin College, where he appointed three Black coaches and expanded women's athletics. Following his UW and professional football career, Tom Greenlee was inducted into the Husky Hall of Fame in 1987.

13. Leaflet, *Monday Morning Wash*, Mar. 8, 1971, in possession of author. The editors wrote, "Caution: This paper does not pretend to conform to objective standards of the *Seattle Times* or KIRO. Trust our facts but beware of our opinions. We hope you had more fun reading it than we had writing it."

14. Regretfully, I realize that younger generations may not know that Billie Jean King is one of the most important American sports figures of the twentieth

century, along with Muhammad Ali and Arthur Ashe. She is not just the former number one US tennis player, with thirty-nine Grand Slam titles, but a champion of racial, gender, and sexual equality and social justice. A founder of the Women's Sports Foundation, she played a leading role in the passage of Title IX, which provided for equal educational opportunities for women. She was named *Sports Illustrated* Sports*man* (?) of the Year in 1972. King was awarded the Presidential Medal of Freedom and elected to the national Women's Hall of Fame. The United States Tennis Association honored her by calling its stadium the Billie Jean King National Tennis Center. See Ware, *Game, Set, Match*; and Collins, "Battle of the Sexes."

15. *Seattle Post-Intelligencer*, Apr. 10, 1971.

16. See Winslow, "Impact of Title IX."

17. The ERA was originally introduced by Senator Charles Curtis, a Republican from Kansas who was of Native American (Kaw) descent, and Representative Daniels R. Anthony Jr., also a Republican from Kansas, who was the nephew of Susan B. Anthony.

18. Cobble, "Labor Feminists," analyzes the debate between "labor feminists" who opposed the ERA and "social feminists" who believed that equal treatment under the law would best advance women's equality.

19. *And Ain't I a Woman* 1, no. 5, n.d. (probably Oct. 1970).

20. *Seattle Post-Intelligencer*, Nov. 13, 1968.

21. Melba Windoffer on the Equal Rights Amendment, Spring 1971, Radical Women Papers, UW #1180, #1492.1774, 2, 3.

22. *Sabot*, Oct. 16, 1970.

23. *And Ain't I a Woman* 1, no. 5, n.d. (probably Oct. 1970).

24. *Sabot*, Oct. 14, 1970; 6.

25. *And Ain't I a Woman* 1, no. 5, n.d. (probably Oct. 1970).

26. *And Ain't I a Woman* 1, no. 7, n.d. (probably Jan.–Feb. 1971).

27. The Farah strike, which lasted from 1972 to 1974, was a massive walkout by the employees of the Willie Farah Manufacturing Company, which employed Latinx workers to make clothing in plants in Texas and New Mexico. The strike started at the Farah plant in San Antonio, Texas, when workers led by Sylvia M. Trevino demanded a union and fought for better working conditions. The strike involved four thousand workers, the majority of whom were women. A former Farah worker was a member of WL-S. See Honig, "Women at Farah Revisited."

28. Toilets have always been a touchstone of the right wing. In the 1940s and 1950s, racist right-wingers railed against desegregating the military by saying that Black and White men would have to share toilets. Similarly, unisex toilets aroused racial and gendered fears about bodily intimacy and issues of gender ambiguity.

29. See Morris, "Equal Rights on the Ballot"; Morris, "From Women's Rights to Women's Liberation"; and Parry, "Putting Feminism to a Vote."

30. William Grimes, "Rosalyn Baxandall, Feminist Historian and Activist, Dies at 76," *New York Times*, Oct. 15, 2015, https://www.nytimes.com/2015/10/15/nyregion/rosalyn-baxandall-feminist-historian-and-activist-dies-at-76.html.

31. Margalit Fox, "Ellen Willis, 64, Journalist and Feminist, Dies," *New York Times*, Nov. 10, 2016, http://www.nytimes.com/2006/11/10/arts/10willis.html.

32. Baxandall, "Catching the Fire."

33. Baxandall, "Re-visioning the Women's Liberation Movement Narrative," 209.

34. Dixon, *My People Are Rising*, 178.

35. Spencer, *Revolution Has Come*; Huggins and LeBlanc-Ernest, "Revolutionary Women, Revolutionary Education."

36. UW *Daily*, May 21, 1971.

37. For an overview, see Michel, *Children's Interests/Mothers' Rights*. Fousekis, *Demanding Child Care*, examines not only wartime day care centers in California but also the struggle to keep them open between the end of World War II and the onset of the War on Poverty.

38. See Sonya Michel, "The History of Child Care in the U.S.," Social Welfare History Project, Virginia Commonwealth University Libraries, 2011, https://socialwelfare.library.vcu.edu/programs/child-care-the-american-history/.

39. Engels, *Origin of the Family, Private Property, and the State*, 92.

40. Freedom Socialist Party platform, 1970, in possession of author.

41. Dotty DeCoster with Heather MacIntosh, "The Women's Movement and Radical Politics in Seattle, 1964–1980," HistoryLink.org, Apr. 15, 2000, http://www.historylink.org/File/2438.

42. Barbara Winslow, handwritten proposal for a Radical Women campaign for child care at the UW, sometime in the fall of 1968, in possession of author.

43. UW *Daily*, Nov. 20, 1968.

44. Leaflet for 1969 International Women's Day, in possession of author.

45. UW *Daily*, Feb. 26, 1970.

46. UW *Daily*, Mar. 3, 1970.

47. *And Ain't I a Woman* 1, no. 1, n.d. (probably Mar. 1970).

48. UW *Daily*, May 15, 1970.

49. UW *Daily*, Aug. 6, 1970.

50. Wanda Adams, *Sabot*, Oct. 23, 1970.

51. UW *Daily*, Sept. 29, 1970.

52. Radical Organizing Committee leaflet, n.d., but sometime in the fall of 1970, George Arthur Collection, UW, Box 1, C0960B/5.

53. UW *Daily*, Oct. 15, 1970; *Seattle Post-Intelligencer*, Oct. 15, 1970.

54. UW *Daily*, Dec. 1, 1972.

55. *Pandora* 1, no. 11 (Mar. 8, 1971).

56. See Winslow, *Shirley Chisholm*. Chisholm was a certified educator, had directed a childcare center, and served as consultant to a public child welfare agency in New York City.

57. "Seattle Woman's Position Paper," 1972, in possession of author. Later in 1972, bowing to feminist pressure, WONAAC came out against coercive sterilization.

58. *And Ain't I a Woman* 2, no. 3 (n.d. [probably fall 1971]).

59. *Pandora*, Oct. 5, 1971, 3.

60. "Abortion Project Proposal," Sept. 27, 1971, in possession of author.

Chapter Six. Antiwar, Antidraft, and Anti-imperialist Feminist Activism

1. Wu, *Radicals on the Road*. On imperial feminism, see Antoinette Burton, "Race, Empire, and the Making of Western Feminism," Routledge History of Feminism, Aug. 3, 2016, https://www.routledgehistoricalresources.com/feminism/essays/race-empire-and-the-making-of-western-feminism.

2. Swerdlow, *Women Strike for Peace*; Alonso, *Peace as a Women's Issue*.

3. Appy, *Working-Class War*.

4. Black resistance to the draft began during World War II with the Nation of Islam and Black members of the Fellowship for Reconciliation; many were imprisoned. See Felber, *Those Who Know Don't Say*, 21–27.

5. See Jessie Kindig, "Draft Resistance in the Vietnam Era," Civil Rights and Labor History Consortium, 2008, http://depts.washington.edu/antiwar/gi_timeline.shtml.

6. The Seattle Draft Resistance papers are in the GI Press Collection, 1964–1977, WHS.

7. Jill Severn, "Women and Draft Resistance: Revolution in the Revolution," on behalf of Radical Women, Apr. 1968, p. 9, in possession of the author and in the George Arthur Papers, UW #1619, C09606, Box 6. Homosexuals have historically been excluded from military service as well. During the Vietnam War, some heterosexual men claimed to be homosexual in order to avoid the draft. Severn's article was written before the emergence of the lesbian and gay liberation movements; had it been written in 1970, she would have included gays and lesbians in her critique of the draft.

8. Judith Bissell, "Women and the Draft," *Lilith*, Fall 1968, 17.

9. Stephanie Coontz, interview by author, Seattle, WA, June 2, 1992.

10. Stephanie Coontz, interview by author, Seattle, WA, June 2, 1992.

11. See "Megan Cornish," Seattle Civil Rights and Labor History Project, University of Washington, accessed Sept. 6, 2022, http://depts.washington.edu/civilr/cornish.htm.

12. This antiwar show originally toured military sites overseas. In conversation Fonda told me that she was inspired by the actress Vanessa Redgrave, then an active member of the Trotskyist Workers' Revolutionary Party in England, who put on similar theatrical shows at factory gates. The title, *FTA*, was generally understood as "Fuck the Army," although the organizers insisted it meant "Free the Army."

13. Op-ed, *And Ain't I a Woman* 1, no. 7, n.d. (probably Jan.–Feb. 1971).

14. Radical Women leaflet, May 12, 1970, in possession of author.

15. *Sabot*, Nov. 12, 1970. See Kathy Naughton, interview with author, Seattle, WA, June 30, 1992; and Anne Schweisow, interview with author, Seattle, WA, Sept. 1, 1993.

16. "OPPOSE THE WARMAKERS, OPPOSE THE WAR ON WOMEN," leaflet handed out at the Oct. 31, 1970, march against the US war in Vietnam in Seattle, in possession of author.

17. International Women's Day Celebration song sheet, Mar. 9, 1974, in possession of author.

18. Letter to the *Seattle Times*, Nov. 17, 1968, original draft in possession of author.

19. Wu, *Radicals on the Road*. For more information about the two conferences, see Liz Briemburg, "Indo-Chinese Women's Conference," Vancouver Women's Caucus, accessed Sept. 6, 2022, https://www.vancouverwomenscaucus.ca/key-issues/indo-chinese-womens-conference/; and Kathleen Gough Aberle, "An Indochinese Conference in Vancouver," Vancouver Women's Caucus, accessed Sept. 6, 2022, https://www.vancouverwomenscaucus.ca/wp-content/uploads/2018/04/An-Indochinese-Conference-in-Vancouver-by-Kathleen-Aberle..pdf.

20. Briemburg, "Indo-Chinese Women's Conference."

21. *And Ain't I a Woman* 1, no. 5, n.d. (probably Oct. 1970).

22. "They're All Fuckin' Trots," April 9, 1971, 2, dittoed manuscript in possession of author.

23. Briemburg, "Indo-Chinese Women's Conference."

24. Briemburg, "Indo-Chinese Women's Conference."

25. Grey Osterud Diary, 1970, Grey Osterud Papers, SL.

Chapter Seven. The Multiplicity of Us

1. See Roth, *Separate Roads to Feminism*; Brown, Castledine, and Valk, *U.S. Women's History*; Mihesuah, *Indigenous American Women*; Evans, "Women's Liberation"; Thompson, "Multiracial Feminism"; Blackwell, *Chicana Power!*; Shah, *Dragon Ladies*; "Lessons from the Damned," Black Ink, Mar. 28, 2020, https://black-ink.info/2020/0328/lessons-from-the-damned; Robinson, *Poor Black Women*; Gerber-Freid et al., *Undivided Rights*; Springer, *Still Lifting, Still Climbing*; Kelley, *Freedom Dreams*; Bambara, *Black Woman*; Polatnik, "Diversity"; Williams, *Concrete Demands*; and Guy-Sheftall, *Words of Fire*. For earlier Black women's activism, see Jones, *Vanguard*. Orleck, *Rethinking American Women's Activism*, offers a multiracial, cross-class account of women's struggles from the turn of the twentieth century to the present.

2. Michelle Moravec, "How Did We Get to Feminism So White?," *Medium*, Jan. 7, 2008, https://professmoravec.medium.com/how-did-we-get-to-feminism-so-white-648218277b54.

3. The sources spell her full first name as Florasina or Florestine, but in Seattle she was always known as Flo.

4. Singler et al., *Seattle in Black and White*. See also Joan Singler, "Seattle CORE Timeline 1961–1968," Seattle Civil Rights and Labor History Project, University of Washington, accessed Sept. 7, 2022, https://depts.washington.edu/civilr/CORE _timeline.htm.

5. The university did not record students' ethnicity except for Black, White, Chicano/a, and Indigenous, and even those totals were not exact.

6. Kathy Mack, "Black Women Tell Ordeals," UW *Daily*, Apr. 22, 1969, 16–17.

7. Jeri Ware, interview by author, Seattle, WA, June 26, 1992.

8. "Panther Sisters on Women's Liberation," *Movement*, Sept. 1969, https:// wams.nyhistory.org/growth-and-turmoil/feminism-and-the-backlash/panther -sisters-womens-liberation/.

9. Nina Harding, "Interrelationship of the Black Struggle and the Woman Question," discussion draft, Radical Women's Conference, University of Washington, Feb. 23, 1970, in possession of author.

10. Combahee River Collective, "Black Feminist Statement."

11. See Oscar Rosales Castaneda, "Chicano/Latino Activism in Seattle, 1960s– 1970s," HistoryLink.org, Nov. 24, 2006, https://www.historylink.org/File/8013.

12. "Third World Women Fight Triple Oppression," UW *Daily*, May 21, 1971

13. "Third World Women Fight Triple Oppression," UW *Daily*, May 21, 1971.

14. Much has been written about the connections between the Red Scare and the Lavender Scare, as well as the repressed or hidden homosexuality of some of its most virulent homophobes. Johnson, *Lavender Scare*. On homosexuality and homophobia on the left, see Phelps, "Closet in the Party"; and Phelps, "Neglected Document."

15. See Atkins, *Gay Seattle*.

16. Chrystie Hill, "Queer History in Seattle, Part 1: To 1967," HistoryLink.org, Apr. 12, 2003, https://www.historylink.org/File/4154. Del Martin and Phillis Lyon, who founded the first lesbian rights organization, Daughters of Bilitis, in 1955, originally met in Seattle.

17. *Helix*, July 10, 1969, 7.

18. UW *Daily*, Mar. 4, 1968.

19. On the UW YWCA, see the chapter "Chautauquas of Feminism and Lesbianism" in Atkins, *Gay Seattle*, 129–56.

20. See Atkinson, *Amazon Odyssey*; and Jay, *Tales of the Lavender Menace*.

21. See Shelley Crites, interview by author, Seattle, WA, June 1, 1992; Jody Olvera, interview by author, Seattle, WA, Aug. 15, 1991; Theresa Ivy Williams, interview by author, Seattle, WA, July, 1991; and Mary Logan Rothschild, interview by author, email, Oct. 13, 2020.

22. *And Ain't I a Woman* 1, no. 5, n.d. (probably Oct. 1970).

23. Harlan G. Kerr Jr. to Women's Liberation–Seattle, Oct. 21, 1970, in possession of author.

24. Clara Fraser did not write anything on lesbian and gay issues until 1974; see Fraser, *Revolution, She Wrote*. Gloria Martin said nothing about support for lesbian and gay liberation until 1973; see Martin, *Socialist Feminism*.

25. Grey Osterud, email conversation with author, Nov. 11, 2020.

26. Susan Brownmiller, "Sisterhood Is Powerful: A Member of the Women's Liberation Movement Explains All," *New York Times Magazine*, Mar. 15, 1970.

27. UW *Daily*, May 23, 1970; Mary Logan Rothschild, conversation with author, Aug. 2020. In *The World Split Open* and "When Women Spied on Women," Ruth Rosen quotes Friedan's charge that the Seattle demonstrators were paid agents. Rothschild told Rosen the charge was false. I wrote a letter to the *Nation* disputing Friedan's charges as well.

28. See Howe, *Politics of Women's Studies*.

29. Mary Logan Rothschild, interview by author, email, Oct. 13, 2020. Disclosure: Aldon Bell was my PhD dissertation adviser. The UW History Department offers the Aldon Duane Bell Award in Women's History in memory of his longstanding commitment to women's history.

30. Jacobs, "Has It Really Been Thirty Years?," 309.

31. The courses included Independent Study: Peoples and Topics in Women's Studies; Twentieth Century British and American Women Novelists; Psychology of Sex Differences; Social History of American Women; The Woman in Spain: Survey of Spanish Culture and Literature; Patriarchal Politics, Women and the Law; Sex Differentiation in the Public Schools; Seminar in Economics: Discrimination; The Language of Sexism; History of Women's Rights and Feminism in America; and Women and Mental Illness. UW Arts and Sciences Collection, Women's Studies Papers, #80–100, Box 5, Folders 1–60. In the 1960s, the UW, like most of academia, did not require faculty or students to self-identify except by sex/gender. It is problematic to determine a person's race, ethnicity, or nationality by photographs or surnames.

32. Antonia Castañeda, interview by author, telephone, Nov. 21, 2020.

33. *And Ain't I a Woman* 1, no. 7, n.d. (probably Jan.–Feb. 1971).

34. *Newsletter* 1, no. 2 (July 1972). The newsletter's original name, *Staff Forum*, was changed when the group changed its name from the Staff Forum Association to the Staff Women's Forum.

35. Draft for leaflet, Staff Women's Forum, Feb. 16, 1972, UW #5061 73-14.

36. AFSCME organizes public employees. SEIU organizes public-sector employees along with private-sector workers in hospitals, home health care, and property service. See Windham, "9 to 5."

37. Dixon, *My People Are Rising*, 179. The clinic was named for Sidney Miller, a young Black man who was shot and killed by the police in 1968.

38. Elaine Schroeder, interview by author, Juneau, AK, Nov. 17, 1993.

39. Elaine Schroeder, interview by author, Juneau, AK, Nov. 17, 1993.

40. UW *Daily*, Jan. 22, 1971.

41. UW *Daily*, Feb. 22, 1972.

42. Nelson, *More Than Medicine*, 98.

43. Proposal for a Third World Women's Resource Center, n.d., UW, YWCA Papers, Box 12, Folder "Third World Women's Clinics 1920–1973."

44. Proposal for a Third World Women's Resource Center.

45. Boston Women's Health Collective, *Our Bodies, Ourselves.*

46. Lynn K. Hansen, Barbara Reskin, and Diana Grey, *How to Have Intercourse without Getting Screwed*, 1, 55. Seattle: ASUW Women's Commission, 1972. Pamphlet in possession of author.

47. Py Bateman, interview by author, Seattle, WA, Oct. 8, 1991.

48. UW *Daily*, Oct. 20, 1972, 8.

49. UW *Daily*, Oct. 20, 1972.

50. Reprinted in *And Ain't I a Woman* 1, no. 3, n.d. (probably May–June 1970).

Chapter Eight. Flow and Ebb

1. Radical Women membership list, n.d., but probably 1972, in possession of author.

2. Martin, *Socialist Feminism*, 126. Most of the Trotskyist organizations have continued; see https://www.marxists.org/history/etol/trees/u, accessed Oct. 5, 2022.

3. UW *Daily*, Feb. 15, 1972.

4. UW *Daily*, Mar. 12, 1969.

5. ASUW Women's Commission, *Report on the Status of Women*, Part II, Students. Women students entered the UW with higher grades than men and graduated with higher GPAs. The report also demolished the myth that women dropped out because of marriage, children, work, loss of interest, or inability to compete with men. Examples of the blatant gender discrimination women encountered included the Dental School refusing to admit women, asking them, "Why don't you find a rich husband and give all this up?" Other administrators and faculty chairs made such comments as, "Women don't go into math; it's too masculine," and "The Admission Committee didn't do its job. There's not one good looking girl in the entering class." (Quotations on p. 19.)

6. *Pandora* 1, no. 14 (Apr. 20, 1971).

7. See "Gayton, Carver Clark (b. 1938)," HistoryLink.org, May 28, 2004, https://www.historylink.org/File/4305.

8. *Pandora* 1, no. 14 (Apr. 20, 1971).

9. See "UW Coalition Faces Difficulty," *Pandora* 1, no. 12 (Mar. 22, 1971): 1, https://www.jstor.org/stable/community.28042429?seq=1#metadata_info_tab_contents.

10. "Third World Women's Exit Statement," UW *Daily*, Mar. 23, 1971.

11. UW *Daily*, Mar. 31, 1971.

12. "Forum on the Office of Equal Opportunity for Women," leaflet, June 2, 1972, in possession of author.

13. "Statement of Women's Liberation Seattle to the Peace-Pipe Proposal," n.d., in possession of author. There is no evidence of who wrote this racially insensitive proposal.

14. Mayfield, "Opening Talk," 5–7.

15. Mayfield, "Opening Talk," 5–7.

16. Jody Olvera, interview by author, Seattle, WA, Aug. 15, 1991.

17. *From the Ground Up: Seattle Feminist Newspaper* 1, no. 2 (July–Aug. 1974).

18. Py Bateman, interview by author, Seattle, WA, Oct. 8, 1991.

19. Enke, *Finding the Movement*, 8.

20. Py Bateman, interview by author, Seattle, WA, Oct. 8, 1991.

21. See Harvey, *Brief History of Neoliberalism*.

22. Dixon, *My People Are Rising*. The liberal Democratic mayor Wes Ulman, for example, refused a Nixon directive to mount an armed assault on the Black Panther headquarters, as happened in Chicago with the murder of Black Panther chair Fred Hampton.

23. See Trevor Griffey, "History," Seattle Civil Rights and Labor History Project, University of Washington, accessed Sept. 7, 2022, https//depts.washington .edu/civilr/ucwa_history.htm.

24. The Reproductive Rights National Network formed in 1978 in response to the national abortion debate, in particular the racist and class-based Hyde Amendment, which denied federal funding for poor women needing abortions. The network included numerous feminist organizations, including one in Seattle, and focused on making reproductive choices available for all women. It campaigned for free, safe, and legal abortions; accessible contraception; the right of lesbian and gay couples to adopt and raise children; an end to coercive sterilization; and day care. In 1984 the Women of Color Caucus of the Reproductive Rights National Network criticized the network for not adequately dealing with racism and walked out. The remaining activists decided they could not go on as a mainly White women's organization, so the group disbanded. The reproductive justice organization with the longest life has been SisterSong, founded in 1997 "by 16 organizations of women of color from four mini-communities (Native American, African American, Latina and Asian American) who realize that we have the right and responsibility to represent ourselves and our communities, and the equally compelling need to advance the perspectives and needs of women of color." SisterSong website, accessed Sept. 7, 2022, https://www.sistersong.net /mission.

25. Reddick, "Opening Talk," 7–10. See Shelly Reddick, interview by author, Seattle, WA, July 11, 1991.

26. Romney, *We Were There*, 131–33

27. The January 7, 1977, Washington State Supreme Court ruling was an important victory for the feminist cause of gender equality before the law. See Thuma, *All Our Trials*.

28. Jacobs, "Has It Really Been Thirty Years?," 314.

Epilogue

1. Morris, "A Dream of John Ball," accessed Oct. 6, 2022, https://www.marxists .org/archive/morris/works/1886/johnball/chapters/chapter4.htm.

2. Du Bois, *Souls of Black Folk*, 1–2.

3. In 1990 the professor who had headed the History Department when I was an undergrad and grad student and chaired my PhD thesis committee took me into his office after I successfully defended my dissertation. He showed me that picture, which was tacked on his bulletin board. He told me that he had kept it up since 1969. So this picture also creeps me out.

4. See "Ohio Barber Shop Shut in Protests; Students Object to Owner's Refusal to Serve Negroes," *New York Times*, Mar. 16, 1964, https://www.nytimes.com/1964 /03/16/archives/ohio-barber-shop-shut-in-protests-students-object-to-owners -refusal.html.

5. Along with other books and essays, E. P. Thompson wrote *William Morris: From Romantic to Revolutionary*.

6. For a vivid portrait of Black community activism in Cleveland, see Frazier, *Harambee City*.

7. See Barbara Winslow, "How Ladies Against Women Flummoxed Phyllis Schlafly," *Meeting Ground Online* (blog), July 12, 2014, http://meetinggroundonline .org/how-ladies-against-women-flummoxed-phyllis-schlafly/.

8. See William Serrin, "200 Mississippi Women Carry on a Lonely, Bitter Strike," *New York Times*, Feb. 27, 1980, A12; and David Moberg, "Puttin' Down Ol' Massa: Laurel, Mississippi, 1979," accessed Oct. 12, 2022, https://www.facingsouth .org/2022/07/david-moberg-sanderson-chicken-workers-strike-mississippi-1979.

9. Bynam, *Free State of Jones*; Wilkie, *When Evil Lived in Laurel*; and Gary Ross, dir., *The Free State of Jones* (Universal City, CA: Universal Pictures, 2016). Laurel has become known today through the HGTV show *Home Town*, starring a White couple who rehab buildings.

10. Bethel, "What Chou Mean We White Girl?"

11. Hartman and Banner, *Clio's Consciousness Raised*.

12. Ramos, *Campañeras*.

13. Juanita Ramos, email conversation with author, Apr. 10, 2021. Grey Osterud also told me that a number of Jewish women protested having Berkshire events on the Jewish sabbath.

14. Juanita Ramos, email conversation with author, Apr. 10, 2021.

15. At the 1990 Berks, there were 152 panels; 20 panels (almost 8 percent) dealt specifically with Black women or women of color, including international panels. I am indebted to Kathleen Sheldon for sending me her 1990 Berks program.

16. Weiner, "Conference Report," 2.

17. See Janell Hobson and Karon Jolme, "Transformation of Conscious- ness," *Ms.*, Oct. 24, 2017, https://msmagazine.com/2017/10/24/transformation-of -consciousness.

18. Angela Davis speaking at the 2019 Annual Conference of the National Women's Studies Association, Nov. 16, 2019. On the younger generation of Black feminists, see Springer, "Third Wave Black Feminism."

19. See Collins, "Battle of the Sexes"; and Welch, "'Up against the Wall Miss America.'"

20. Carol Hanisch, "What Can Be Learned," *Redstockings Newsletter*, Nov. 11, 1968.

21. Angela Davis, "Reflections on the Black Woman's Role."

22. While looking for photographs for this book, I found pictures of my father with the winners of the 1963 Miss Universe and Miss USA pageants, which my father's company ran from the 1950s until 1975. In 1962, just six years before the *Playboy* protest, I was photographed in my father's office with Miss Universe, Norma Nolan from Argentina, and Miss USA, Hawaiian Macel Leilani Wilson, the first Asian American to be chosen.

23. Carole Joffe, "Failing to Embed Abortion Care in Mainstream Medicine Made It Politically Vulnerable," *Washington Post*, Jan. 11, 2022, https://www.washingtonpost.com/outlook/2022/01/11/failing-embed-abortion-care-mainstream-medicine-made-it-politically-vulnerable/.

24. For a collection of timely pieces from advocates for abortion access and reproductive rights, see Adler et al., *We Organize*. This e-book includes Barbara Winslow, "What We Need Now Is More of What We Did Then: The Militant Multiracial Coalition Grassroots Campaign That Won Abortion by Popular Referendum in Washington State—in 1969."

Glossary

Anarchism is a political philosophy that opposes almost all forms of authority, rejects coercion, and calls for the abolition of the state, which it holds to be harmful as well as unnecessary. In the 1960s, feminists identified with the early twentieth-century anarchist Emma Goldman, who organized working women, advocated women's sexual freedom, and defended freedom of speech.

Anti-imperialism is a political position that opposes the domination and control of peoples by foreign nation-states. It condemns wars of conquest, especially those meant to subjugate other peoples and colonize their territory or exploit it economically. The seminal text for Marxist anti-imperialism is Vladimir Lenin's *Imperialism, the Highest Stage of Capitalism* (1917). In the 1960s and 1970s, American activists opposing the US war in Vietnam, as well as supporting anticolonial struggles in Africa, South America, and Asia, defined themselves as anti-imperialists.

The **bourgeoisie** is conventionally defined as the middle class, as distinct from the landed aristocracy, the peasantry, or the working class. Marxists use the term for the capitalist class that owns the means of production and exploits other classes for private profit. The adjective *bourgeois* refers to the materialistic values of those in the middle class.

When spelled with a lower-case *c*, **communism** refers to a philosophical, social, political, and economic ideology. Developed by Karl Marx and others, its ideal is a society in which the means of production are owned by the proletariat (working class) and used for the common good, and class stratification, money, and the state have all withered away. A basic tenet of the communist movement was that socialism, a transitional form, and communism, its more advanced iteration, need to be international to transform the global economic and political order.

A **Communist**, usually with a capital *C*, is a person who advocates the overthrow of the capitalist ruling class (bourgeoisie), replacing capitalism with socialism and eventually establishing a communist society.

The **Communist Party** was founded after the Bolshevik Party took power in Russia and ruled the Soviet Union until 1991. It also had an international organization with affiliates in many countries.

The **Communist Party of the United States of America**, founded in 1917, played a major role in left-wing politics in the 1930s and 1940s, defending the rights of Black Americans and labor unions and organizing against fascism. After being persecuted and prosecuted during the Red Scare of the late 1940s and early 1950s, it had little impact on the Left during the 1960s and 1970s.

A **faction** is a small dissenting group within a larger political organization. Factions organize and promote a dissenting position in order to win a majority or leave the organization. **Factionalism** is the tendency of political groups to split into warring subgroups, often paralyzing or destroying them.

Feminism is the advocacy of women's rights, and in the early twentieth century it subsumed earlier terms such as *the emancipation of women*. With the emergence of women's liberation movements in the 1960s, especially with the leadership of Black feminists, feminism was understood as a political theory and practice that supported the struggles of *all* women—women of color as well as White women, of all sexual and gender identities, and of all classes, abilities, ethnicities, faith traditions, and nationalities—to abolish all oppressive hierarchies and forms of domination.

The **Freedom Socialist Party**, a Trotskyist political organization based in Seattle, Washington, was formed in 1966 when the city's branch of the Socialist Workers Party left the national organization. The FSP's most serious disagreements with the Socialist Workers Party turned on its lack of attention to women's issues. In 1967 the FSP split into two factions, which were dubbed the FSP Bolshevik and FSP Menshevik. Members of the former were in Radical Women; those in the latter were in Women's Liberation–Seattle.

Mao Zedong was the leader of the 1949 Chinese Revolution, the Peoples' Republic of China, and the Communist Party of China until his death in 1976. **Maoism**, a variant of Marxist and Leninist theory, argued that social classes beyond the proletariat can make a revolution; in China, revolutionary communism took root among peasants as well as wage workers in industry. Maoism posited that bourgeois ideology must be continuously combatted even under socialism through ongoing cultural revolutions. In addition, it developed the model of three worlds: the US and the USSR were the imperialist powers of the First World; the Second World included the less powerful but economically developed nations; and the Third World comprised the nations that were subject to imperialist domination and underdevelopment. According to Mao, Third World nations were the most revolutionary. This view resonated powerfully during the 1960s and early 1970s, when African nations were emerging from colonialism and national liberation movements were burgeoning across Asia. Today, the Third World is referred to as the global South.

Marxism is a political-economic theory developed in the mid-nineteenth century by Karl Marx and Friedrich Engels that has influenced progressives throughout the world. It posits that the struggle between social classes is the major force in history; that capitalism created the economic, political, and social conditions for a global working-class revolution; and that under socialism and eventually communism there would be a classless society free from inequality. Marx and Engels wrote about the subordination of women in class societies and supported women's emancipation. Since then, the relationship between Marxism and feminism has been subject to debate.

Neoliberalism refers to the ideology of market-oriented liberalism and to policies that privatize public economic sectors and services, deregulate corporations and banks, sharply reduce expenditures on public infrastructure, cut taxes on the wealthy and on corporations, impose austerity on public social programs and services, and promote militarization, policing, and mass incarceration. Beginning in the 1970s, Republicans campaigned to dismantle Franklin D. Roosevelt's New Deal and Lyndon Johnson's Great Society. Presidents Jimmy Carter and Bill Clinton, both Democrats, as well as Republican presidents George H. W. Bush and George W. Bush, advanced the neoliberal agenda by deregulating many industries and weakening regulatory agencies.

The **Peace and Freedom Party** grew out of the civil rights and antiwar movements and broke with the Democratic Party because of its support for the US war in Vietnam and its failure to effectively advance civil rights. The Peace and Freedom Party ran its first candidates for office in 1966. Those leftists who believed that electoral campaigns had educational value tended to support it, while many members were also active in other, issue-oriented groups, including women's liberation.

The **proletariat** is the working class in a capitalist society, which produces all wealth through its labor but does not share in the wealth it creates. According to Marxist theory, the proletariat is *the* revolutionary class because of its exploitation and because of the solidarity it develops in large-scale workplaces; its main political weapon is the general strike.

A **sect** is a subgroup or offshoot of a religious or political organization. Although the term was originally used for religious groups, it now refers to any group that separates from a larger one to follow a different set of rules. Members of sects are bound together by a high level of unquestioning participation, the belief that their group alone holds the truth, and the notion that opponents and enemies are everywhere. Those who challenge the leadership or ideas of the sect are expelled and banished. **Sectarianism** is the tendency of relatively small groups to foment conflict within them and is closely related to factionalism.

Social democracy is a tendency within socialism that supports political and economic democracy, which is decentralized and features popular participation and control. In contrast to Leninists, social democrats do not advocate a vanguard party of professional revolutionaries but support the idea of a constitutional or electoral path toward socialism.

Socialism is a political-economic philosophy encompassing a range of social systems characterized by popular and social ownership of the means of production. For orthodox Marxists, socialism is a transitional stage leading to communism.

The **Socialist Workers Party**, founded in 1938 by US supporters of Leon Trotsky, was dominant on the Left in Seattle and played a central role in the anti–Vietnam War movement and after 1970 in the women's liberation movement.

Joseph Stalin, one of the leaders of the 1917 Bolshevik revolution, became the ruler of the USSR after Vladimir Lenin's death in 1924. He advocated socialism in one country to protect the revolution from foreign enemies, rejecting the principle of internationalism. Stalin persecuted and murdered his opposition within the party, which prompted many people to leave the Communist Party. **Stalinism** refers to the political and organizational methods associated with Stalin.

Students for a Democratic Society was a nationwide activist organization in the US in the 1960s, which grew out of a small social democratic organization. Rather than adopting a hierarchical leadership structure, the founders conceived of the organization as a broad exercise in participatory democracy. It grew rapidly, with over three hundred campus chapters and thirty thousand supporters by 1969. In the late 1960s, it turned to anti-imperialist and revolutionary politics. Factional splits led to its dissolution.

Third World women included all women of color around the globe. Those who used this term in the 1960s believed that women of color in United States were part of internal colonies of Indigenous, African-descended, and Latinx people and thus were natural allies of women in the Third World who were struggling against colonialism and imperialism.

Leon Trotsky was one of the leaders of the 1917 Bolshevik revolution and served in the Communist government until 1924. He argued that the Russian Revolution could not succeed in isolation; it needed to be defended by revolutions in Europe and required a global economic transformation. As Trotsky grew more critical of Joseph Stalin's leadership, he and his followers were persecuted, and Stalin had Trotsky murdered in Mexico in 1940. In 1938 Trotsky's supporters founded the Socialist Workers Party in the United States.

The **women's liberation movement** was anticapitalist, antiracist, and anti-imperialist and called for cultural and sexual liberation from all forms of White male patriarchy. Its organizations were local, organized at the grassroots level, and tried to be nonhierarchical.

The **women's movement** refers to the mainstream, moderate, reformist, liberal, or bourgeois women's movement, best exemplified by hierarchical organizations such as the National Organization for Women, National Abortion Rights Action League, Coalition of Labor Union Women, and National Women's Political Caucus.

Bibliography

Primary Sources in Possession of Barbara Winslow

And Ain't I a Woman, journal published by Women's Liberation–Seattle

Arthur, George. Mimeographed letter, n.d. "Ask Any Fringe: Being an Account of Certain Events Taking Place in the City of Seattle prior to 1972 or Thereabouts Told by a Native Born Son of the Pacific Northwest Marooned on the Island of Manhattan."

Fraser, Clara. "Which Road towards Women's Liberation—the Movement as a Radical Vanguard or a Single Issue Coalition?" Discussion draft for Radical Women conference, Feb. 23, 1970.

Lilith, journal published by the Women's Majority Union

Monday Morning Wash, a left-wing publication

Peace and Freedom Party: minutes, leaflets, posters, and pictures

Radical Women: leaflets, position papers, and other ephemera

Revolutionary Age, a left-wing periodical

Students for a Democratic Society: minutes and leaflets

Women's Liberation–Seattle: buttons, leaflets, letters, minutes of meetings, photographs, and transcripts of speeches

Primary Sources in Repositories

Schlesinger Library at the Radcliffe Institute for Advanced Study, Harvard University, Cambridge, MA (SL)

> Grey Osterud Papers

University of Washington Libraries, Special Collections, Seattle (UW)

> Aradia Clinic Papers
> George Arthur Papers

Feminist Coordinating Council Records, 1971–1977
Erika Gottfried Papers
Radical Women Papers
Susan Stern Papers
Dorothy Strawn Papers
University of Washington Women's Studies Papers
Washington State Committee on Abortion Reform Papers
Young Women's Christian Association Papers

Washington State Archives, Olympia (wsa)

Governor Dan Evans Papers

Wisconsin Historical Society, Madison (whs)

GI Press Collection, 1964–1977

Oral History Interviews Conducted by Barbara Winslow

Py Bateman, Seattle, WA, Oct. 8, 1991, and June 1, 1992
Antonia Castañeda, telephone, Nov. 21, 2020
Johnetta Cole, Wellesley, MA, May 28, 1993
Stephanie Coontz, Seattle, WA, June 2, 1992
Linda Corr, Seattle, WA, June 2, 1992
Shelley Crites, Seattle, WA, June 1, 1992
Lisa DiCaprio, New York, NY, May 14, 2014
Karen Foreit, email, July 1, 1991
Clara Fraser, Seattle, WA, May 8, 1991, and July 5, 1991
Nina Harding, Seattle, WA, June 30, 1992
Anci Koppel, Seattle, WA, July 6, 1991
Jan Knudson Krause, Seattle, WA, Jan. 19, 1993
Gloria Martin, Seattle, WA, June 8, 1991
Lee Mayfield, Seattle, WA, July 9, 1991, June 25, 1992, and June 30, 1992
Lee Minto, Seattle, WA, June 9, 1992
Ed Morman, email, Feb. 7, 1998
Kathy Naughton, Seattle, WA, June 30, 1992
Jody Olvera, Seattle, WA, Aug. 15, 1991
Shelly Reddick, Seattle, WA, July 11, 1991
Mary Logan Rothschild, email, Oct. 13, 2020
Elaine Schroeder, Juneau, AK, Nov. 16 and 17, 1993
Anne Schweisow, Seattle, WA, Sept. 1, 1993
Nancy Stokely, Seattle, WA, June 30, 1992
Jeri Ware, Seattle, WA, June 26 and 29, 1992
Theresa Ivy Williams, Seattle, WA, July 9, 1991

Newspapers

La Chispa, 1972
City Collegian, 1965–75
Daily, published by the Associated Students of the University of Washington,
1965–75
Daily Olympian, 1966–73
Fact, 1965–75
From the Ground Up: Seattle Feminist Newspaper (undated)
Helix, 1967–70
Medium, 1965–75
New York Times, 1965–75
Pandora, 1970–76
Sabot, 1969–70
Seattle Barb, 1967
Seattle Post-Intelligencer, 1965–75
Seattle Times, 1965–75
University Herald, 1965–76
Washington State Service Employee, 1967–70
Western Front, 1969
Workers' Power, 1970–73

Published Sources

Adler, Natalie, Marian Jones, Jessie Kindig, Elizabeth Navarro, and Anne Rumberger,
eds. *We Organize to Change Everything: Fighting for Abortion Access and Reproductive Justice*. Brooklyn, NY: *Lux* Magazine and Verso, 2022. E-book.

Alonso, Harriet Hyman. *Peace as a Women's Issue: A History of the U.S. Movement
for World Peace and Women's Rights*. Syracuse, NY: Syracuse University
Press, 1993.

Angelou, Maya. *I Know Why the Caged Bird Sings*. New York: Random House, 1970.

Appy, Chris. *Working-Class War: American Combat Soldiers and Vietnam*. Chapel
Hill: University of North Carolina Press, 1993.

Associated Students of the University of Washington (ASUW) Women's Commission. *Report on the Status of Women at the University of Washington, Part I,
Faculty and Staff, Part II, Students*. Oct. 1970.

Atkins, Gary. *Gay Seattle: Stories of Exile and Belonging*. 2nd ed. Seattle: University of Washington Press, 2003.

Atkinson, Ti Grace. *Amazon Odyssey*. New York: Links Books, 1974.

Bakke, Kit. *Protest on Trial: The Seattle Conspiracy*. Pullman: Washington State
University Press, 2018.

Bambara, Toni Cade, ed. *The Black Woman: An Anthology*. New York: New American Library, 1970.

Baxandall, Rosalyn. "Catching the Fire." In *The Feminist Memoir Project: Voices from Women's Liberation*, edited by Rachel Blau Duplessis and Ann Snitow, 218–24. New York: Three Rivers, 1998.

Baxandall, Rosalyn. "Re-visioning the Women's Liberation Movement's Narrative: Early Second Wave African American Feminists." *Feminist Studies* 27, no. 1 (Spring 2001): 225–45.

Baxandall, Rosalyn, and Linda Gordon, eds. *Dear Sisters: Dispatches from the Women's Liberation Movement*. New York: Basic Books, 2001.

Beal, Frances M. "Double Jeopardy: To Be Black and Female." Original pamphlet, titled "Black Women's Manifesto; Double Jeopardy: To Be Black and Female," published by the Third World Women's Alliance, New York, in 1969; revised version in *The Black Woman: An Anthology*, edited by Toni Cade Bambara, 109–22. New York: New American Library, 1970.

Bethel, Lorraine. "What Chou Mean We, White Girl? Or, the Cullud Lesbian Feminist Declaration of Independence (Dedicated to the Proposition That All Women Are Not Equal, i.e. Identical/ly Oppressed)." In "The Black Women's Issue," *Conditions* 5 (Autumn 1979): 86–92.

Blackwell, Maylei. *Chicana Power! Contested Histories of Feminism in the Chicano Movement*. Austen: University of Texas Press, 2011.

Blain, Keisha N. *Until I Am Free: Fannie Lou Hamer's Enduring Message to America*. Boston: Beacon, 2021.

Boggs, Carl. *The Two Revolutions: Gramsci and the Dilemmas of Western Marxism*. Boston: South End, 1984.

Boston Women's Health Collective. *Our Bodies, Ourselves: A Book by and for Women*. New York: Simon and Schuster, 1971.

Brown, Leslie, Jacqueline Castledine, and Ann Valk, eds. *U.S. Women's History: Untangling the Threads of Sisterhood*. New Brunswick, NJ: Rutgers University Press, 2017.

Buhle, Paul, Mari Jo Buhle, and Dan Georgakas, eds. *Encyclopedia of the American Left*. 3rd ed. New York: Verso, 2022.

Bynam, Victoria. *The Free State of Jones: Mississippi's Longest Civil War*. Chapel Hill: University of North Carolina Press, 2003.

Chaudhuri, Nupur, Sherry J. Katz, and Mary Elizabeth Perry, eds. *Contesting Archives: Finding Women in the Sources*. Urbana: University of Illinois Press.

Cleaver, Eldridge. *Soul on Ice*. New York: Dell, 1968.

Clifford, Kate. *Walk with Me: A Biography of Fannie Lou Hamer*. New York: Oxford University Press, 2021.

Cobbins, Quin'Nita F. "Black Emeralds: African American Women's Political Activism and Leadership in Seattle, 1941–2000." PhD diss., University of Washington, 2018.

Cobble, Dorothy Sue. "Labor Feminists and President Kennedy's Commission on Women." In *No Permanent Waves: Recasting Histories of US Feminism*, edited by Nancy Hewitt, 144–67. New Brunswick, NJ: Rutgers University Press, 2010.

Cobble, Dorothy Sue. *The Other Women's Movement: Workplace Justice and Social Rights in Modern America*. Princeton, NJ: Princeton University Press, 2004.

Collins, Gail. "The Battle of the Sexes." In "Turning Points in American Sports," special issue, *History Now* 23 (Spring 2010). https://www.gilderlehrman.org /history-resources/essays/battle-sexes.

Combahee River Collective. "A Black Feminist Statement." Reprinted in *Women's Liberation! Feminist Writings That Inspired a Revolution and Still Can*, edited by Alix Kates Shulman and Honor Moore, 345–53. New York: Library of America, 2021.

Crowley, Walter. *Forever Blue Moon*. Seattle: Three Fools, 1992.

Crowley, Walter. *Rites of Passage: A Memoir of the Sixties in Seattle*. Seattle: University of Washington Press, 1995.

Davidson, Alastair. *Antonio Gramsci: Towards an Intellectual Biography*. Chicago: Haymarket Books, 2018.

Davis, Amiri. *"Watch What We Do": The Politics and Possibilities of Black Women's Athletics, 1910–1970*. Baltimore: Johns Hopkins University Press, 2016.

Davis, Angela. "Reflections on the Black Woman's Role in the Community of Slaves." *Black Scholar* 3, no. 4 (1971): 2–15.

Dixon, Aaron. *My People Are Rising: Memoir of a Black Panther Party Captain*. Chicago: Haymarket Books, 2012.

Du Bois, W. E. B. *The Souls of Black Folk*. 1903. New York: Penguin, 1996.

Edwards, Harry. *The Revolt of the Black Athlete*. New York: Free Press, 1968.

Engels, Friedrich. *The Origin of the Family, Private Property and the State*. Translated by Ernest Untermann. Chicago: Kerr, 1884.

Enke, Anne. *Finding the Movement: Sexuality, Contested Space, and Feminist Activism*. Durham, NC: Duke University Press, 2007.

Evans, Sara. *Personal Politics: The Roots of Women's Liberation in the Civil Rights Movement and the New Left*. New York: Alfred Knopf, 1979.

Evans, Sara. "Women's Liberation: Seeing the Revolution Clearly." *Feminist Studies* 41, no. 1 (2015): 138–49.

Ezekiel, Judith. *Feminism in the Heartland*. Columbus: Ohio State University Press, 2002.

Felber, Garrett. *Those Who Know Don't Say: The Nation of Islam, the Black Freedom Movement, and the Carceral State*. Chapel Hill: University of North Carolina Press, 2020.

Femia, Joseph. *Gramsci's Political Thought: Hegemony, Consciousness and the Revolutionary Process*. Oxford: Oxford University Press, 1981.

Flexner, Eleanor. *Century of Struggle: The Women's Rights Movement in the United States*. Cambridge, MA: Belknap Press of Harvard University Press, 1959.

Fousekis, Natalie M. *Demanding Child Care: Women's Activism and the Politics of Welfare, 1940–1971*. Urbana: University of Illinois Press, 2013.

Fraser, Clara. *Revolution, She Wrote*. Seattle: Red Letter, 1998.

Frazier, Nishani. *Harambee City: The Congress of Racial Equality in Cleveland and the Rise of Black Power Populism*. Fayetteville: University of Arkansas Press, 2017.

Freeman, Jo. *The Politics of Women's Liberation: A Case Study of an Emerging Social Movement and Its Relation to the Policy Process*. Philadelphia: David McKay, 1975.

Friedan, Betty. *The Feminine Mystique*. New York: W. W. Norton, 1963.

Gerber-Freid, Marlene, Elena Gutierrez, Loretta Ross, and Jael Silliman. *Undivided Rights: Women of Color Organize for Reproductive Justice*. Boston: South End, 2004.

Giardina, Carol. *Freedom for Women: Forging the Women's Liberation Movement, 1953–1970*. Gainesville: University Press of Florida, 2010.

Gilmore, Stephanie. *Groundswell: Grassroots Feminist Activism in Postwar America*. New York: Routledge, 2013.

Gordon, Linda. "Intersectionality, Socialist Feminism and Contemporary Activism." *Gender and History* 28, no. 2 (2016): 340–57.

Gordon, Linda. "The Women's Liberation Movement." In *Feminism Unfinished: A Short Surprising History of American Women's Movements*, edited by Astrid Henry, Dorothy Sue Cobble, and Linda Gordon, 69–145. New York: Liveright, 2014.

Gordon, Linda, and Rosalyn Baxandall. "Second-Wave Soundings." *Nation*, June 15, 2000.

Gramsci, Antonio. *Selections from the Prison Notebooks*. Edited and translated by Quintin Hoare and Geoffrey Noel Smith. New York: International Publishers, 1971.

Guy-Sheftall, Beverly, ed. *Words of Fire: An Anthology of African-American Feminist Thought*. New York: New Press, 1995.

Haarsager, Sandra. *Bertha Knight Landes: Big City Mayor*. Norman: University of Oklahoma Press, 1994.

Hanson, Henry, ed. *World Almanac and Book of Facts*. New York: *New York World-Telegram* and *Sun*, 1965.

Hartman, Mary S., and Lois F. Banner, eds. *Clio's Consciousness Raised: New Perspectives on the History of Women*. New York: Harper and Row, 1974.

Harvey, David. *A Brief History of Neoliberalism*. Oxford: Oxford University Press, 2007.

Hewitt, Nancy, ed. *No Permanent Waves: Recasting Histories of U.S. Feminism*. New Brunswick, NJ: Rutgers University Press, 2010.

Holsaert, Faith S., Martha Prescod Norman Noonan, Judy Richardson, Betty Garman Robinson, Jean Smith Young, and Dorothy M. Zellner, eds. *Hands on the Freedom Plow: Personal Accounts by Women in SNCC*. Urbana: University of Illinois Press, 2010.

Honig, Emily. "Women at Farah Revisited: Political Mobilization and Its Aftermath among Chicana Workers in El Paso, Texas, 1972–1992." *Feminist Studies* 22, no. 2 (Summer 1996): 425–52.

Horowitz, Daniel. *Betty Friedan and the Making of "The Feminine Mystique": The American Left, the Cold War, and Modern Feminism.* Amherst: University of Massachusetts Press, 1998.

Howe, Florence, ed. *The Politics of Women's Studies: Testimony from 30 Founding Mothers.* New York: Feminist Press, 2000.

Huggins, Erika, and Angela D. LeBlanc-Ernest. "Revolutionary Women, Revolutionary Education." In *Want to Start a Revolution? Radical Women in the Black Freedom Struggle,* edited by Dayo F. Gore, Jeanne Theoharis, and Komozi Woodward, 161–84. New York: New York University Press, 2009.

Jacobs, Sue-Ellen. "Has It Really Been Thirty Years?" In *The Politics of Women's Studies: Testimony from Thirty Founding Mothers,* edited by Florence Howe, 307–15. New York: Feminist Press, 2000.

Jay, Karla. *Tales of the Lavender Menace.* New York: Basic Books, 1999.

Johnson, David K. *The Lavender Scare.* Chicago: University of Chicago Press, 2004.

Jones, Martha. *Vanguard: How Black Women Broke Barriers, Won the Vote and Insisted on Equality for All.* New York: Basic Books, 2020.

Kaplan, Temma. "On the Socialist Origins of International Women's Day." *Feminist Studies* 11, no. 1 (Spring 1985): 163–71.

Kelley, Robin D. G. *Freedom Dreams: The Black Radical Imagination.* Boston: Beacon, 2002.

King, Billie Jean. *All In: An Autobiography.* New York: Alfred Knopf, 2021.

Koedt, Anne. *The Myth of the Vaginal Orgasm.* Boston: New England Free Press, 1970.

Lader, Lawrence. *Abortion II: Making the Revolution.* Boston: Beacon, 1973.

Martin, Gloria. *Socialist Feminism: The First Decade, 1966–1976.* Seattle: Freedom Socialist Publications, 1978.

May, Elaine Tyler. *Homeward Bound: American Families in the Cold War Era.* New York: Basic Books, 2008.

Mayer, Serena. *Reasoning from Race: Feminism, Law and the Civil Rights Revolution.* Cambridge, MA: Harvard University Press, 2014.

Mayfield, Lee. "Opening Talk." In *Strong Women's Conference: Follow Up Booklet.* Seattle: Planning Committee of the Strong Women's Conference, 1977.

McNally, Mark, ed. *Antonio Gramsci.* Basingstoke, UK: Palgrave Macmillan, 2015.

Meggyesy, Dave. *Out of Their League.* Lincoln: University of Nebraska Press, 2005.

Michel, Sonya. *Children's Interests/Mothers' Rights: The Shaping of America's Child Care Policy.* New Haven, CT: Yale University Press, 1997.

Mihesuah, Devon Abbot. *Indigenous American Women: Decolonization, Empowerment, Activism.* Omaha: University of Nebraska Press, 2003.

Morgan, Robin. "Goodbye to All That." *Liberated Rat,* Jan. 1970, reprinted in *Dear Sisters: Dispatches from the Women's Liberation Movement,* edited by Rosalyn Baxandall and Linda Gordon, 53–55. New York: Basic Books, 2001.

Morris, Hope. "Equal Rights on the Ballot: The 1972–73 Campaign for the Washington State ERA." Seattle Civil Rights and Labor History Project, University of Washington, 2021. http://depts.washington.edu/civilr/ERAcampaign.htm.

Morris, Hope. "From Women's Rights to Women's Liberation: An Overview of the Second-Wave Feminist Movement in Washington State." BA thesis, University of Washington, 2022. Seattle Civil Rights and Labor History Project, University of Washington, 2022, http://depts.washington.edu/civilr/feminism.htm.

Morrison, Robert G. "Choice in Washington: The Politics of Liberalized Abortion." MA thesis, University of Virginia, 1982.

Nelson, Jennifer. *More Than Medicine: A History of the Feminist Health Movement*. New York: New York University Press, 2015.

O'Connor, Harvey. *Revolution in Seattle: A Memoir*. Chicago: Haymarket, 2009.

Orleck, Annelise. *Rethinking American Women's Activism*. New York: Routledge, 2015.

Parry, Janine A. "Putting Feminism to a Vote: The Washington State Women's Council, 1963–1978." *Pacific Northwest Quarterly* 4 (Fall 2000): 171–82.

Payne, Cril. *Deep Cover: An FBI Agent Infiltrates the Radical Underground*. New York: Newsweek Books, 1979.

Petchesky, Rosalind Pollack. *Abortion and Woman's Choice: The State, Sexuality, and Reproductive Freedom*. Boston: Northeastern University Press, 1984.

Phelps, Christopher. "The Closet in the Party: The YSA, the SWP and Homosexuality, 1962–1970." *Labor: Studies in Working-Class History in the Americas* 10, no. 4 (2013): 11–38.

Phelps, Christopher. "A Neglected Document: Socialism and Sex." *Journal of the History of Sexuality* 16, no. 1 (Jan. 2007): 1–13.

Piercy, Marge. "The Grand Coolie Dam." *Leviathan*, [Nov.?] 1969. Reprinted, Boston: South End Press, 1969.

Polatnik, M. Rivka. "Diversity in Women's Liberation Ideology: How a Black and a White Group of the 1960s Viewed Motherhood." *Signs* 21, no. 3 (1996): 679–706.

Presidential Commission on the Status of Women. *American Women*. Washington, DC: US Government Printing Office, 1963.

Ramos, Juanita, ed. *Compañeras: Latina Lesbians*. New York: Routledge, 1987.

Randolph, Sherie M. *Florynce "Flo" Kennedy: The Life of a Feminist Radical*. Chapel Hill: University of North Carolina Press, 2015.

Reddick, Shelly. "Opening Talk." In *Strong Woman's Conference: Follow Up Booklet* Seattle: Planning Committee of the Strong Women's Conference, 1977.

Robinson, Patricia. *Poor Black Women*. Boston: New England Free Press, 1968. https://library.duke.edu/digitalcollections/wlmpc_wlmms01008/.

Romney, Patricia. *We Were There: The Third World Women's Alliance and the Second Wave*. New York: Feminist Press, at the City University of New York, 2021.

Rosellini, Albert D. *Report of the Governor's Commission on the Status of Women*. Olympia, WA: Office of the Secretary of State, 1963.

Rosen, Ruth. "The Female Generation Gap: Daughters of the Fifties and the Origins of Contemporary American Feminism." In *U.S. History as Women's His-*

tory: New Feminist Essays, edited by Linda Kerber and Kathryn Kish Sklar, 313–32. Chapel Hill: University of North Carolina Press, 1995.

Rosen, Ruth. "When Women Spied on Women." *Nation*, Sept. 20, 2000.

Rosen, Ruth. *The World Split Open: How the Modern Women's Movement Changed America*. New York: Penguin, 2000.

Roth, Benita. *Separate Roads to Feminism: Black, Chicana, and White Feminist Movements in America's Second Wave*. Cambridge: Cambridge University Press, 2004.

Rowbotham, Sheila. *A Century of Women: The History of Women in Britain and the United States in the Twentieth Century*. Harmondsworth, UK: Viking/ Penguin, 1997.

Santos, Bob, and Gary Iwamoto. *The Gang of Four: Four Leaders, Four Communities, One Friendship*. Seattle: Chin Music, 2015.

Shah, Sonia. *Dragon Ladies: Asian American Women Breathe Fire*. Boston: South End, 2007.

Shulman, Alix Kates, and Honor Moore, eds. *Women's Liberation! Feminist Writings That Inspired a Revolution and Still Can*. New York: Library of America, 2021.

Singler, Joan, Jean C. Durning, Bettylou Valentine, and Martha (Maid) Adams. *Seattle in Black and White: The Congress of Racial Equality and the Fight for Equal Opportunity*. Seattle: University of Washington Press, 2010.

Slonecker, Blake. "'It's with Tokens': Women's Liberation and Toxic Masculinity in Seattle's Underground Press." *Pacific Historical Review* 89, no. 3 (Summer 2020): 402–32.

Spencer, Robyn. *The Revolution Has Come: Black Power, Gender, and the Black Panther Party in Oakland*. Durham, NC: Duke University Press, 2016.

Springer, Kimberly. *Still Lifting, Still Climbing: Contemporary African American Women's Activism*. New York: New York University Press, 1999.

Springer, Kimberly. "Third Wave Black Feminism." *Signs* 27, no. 4 (Summer 2002): 1059–82.

Stern, Susan. *With the Weathermen: The Personal Journal of a Revolutionary Woman*. Garden City, NY: Doubleday, 1975.

Swerdlow, Amy. "The Congress of American Women: Left-Feminist Peace Politics in the Cold War." In *U.S. History as Women's History: New Feminist Essays*, edited by Linda Kerber and Kathryn Kish Sklar, 296–332. Chapel Hill: University of North Carolina Press, 1995.

Swerdlow, Amy. *Women Strike for Peace: Traditional Motherhood and Radical Politics in the 1960s*. Chicago: University of Chicago Press, 1993.

Taylor, Quintard. *The Forging of a Black Community: Seattle's Central District from 1870 through the Civil Rights Era*. Seattle: University of Washington Press, 1994.

Thompson, Becky. "Multiracial Feminism: Recasting the Chronology of Second Wave Feminism." In *No Permanent Waves: Recasting Histories of US Feminism*, edited by Nancy Hewitt, 39–60. New Brunswick, NJ: Rutgers University Press, 2010.

Thuma, Emily M. *All Our Trials: Prisons, Policing and the Feminist Fight to End Violence*. Urbana: University of Illinois Press, 2019.

Trotsky, Leon. *History of the Russian Revolution*. Vol. 1. Translated by Max Eastman. London: Victor Gollancz, 1965.

Ware, Cellestine. *Womanpower: The Movement for Women's Liberation*. New York: Tower Books, 1970.

Ware, Susan. *Game, Set, Match: Billie Jean King and the Revolution in Women's Sports*. Chapel Hill: University of North Carolina Press, 2011.

Weiner, Lyn. "Conference Report: The Eighth Berkshire Conference on the History of Women." *Journal of Women's History* 2 (Fall 1990): 174–76.

Welch, Germaine Paige. "'Up against the Wall Miss America': Women's Liberation and Miss Black America in Atlantic City, 1968." *Feminist Formations* 27, no. 2 (Summer 2015): 70–97.

White, Deborah Grey, ed. *Telling Histories: Black Women Historians in the Ivory Tower*. Chapel Hill: University of North Carolina Press, 2008.

Wilkie, Curtis. *When Evil Lived in Laurel: The "White Knights" and the Murder of Vernon Dahmer*. New York: W. W. Norton, 2021.

Williams, Rhonda Y. *Concrete Demands: The Search for Black Power in the 20th Century*. New York: Routledge, 2014.

Windham, Lane. "9 to 5: Framing a New Doorway." In *Knocking on Labor's Door: Union Organizing in the 1970s and the Roots of the New Economic Divide*, 152–77. Chapel Hill: University of North Carolina Press, 2017.

Winslow, Barbara. "Activism and the Academy." In *Voices of Women Historians: The Personal, the Professional the Political*, edited by Eileen Boris and Nupur Chaudhury, 218–33. Bloomington: University of Indiana Press, 1999.

Winslow, Barbara. "The Impact of Title IX." In "Turning Points in American Sports," special issue, *History Now* 23 (Spring 2010), https://www.gilderlehrman.org/history-resources/essays/battle-sexes.

Winslow, Barbara. "Primary and Secondary Contradictions in Seattle, 1967–1969." In *The Feminist Memoir Project: Voices from Women's Liberation*, edited by Rachel Blau DuPlessis and Ann Snitow, 225–48. New York: Three Rivers, 1998.

Winslow, Barbara. *Shirley Chisholm: Catalyst for Change*. New York: Routledge, 2013.

Wu, Judy Tzu-Chun. *Radicals on the Road: Internationalism, Orientalism and Feminism during the Vietnam Era*. Ithaca, NY: Cornell University Press, 2013.

Index